A GOLDEN ADVENTURE

A rig on the Mercedes field in Venezuela in the 1940s

# A GOLDEN
# ADVENTURE

The First 50 Years of ULTRAMAR

*LONDON*
HURTWOOD PRESS
1985

First published in Great Britain 1985
by Hurtwood Press Silversted Westerham Hill Kent

Written by Paul Atterbury and Julia MacKenzie
General Editor R. S. Atterbury
Computer typeset by C.R. Barber and Partners, Wrotham
Photographic work by Photocare, Sevenoaks
Platemaking by Hyway, London
Jacket design by Dennis Bailey, R.D.I.
Printed in England by Alan Pooley, Tonbridge
Bound by Butler and Tanner, Frome


British Library Cataloguing in Publication Data
Atterbury, Paul
A golden adventure : the first fifty years of Ultramar
1. Ultramar PLC - History
I. Title      II. MacKenzie, Julia
338.7'6223382'0941      HD9571.9.U4

ISBN   0-903696-35-5

# CONTENTS

Foreword by Arnold Lorbeer      *page* 7

Acknowledgements      9

1. The Start of a Business      11

2. The Early Years, 1935-40      29

3. The Texaco Partnership      43

4. Post-War Problems      59

5. The 1950s: Consolidation and Expansion      77

6. An Integrated Oil Business      101

7. Caribbean Conclusion      125

8. The Quebec Refinery      139

9. Marketing      159

10. Exploration and Production      193

11. Shipping      227

12. Diversification      245

13. Ultramar Life      255

14. The Next Fifty Years      269

Chart — Fifty Years of Financial Growth      274

Directors Past and Present      275

Index      277

# FOREWORD

In the 1920s and early 1930s, a small group of British financiers and mining men joined hands with an American banker and oil entrepreneur to consummate some successful oil ventures in South America. These were the forerunners of Ultramar, which was formed in London in 1935 as a British-financed public company to trade overseas. Ultramar today, 50 years later, is broadly the same. It is still a British-owned oil investment company, but the scale and the range of its business have increased many times. Initially an exploration company in Venezuela, now an oil and gas producer on four continents. Then a seller of crude oil, now an integrated oil company with world-wide refining, marketing and shipping interests. From no sales revenue and no income in 1935 to revenue of £3,260 million and net income of £127 million in 1984.

Fifty years of Ultramar is largely the story of its men and women. For some, it was the cornerstone of their life's work and achievements; for others, it was a way-station on the road of life. Lasting friendships were made and, in a few cases, antagonisms developed.

To the handful of us who have been on the scene for almost all of Ultramar's first half century, it seemed that its story should be written. This history is based on the files of Ultramar, of its founders and of its associates, but perhaps equally important are the recollections of many of us who were there. As we look back over the events of the past five decades, we see our mistakes; but we also see the successes, and for these we thank all those in Ultramar who have helped make it what it is today.

*Arnold Lorbeer*

April 1985

# PHOTOGRAPH CREDITS

Amoco (U.K.) Exploration Company: pages 204, 205 top left; BBC Hulton Picture Library: page 14 top; Gulf Oil Corporation: page 12; Petróleo Internacional: page 48 lower; Popperfoto: pages 36 centre, 61 top, 80 lower; Texaco: frontispiece, pages 46, 73, 78, 107

# ACKNOWLEDGEMENTS

We are grateful to the Chairman and Directors, and to all the employees of Ultramar past and present who have been generous with their time, and have assisted in so many ways with the preparation and writing of this history. Particular thanks are due to Arnold Lorbeer and Campbell Nelson who, as well as being vital sources of information themselves, displayed endless patience and offered continual encouragement during our search for Ultramar's past. It is not possible to list all those who have helped but among those who gave us their time and corrected many a misapprehension, we must mention James Allan, Joseph Ament, Virgil Anderson, Dale Austin, the late Blaine Beal, Lloyd Bensen, Robert Bland, Jean Gaulin, Robert Haddow, Edward Hall, W. C. Ings, Charles Irwin, George Mottershead, Howard Pearl, Peter Raven, William Sheptycki, Frank Sisti, and Laurie Woodruff. In addition David Elton supplied constant support in London. Eugene O'Shea, not for the first time, kept a sharp eye on the legal boundaries and John Shaheen discussed the early history of Golden Eagle.

We are particularly appreciative of those who loaned photographs from their personal collections or allowed us to print extracts from personal memoirs. These include Max Bayer, Sir Kenneth Barrington, Edna Bensen, Roy Brotherhood, Keith Cullingham, Richard Finder, Burl Freeman, Mrs F. M. Ffoulkes-Jones, Hans Garde-Hansen, Malcolm Haigh, John Hawco, George Higgins, G. D. Hobson, Leslie Illing, Maurice Kamen-Kaye, Frank Kay, Arthur Lundrigan, Ruth Marks, C. J. May, John Pepper, Frank Prebble, Charles Quigley, Mrs Hilary Robinson, Lady Gwen Tangley and Dorothy Tom.

Thanks are due to David Willoughby, Judi Burton and Helen Williams of Ultramar Exploration who drew maps, to Kay Leeson who tracked down many of the photographs and to all the staff of Ultramar PLC who tolerated our invasion of the London office and encouraged us in many ways. Similarly, Ruth Brenner and Anissa Brandt ensured constant support from Mount Kisco. We also wish to thank Janet Dann, Debbie Groombridge and Beryl Walden who typed and retyped the manuscript.

Finally we owe a special debt to the late John Owers, whose work during the early days of the project made it possible for us, relative outsiders, to write the history of Ultramar.

The story of Ultramar is above all the story of people. The support and help we received at all levels is indicative of the character of this great company.

P.R.A. & J.M.

Alfred Meyer

# THE START OF A BUSINESS 1

The Ultramar Exploration Company Limited was formed in London on 30 May 1935. A small company with no full-time staff and no offices, Ultramar was established principally to raise finance to fund the development of oil fields in Venezuela. Its formation was the logical conclusion of a series of previous attempts by British, French and American finance and mining houses to realise the great wealth waiting to be tapped in Venezuela, and so the story of Ultramar actually starts many years before 1935.

The early history of Ultramar is so closely related to Venezuela that it is necessary to examine the latter to understand the former. The development of Venezuela as a major oil-producing country is a recent phenomenon. In 1937, 20 million tons of oil were produced but by 1946 this had risen to 90 million tons, making Venezuela one of the leading oil-producing countries in the world. Between the late 1940s and 1970, Venezuela was the most important exporter of oil in the world. However, the history of Venezuela's oil fields is actually far older. The existence of oil had been known for hundreds of years through surface seepages and naturally-occurring tar lakes and deposits. In the pre-Columbian period, these oils and tars were used in many ways, for example for making fires, for caulking boats and water barrels and for a variety of medicinal uses. During the period of Spanish domination, there was little interest in the oil, but at least one conquistador, Gonzalo de Oviedo y Valdés, saw fit to mention the oil stains in the sea and the seepages to be seen in the Lake Maracaibo region. In 1669 the English pirate Henry Morgan used the oils to create a fire ship that he sent among the Spanish naval force that had trapped him in the narrow channel that links Lake Maracaibo with the sea. In the resultant confusion, Morgan made good his escape.

Another two centuries were to pass before there was any significant development of Venezuela's oil reserves. In 1878, inspired by the world's new and increasing interest in sources of petroleum, the first wells were drilled, in the Province of Táchira. These were small affairs going down no more than 60 feet, yet their output was sufficient to attract the attention of oil companies and speculators from outside Venezuela. The same year the Venezuelan Government granted its first oil concessions. However, for some years development only took place in those areas where surface seepages indicated the presence of oil. In 1904 a system of licences was introduced, to encourage prospecting for oil, gas and minerals in other areas. At first these licences were only issued to Venezuelan

Lake Maracaibo, the centre of early oil exploration
and production in Venezuela

citizens, but they were free to sell them to outsiders. By this means British and American companies started to operate in Venezuela. The true oil potential of the region was realised in 1922 when Barroso 2, a well drilled by Shell interests on the shores of Lake Maracaibo, blew wild for nine days at the rate of 100,000 barrels per day. This event effectively launched Venezuela as an oil-producing country.

Foreign companies were actively encouraged to operate in Venezuela by General Juan Vicente Gómez, the dictator who had been in power since 1908. Gómez had long realised that, while his country's needs for oil were small and likely to remain so, the Venezuelan economy could be greatly stimulated by attracting investments from overseas. In 1920 the concession legislation had been simplified by the passing of the first Petroleum Law, which allowed existing landowners to obtain for one year a permit to explore for oil on their own land and subsequently to obtain an exploitation concession for the same land. More important still was the provision which established the right of the landowner to sell his concession to third parties, including foreigners. This law, which remained in force for many years, encouraged large-scale speculation in concessions as many landowners were keen to sell their rights. At this time Venezuela was poorly mapped, and there was only a limited understanding of its geology. As a result, many worthless concessions were sold to investors in London and New York alongside legitimate sales of potentially valuable lands. Gómez, as well as having a considerable personal stake in the successful development of Venezuelan oil, was astute enough to realise that the future of the industry could be threatened by unscrupulous trading in worthless concessions. He saw that the long-term stability and future growth of the Venezuelan economy was dependent upon control of the oil revenues, resulting from major investments by overseas companies. Gómez actually wanted to keep the effect of the oil revenues on the economy to a minimum, in the belief that a backward, agricultural nation was more governable. Thus between 1919 and 1936 the Venezuelan Government took only 7% of the profits of the foreign oil companies.

As a dictator, Gómez enjoyed a fairly unsavoury reputation, being known as tyrant of the Andes, but his development and control of the Venezuelan oil industry were both sound and foresighted. Ironically, his death, in December 1935, came too soon for him to see the fulfilment of his plans. After some initial uncertainty, the foreign oil companies continued under a succession of governments which were for a time benevolently inclined towards the industry. Although Shell and some other companies were by this time producing large quantities of Venezuelan oil, the real growth was to occur after 1938, a period coinciding with Ultramar's entry into the field. In 1938, the oil industry in Mexico was nationalised, with the oil companies being expelled and their assets seized. Major companies like Shell and Esso quickly wanted to find an alternative Latin-American source for the 15 million tons they had been extracting each year from Mexico and so they turned to Venezuela. From that moment the Venezuelan oil industry came of age and production rapidly increased. An even greater stimulus occurred a few years later, when the United States entered the Second World War. Wartime demands stretched the domestic oil industry in the United States and many companies looked for new sources of supply. With Mexican oil embargoed following nationalisation, Venezuela was the nearest large source of oil for the United States. With this stimulus, Venezuela was able to rise rapidly up the world league table of oil-producing countries.

By the 1930s a legislative pattern had been established whereby exploration concessions were granted for three years. During this period, the company operating the concession had to carry out the necessary surveying, mapping and geological assessments and then, at the end of the period, it was able to apply for an exploitation licence for 50% of the concession, the other 50% reverting to the government. The concessionaire and the Venezuelan Government took alternate parcels with the initial choice decided by spinning a coin. Gómez's attempts at controlling and regulating the concessions market also led him to engage a number of men with international reputations who appeared to him to be trustworthy and reliable to act as agents for concession selling.

Foremost among those operating as a concession agent for General Gómez was Alfred Meyer. A banker by profession, Meyer was deeply involved in trading in Venezuelan land concessions between 1922 and 1935, when he played the major role in the formation of Ultramar. Before 1929 he had handled, in his own name, more than 5 million hectares of property in Venezuela. (A hectare of land is equal to 2.47 acres.)

General Juan Vicente Gómez, ruler of Venezuela 1908-35

| No. SERIAL | NOMBRE DE LA CONCESION | UBICACION | CONCESIONARIO |
|---|---|---|---|
| 10.750 | MEYER "C" | Monagas. | Simón Izaguirre. |
| | | Cedeño, & | |
| | | Caicara,& | |

PERIODO DE EXPLORACION:
Título, G. O. fecha: 2-12-26.
Vencimiento:
Prorrogada hasta
Tipo del Impuesto: Bs. 0.10 por Ha.
Superficie. 10.000.- Ha.

| INICIAL | SUPERFICIAL | | | % EXPLOTACION |
|---|---|---|---|---|
| | 3 AÑOS | 27 AÑOS | 10 AÑOS | |
| Bs. 2.- | Bs. 2.- | Bs. 4.- | Bs. 5.- | 10. |

PERIODO DE EXPLOTACION:
Plano aprobado, G. O. fecha: 1-10-28.
Certificado de Explotación, fecha: 13-10-28.
IMPUESTOS (Superficie Parcelas=4.924.77 Ha.)

IMPUESTOS RESERVAS NACIONALES
Título, G. O. fecha: 27-10-28.
(SUPERFICIE 4.924.77 Ha.)

| INICIAL | SUPERFICIAL | | | % EXPLOTACION |
|---|---|---|---|---|
| | 3 AÑOS | 27 AÑOS | 10 AÑOS | |
| Bs. 2.- | Bs. 2.- | Bs. 4.- | Bs. 5.- | 10. |

Caduca o Renunciada, G. O. fecha:
TIP. AMERICANA

A concession certificate granted to Alfred Meyer by the Venezuelan Government in 1926

14

## THE START OF A BUSINESS

Born in Hamburg in 1877, Meyer worked first for Deutsche Bank, becoming an officer in the Havana branch in 1900. A few years later he gave up banking to become a tobacco farmer and trader in Cuba, a successful venture that made him a millionaire by 1908. He returned to banking, as head of the Anglo South American Bank in Latin America, a position he held until the outbreak of war in 1914. A German citizen, he took up permanent residence in the United States, and became an American citizen in 1919. Helped by associates and friends from his pre-war banking days, Meyer next became president of the Mercantile Bank, a South American affiliate of Guaranty Trust with over 90 branches in Central and South America. In 1921 Guaranty Trust sold the Mercantile to the Royal Bank of Canada, and Meyer resigned, along with several of his leading branch managers, some of whom later were to join Ultramar.

During his banking days, Meyer had worked extensively in Venezuela and had become friendly with a number of prominent Venezuelans, including General Gómez. Following his resignation from the Mercantile Bank, he was quickly persuaded by these friends to open an office in Caracas and renew his association with Gómez. This was the time Gómez was looking for men to help him control the new market in oil concessions, and he asked Meyer to assist in interesting established and reliable overseas oil companies in concessions in the Lake Maracaibo region, an area where extensive oil deposits were later discovered. After one major oil company, no longer in existence, rejected Meyer's advances, calling him unscrupulous for trying to sell a worthless 'muddy lake', he was successful in selling concessions to another major oil company at a price higher than Gómez had expected and without charging an exorbitant commission. As a result, within a year of opening his office, Meyer had become Gómez's principal concession agent.

Encouraged by his success, Meyer decided to trade in concessions in his own right, knowing that his connections in the Venezuelan Government would help him through the minefield represented by the new oil concession laws. By the mid 1920s, Meyer had achieved a solid position within the Venezuelan oil business. The second largest concession holder in the country, he organised various trading and exploration companies using American, French and British finance. Branch offices were opened in New York, London, Paris, Bogotá and Lima, and concession trading was carried on in Colombia, Peru, the Dominican Republic and other countries as well as in Venezuela. His interests were wide-ranging. Much of his activity was concentrated around the already proven Lake Maracaibo region in western Venezuela, but he also held concessions in the still unexplored eastern part of the country. Many of his prominent Venezuelan friends, such as Alfredo Brandt, Nicomedes Zuloaga and Lorenzo Mendoza, were closely involved in these activities, establishing in the process associations with Meyer that were to last for many years. Some became directors of Caracas Petroleum Corporation and subsequently of Caracas Petroleum Sociedad Anónima, with considerable shareholdings in Ultramar. Zuloaga and his company were to become Ultramar's Venezuelan attorneys in 1935, a position they retained until nationalisation in 1975.

However, a more significant figure was Alfredo Brandt, who appears to have acted as

15

The Caribbean area and the West Indies in the 1930s

Meyer's agent or partner on many concession deals. One such deal is typical of the concession business at this period. In 1926, Brandt acquired concession rights over 48,000 hectares in Anzoátegui for 53,362 Bolivars (the Venezuelan currency unit). Three years later he sold the concession to the Venezuelan American Corporation for 130,625 Bolivars, who in turn transferred it soon afterwards to Caracas Petroleum Corporation. In 1934 Caracas sold the block to Orinoco Oilfields Limited for 1,149,225 Bolivars. Meyer was represented at all stages in this dramatic progression, first through his association with Brandt, second through his ownership of Venezuelan American, third as president of Caracas Petroleum, and fourth as a major shareholder in Orinoco Oilfields. Meyer owned or operated many concession companies during the 1920s, some rather obscure and some significant enough to survive to be incorporated into, or trade with, Ultramar. One of the earliest of these was the Venezuelan American Corporation. Organised under the laws of Delaware, this company had received a Certificate of Authority to do business in New York in February 1924. Others included the Oriental Oil Company and Algeo Oil Concessions Corporation, both of which were actually owned by Mrs Meyer. Meyer had married his French wife Georgette in 1913 and had used their two Christian names in Algeo Oil. As well as trading and exploration, Meyer's activities were gradually expanded to include exploitation and development. One of the companies he acquired was the Société Française de Recherches au Venezuela. This operated an exploitation concession near Lake Maracaibo and drilled the Cacuz well which found heavy gravity oil, considered to be uncommercial at the time.

16

Venezuela, showing the States as they were in the late 1930s

However, the most important of Meyer's companies was the Caracas Petroleum Corporation.

Incorporated in March 1929 in Delaware, Caracas Petroleum was owned by a London-based syndicate, the principal members of which were Alfred Meyer, A. Chester Beatty, C. S. Gulbenkian, Cull and Company and New Consolidated Gold Fields. The most important member of the syndicate was the London merchant bank, Cull and Company. Little known today, Cull and Company had been formed in the 1920s by four former stock exchange jobbers, Eric Cull, Hugh Micklem, Gilbert Russell and Hermann Marx. Already familiar with the oil business, and used to working with Meyer, Cull and Marx put together the syndicate that formed Caracas Petroleum. Cull and Company remained the principal merchant bankers for Caracas Petroleum and the other companies, such as Orinoco Oilfields, that preceded the formation of Ultramar in 1935. They then continued as Ultramar's bankers until 1943 when they were absorbed by Morgan Grenfell. It is interesting to note that Morgan Grenfell were themselves involved in the formation of Caracas Petroleum, having acquired 25,000 shares during the original placing in November 1929. Caracas Petroleum immediately purchased oil concessions and options covering over two million hectares in Venezuela, much of which had previously been held by Meyer, and an office was set up in New York under the management of Arthur Lawder, a Canadian who had previously been one of Meyer's branch managers in the old Mercantile Bank. Technicians were hired and sent to Venezuela to begin the long and complex task of conducting geological, geophysical and

17

Certificate of Authority issued by the State of New York in 1924 for the Venezuelan American Corporation, a company owned by Alfred Meyer

Letter written in 1931 by Ebert Boylan, manager of CPC, to Thomas Servello, terminating his contract as a geologist

topographical surveys. The original intention had been for the shares in the new company to be listed in New York and, with this in mind, negotiations were carried on with another company with interests in Venezuela, but these proved to be abortive. In any case, the stock market crash in New York in 1929 made any further action in this direction a waste of time.

During 1930 and 1931, Caracas Petroleum bought more concessions and exercised some of its options, so that by the end of 1931 the company held concessions covering 2,540,000 hectares in Venezuela and 1,000,000 hectares in Santo Domingo. By this time, however, Caracas Petroleum was short of cash. With barely enough funds to meet current overheads, the company was in no position to undertake the expensive surveys necessary to convert their concessions into exploitation parcels, let alone pay the heavy exploitation taxes that would become due. The original syndicate members continued to support the company, but it was Meyer who effectively carried it throughout its early existence. For the first four years he paid out of his own pocket all the costs and salaries associated with the New York office. During the same period, he elected to receive his contracted salary as president of Caracas Petroleum in the form of shares. At the beginning of 1932, Meyer, having been badly hit by the New York stock market crash, announced that he could no longer afford to support Caracas Petroleum in this way, and so the need for extra cash became acute.

The first scheme involved the setting up of a company in France, supported by

# THE START OF A BUSINESS

Gulbenkian, at that time reputed to be the richest man in the world, with the title, Société Petrolière Française de Caracas. Holdings in the American company were to be exchanged for shares in the new French company, which would then be merged with another French company, Société Française de Recherches au Venezuela, which was already trading and owned by Meyer. By this means it was hoped that the French Government would be prepared to grant the Société Petrolière the right to list its shares on the Paris market, and thus help raise the necessary capital to allow Caracas Petroleum to develop. In the event, this scheme came to naught, apparently because continual disagreement among the French directors of the two companies caused the French Government to withhold the right for the shares to be listed. During the latter part of 1932, the original syndicate members advanced further financial assistance, but this was not sufficient either to develop existing concessions or to purchase the new ones which were still being secured from the Venezuelan Government by Alfred Meyer on very favourable terms. Fortunately, Meyer was also able to negotiate new exploration titles for the most promising of the concessions already held by Caracas Petroleum, covering about 625,000 hectares, on condition that the remaining concessions were allowed to lapse.

Among its holdings, Caracas Petroleum had an option on about 500,000 hectares in Anzoátegui which appeared to be geologically very promising. In May 1933 the option price became due, but the Company could only raise about a third of the amount required. At this point Caracas Petroleum was not only in danger of collapsing through lack of cash, but also ran the risk of letting its potentially valuable concessions fall into the hands of more powerful companies, such as Standard Oil of New Jersey. It was to overcome this problem that a new company, Orinoco Oilfields Limited, was set up in London. Once again Cull and Company and Alfred Meyer were the prime movers, but New Consolidated Gold Fields now shared the principal shareholding with the other three major South African mining groups, Central Mining and Investment Corporation, Union Corporation and Selection Trust. These same four mining companies were in due course to become the principal shareholders in Ultramar. There were various reasons for these companies to be interested in Venezuela. All were keen to diversify their commercial activities and there was by now a widespread understanding of the future potential of Venezuelan oil. New Consolidated Gold Fields had already invested a considerable sum in Venezuela through their shareholding in Caracas Petroleum and had no desire to see it disappear. Central Mining also had a particular motive; as owners of an oil refinery in Trinidad, they saw Venezuela as a suitable source for future supplies of crude. In any case, they had been actively involved through subsidiaries in Venezuela since the late 1920s, albeit unsuccessfully. Orinoco was established with 330,000 issued shares, of which 80,000 were given to Caracas Petroleum as a bonus. By selling some of these shares, and selling some of its concessions to Orinoco, Caracas was able to raise enough capital to pay off its debts and to continue to operate in the field during 1934.

As far as Orinoco was concerned, its main business was concession trading which was carried out by Alfred Meyer and his associates. Orinoco had no real interest in

Professor Illing on the Rio Memo, Venezuela, in 1929

Geologists in Venezuela in the late 1920s

developing its concessions, partly because of the costs involved and partly because they did not have the technical resources to mount extensive surveying and drilling operations. After an unsuccessful series of negotiations with Anglo Persian Oil, Orinoco was able to conclude a profitable deal with Gulf Oil who bought its concessions in eastern Venezuela for a cash price of U.S.$4 million, plus a contingency payment of a further U.S.$3 million from any oil produced. Gulf quickly drilled a well and discovered a major oil field in the Oficina area, ensuring that the Orinoco shareholders would receive the contingency payment. This represented a 400% profit on the initial investment. Orinoco was liquidated and went out of business but Caracas Petroleum, as a result of its holding in Orinoco, was able to achieve financial security.

The successful sale appeared to justify Meyer's concession trading policy. However, some of the mining group shareholders, who had more experience in oil development and marketing, realised that their profit could have been many times greater if they had financed and controlled the drilling operations themselves. There was a strong feeling that they should now become fully involved in future exploration and drilling operations. Alfred Meyer appears to have had mixed feelings about this, but others clearly supported the idea. It was this change of policy that brought about the founding of Ultramar. At the same time, part of the proceeds from the sale of Orinoco's concessions was used to purchase overriding royalties in the same areas, and these proved to be very profitable for Ultramar in the years to come.

The success of Orinoco was also a reflection on the high quality of the geological and technical research to which the company had access. Orinoco, Caracas Petroleum and ultimately Ultramar were largely dependent upon the skills and experience of Professor Vincent Illing and his associates. A friend of Meyer, Illing had set up the Department of Petroleum Geology, later called the Department of Oil Technology, at the Royal School of Mines in 1913. He understood the importance of all aspects in oil exploration, and was determined that Britain should not surrender to American domination in this field, as had occurred in so many other areas of oil expertise and technology.

During the First World War, he had concentrated on Trinidad, and then in the early 1920s he had turned his attention towards Venezuela. Throughout this period, he spent a part of every summer in Venezuela studying the geology of the central part of the country. It was on Illing's advice that Orinoco Oilfields purchased the concessions in the Oficina area of eastern Venezuela that proved so profitable. With so much experience and knowledge of Venezuela at his fingertips, Professor Illing was clearly destined to be closely involved not only with Orinoco Oilfields and Caracas Petroleum but with Ultramar. When Ultramar was formed the following year, Illing immediately became its consultant geologist.

Illing's expertise appears to have made the process of oil exploration relatively simple, but this was in fact far from the case. While interested by the latest technology, he always believed that a good geologist should be able to identify the nature of the rock thousands of feet below ground from the many clues that a trained eye could see on the surface. Technology was there to back up observation and experience. To many of his

Group of CPC staff photographed in Caracas in 1931. *Left to right:* James Marsh, Hector
Guardia, Mr Hawk, Dr Velutini, Berta Miller, Mr Ferraro, J. Fling, Mr Khan.
*Kneeling:* A. Alfonso, Victor Oronel

contemporaries this method of working may sometimes have appeared intuitive rather
than scientific, but Illing's forceful personality, plus the fact that he was generally right,
usually carried the day. However, his approach was dependent upon very detailed
fieldwork which often had to be carried out in the most adverse circumstances. To say
that conditions in the interior of Venezuela were primitive would be an understatement.
Much of the country where the Caracas Petroleum and Orinoco concessions lay was
unmapped and relatively unexplored. There were few roads or tracks across a landscape
composed of a series of scrub-covered hills. In most areas the only practical form of travel
was by burro or donkey. Initial exploration and surveying was carried out by a small
team of geologists, often led by Professor Illing, and with only limited support facilities.
In many cases the teams would split up, with each geologist making a single-handed
survey of a large area of unknown country, a survey that had to be thorough enough to
supply all the necessary information for the creation of a detailed geological map. In the
early days, there was little seismic equipment available and so the geologists had to rely
on their training and on traditional methods of interpretation. Although the oil business
was by this time already dominated by American technology and expertise, many of the
geologists came from Britain.

One of the most prominent figures introduced to Venezuela by Professor Illing was
Maurice Kamen-Kaye, who worked with Caracas Petroleum through the early 1930s
and then went on to become Ultramar's chief geologist for many years. His dramatic
introduction to the lifestyle of the survey camps, with only the sea voyage to mark the
transition between a comfortable college life in England and the primitive conditions of

22

remote regions, was typical of many of the young people who joined Caracas. Field trips might last for weeks, during which time the geologists had often to be self-supporting. Kamen-Kaye in his unpublished memoirs writes of his experiences in Venezuela in 1932. 'One of the sounds heard in the forest, as we followed the bed of the river upstream, was a descending cadence given out by the pauji, a beautiful crested black turkey. On the second day of the traverse our hunter shot one of these birds, to my mixed feelings, since I had to admit that its meat made a valuable addition to commons. The actual taste of the meat, as I had heard from others, was delicate and rewarding. In the days that followed, however, there was neither fowl nor other living thing for the pot. Finally, and I suppose in desperation, the hunter brought down a monkey. The men seemed rather shamefaced at eating the flesh, and they were hesitant about offering a piece to me. Not being able to recognize the part that they offered me, I was able to taste it gingerly. I do not recommend the viand.

'Conditions sometimes forced us to leave the stream and detour over steep ridges. Progress was then distressingly slow, as the rain fell, as footing became precarious, and as exhaustion frequently overtook the men while cutting trail with packs on their backs. Our guide had been right about the need for additional hands. But the problem of food was quite acute. Along one of the detours, the men found the site of an abandoned hut and a pair of plantain trees with some straggly fruit. The taste of a plantain roasted in wood ashes, at that point, was superlative. Otherwise we were forced to rely mainly on casabe, or cassava, a thin cake of material made from the root that also yields tapioca. The casabe, when freshly made, is dried in the sun, and can be said to have a slight taste. When casabe ages under field conditions, however, it becomes like hardened sawdust, and is then little better than bulk for the stomach. Each would dip that hard stuff in water, and would chew philosophically at the moistened piece.'

Roy Brotherhood, another of the young British scientists who joined Ultramar in the 1930s and who later became part of Ultramar's management team, has described the vital role played by the chicken. 'Our diet consisted of a boiled egg for breakfast, after which the poor hen was killed and boiled to make it tender and at the same time yield soup, then the remains were fried for dinner!' Food and equipment had to be carried vast distances by burro, for many of the survey regions were unapproachable by vehicle. Water was also sometimes a problem, while the constant threat of malaria made camping a precarious operation.

The rather monotonous field work of the geologists was followed by a period back at base while the survey maps were prepared and the geological data assessed. As Kamen-Kaye recalls, 'There was no formal allotment of time for work in the Caracas office, but we knew that we could not dawdle. Maps had to be prepared from my scribbled notes. Letters, comments, text, evaluations and recommendations had to be written. I even coloured my own final geological map. It was not the best map in the world, but to me it seemed an informative and rewarding one.'

Based on the maps, a rather more elaborate exploration could then be carried out in selected areas, involving a larger survey party with several technicians apart from

23

Professor V. C. Illing

Arthur Lawder, manager of CPC New York    Ebert Boylan, manager of CPSA in Caracas

geologists, such as geophysicists and surveyors, supported by up to 50 native labourers. Far more complex were the arrangements involved in establishing seismic and drilling camps, both of which required many more men and a greater degree of permanence. However, neither Caracas Petroleum nor Orinoco Oilfields were in the early stages seriously involved in these activities, which lay beyond the requirements of the business of concession trading.

With the successful conclusion of the deal between Orinoco and Gulf came the need for the major shareholders to reconsider the future. Caracas Petroleum was now clear of any financial difficulties and was in a position to carry on a more elaborate programme of exploration and field work. However, this was concentrated on the concessions that it still held, mainly in the States of Guárico and Portuguesa, and no further purchases were being considered. As already mentioned, the sale of Orinoco's concessions had opened the eyes of the major shareholding companies to the far greater profits that could be made by the process of oil production and marketing. As far as they were concerned, simple concession trading now had a rather limited appeal and it was decided to form a new company to be actively involved in oil exploration and development in Venezuela.

On 30 May 1935, the transition took place; Orinoco Oilfields was no more and Ultramar Exploration Company Limited had been born. The name 'Ultramar' was adopted because it is the Spanish word for 'overseas' and this was to be an overseas investment made by a British company in a Spanish speaking country. The change of title and the new business policy to some extent masked the degree of similarity between the two companies. There were the same principal shareholders, the four mining groups Consolidated Gold Fields, Selection Trust, Central Mining and Union Corporation; the

25

Conditions in the field were often difficult and exploration parties relied on burros or mules

same merchant bankers, Cull and Company; the same lawyers, Freshfields; the same Secretaries, Limebeer; the same consulting geologist, Illing; and the same Board Chairman, Walter Maclachlan. The latter was a Scottish chartered accountant who had been a successful entrepreneur since the early 1900s and who had pioneered the formation of British-Borneo Petroleum Syndicate and Apex Trinidad Oilfields. Maclachlan was to remain Chairman of Ultramar through the early war years until his death in 1944.

Alfred Meyer was apparently not enthusiastic about the move into oil production, but he remained a major shareholder. At the same time, he anticipated the formation of Ultramar by some extensive concession buying in his own name, concessions selected on the advice of Professor Illing that were later to be transferred to Ultramar. These concessions, in the States of Monagas, Guárico and Anzoátegui, were bought very shrewdly and taken over willingly by Ultramar. He also negotiated a number of royalty agreements, which were to prove a useful source of revenue for Ultramar during some of the difficult years that were to follow. The question of royalty holdings caused some debate. They were then a relatively new concept and some shareholders felt that investing in royalty rights was rather a gamble, but the purchase went through. Indeed, the first Ultramar prospectus states that, 'The Company was incorporated ... for the

26

primary purpose of acquiring, either directly, or through holdings in other companies, oil concessions and royalties, or interests in oil concessions and royalties in the Republic of Venezuela.' The royalties covered concessions in Anzoátegui and Guárico and produced considerable revenues into the 1970s. At their peak they contributed £1,487,000 to Ultramar in one year, which made their purchase price of £46,181 in 1935 seem quite a bargain.

In retrospect, perhaps the most remarkable aspect of Ultramar's formation was the personalities involved. Many of those who joined the company in its infancy or who had been associated with its predecessors were to continue to be involved with Ultramar for many years. Apart from Meyer and Illing, others who were to enjoy a long relationship with Ultramar included Maurice Kamen-Kaye, the chief geologist, Ebert Boylan, the manager of Caracas Petroleum, Vahan Djalaloff, who had mastered every aspect of the oil business in Russia before the First World War and who came to Ultramar via the Société Française de Recherches au Venezuela, Arthur Lawder, James Marsh and Douglas Hubbard who came with Meyer from the Mercantile Bank, Richard Thompson who came from Cull and Company to be one of Ultramar's first directors, Campbell Nelson who as a young accountant handled the liquidation of Orinoco Oilfields and became the partner from Limebeer and Company who looked after Ultramar's interests and, last but not least, Ruth Marks, a secretary for Cull and Company from the mid 1920s, who was to become a personal secretary first to Alfred Meyer and then to Professor Illing.

Transport in the field in Venezuela in 1939

# THE
# EARLY YEARS
# 1935-40

# 2

Ultramar Exploration Company held its first Board Meeting on 3 June 1935 at 2 Broad Street Place, London, in offices made available through an arrangement with Walter Maclachlan and rented from Limebeer. The accommodations were limited but adequate, comprising a room for Walter Maclachlan, another shared by a company secretary with Maclachlan's personal secretary, and the use of a board room. The latter was also used by Alfred Meyer during his visits to London. At this meeting the appointment of the first directors was confirmed, Walter Maclachlan, Lieutenant Colonel Ralph Micklem from Selection Trust and Richard Thompson, a manager from Cull and Company. There had been considerable discussion and correspondence concerning the composition of the Board. Some pressure was applied to induce Alfred Meyer, Hermann Marx and Professor Illing, as well as the Chairman or Managing Director of each of the four mining groups, to become directors, but in the end all refused. As a consequence the Board played only a limited part in the early history of Ultramar.

At the first Board Meeting, Maclachlan was confirmed as Chairman, Limebeer's were appointed as Secretaries and Accountants, Jackson Pixley as Auditors, Freshfields as Solicitors and Cazenoves as Brokers. Some of these business relationships established by Ultramar at the start of its existence were to continue to the present, notably those with Limebeer's, Freshfields, Cazenoves and Morgan Grenfell, the successors to Cull and Company from 1943. Ultramar had no staff in London in its own name, a situation which persisted for about ten years after its founding. The overseas business was run by Caracas Petroleum which had an organisation in Venezuela and in the United States as well as representatives in other countries. The administration in London was carried out by Limebeer's and a technical office was opened by Meyer at 15 Throgmorton Avenue, next door to Cull and Company, and managed by an American, John Hicklin.

The close links between Ultramar and Caracas Petroleum were apparent from the start. Caracas Petroleum's major shareholders were offered and took up at par practically all the initial issue of 500,000 shares of Ultramar. At the same time, Caracas Petroleum agreed to provide office accommodations, staff and other facilities in Venezuela and New York for an annual fee of £5,000, an agreement that was to run for five years.

However, the closest link between the two companies was the all-important figure of

Certificate from the first issue of shares by the Ultramar Exploration Company in 1935

Alfred Meyer, the president of Caracas Petroleum. Concessions acquired by him in Venezuela, largely on the advice of Professor Illing, formed the basis of Ultramar's business in Venezuela. Many of these concessions were purchased from companies in which Meyer had a controlling interest, such as Algeo Oil and Valle Grande. At first, Meyer kept himself slightly at a distance from Ultramar, at least on paper, accepting a five-year agreement to serve as Venezuelan manager, but in fact he was deeply involved from the start, along with many of his associates. Indeed, Meyer created a style of management which he passed on to his successors and which has remained Ultramar's policy for its first 50 years. Meyer, while a strong personality, was also a tremendous communicator and believed in sharing the business problems with his associates. This was done by correspondence, by personal visits and by conferences. Meyer, Lawder and others from New York would make constant trips to Venezuela, by sea of course, since there was no air transportation, and, except for the war years, also to London. From the English side Illing and Marx were often in North America and so were a number of the technicians from the Paris and London offices.

In the late 1920s and early 1930s, Alfred Meyer evolved a system of management conferences which were held at least once a year. The early conferences were generally held in Evian, France, a pleasant location for a meeting. This practice of meeting in

30

**ULTRAMAR EXPLORATION COMPANY LIMITED.**

TELEPHONE: NATIONAL 1071 (7 LINES).
CABLES: ULTRAMAR, LONDON.

DIRECTORS:
W. MACLACHLAN (CHAIRMAN).
H. MEYER (U.S.A., GERMAN ORIGIN).
LT. COL. R. MICKLEM, C.M.G.
R. P. L. THOMPSON.

SECRETARIES AND REGISTERED OFFICE:
HUGH LIMEBEER & CO.,
2, BROAD STREET PLACE, LONDON, E.C.2.

15, THROGMORTON AVENUE,
LONDON, E.C.2.

2nd May 1939.

Mr. G.R.Brotherhood,
53 Baker Street,
Stapenhill, Burton-on-Trent.

Dear Sir,
          This letter will serve as an agreement and outline the
conditions of your employment by this Company.

          The Company agrees to employ you as Geophysicist in Venezuela
or wherever required in any other capacity, for a period of three years
commencing from the date on which you sail from England for Venezuela
and at a salary of £50. per month, payable monthly, and living expenses
approved by the Representative of the Company in the country to which
you are assigned. Transportation, salary and reasonable travelling
expenses will be allowed you on outward trip to Venezuela and return
journey to London. Medical expenses will be allowed you in case of
illness contracted during your employment.

          Upon completion of three or more years of active service,
the Company will allow you one month of vacation, with salary, but
without other expenses, for each year of service.

          The Company reserves the right to terminate your employ-
ment in case of any disability, not due to the nature of your work,
which in the Company's opinion renders you incapable of carrying out
your duties. The Company also reserves the right to refuse payment of
return passage, salary, and expenses if you terminate your employment
through your own desire before the end of three years' service.

          Your signature at the foot of this letter will signify your
acceptance of this agreement.
                              Yours faithfully,
                    ULTRAMAR EXPLORATION COMPANY LIMITED,

                                                  Assistant Manager.

Gerald Roy Brotherhood.

Ultramar Exploration Company's first Annual Report and Accounts, for the year ended 31 December 1935

Roy Brotherhood's letter of employment with Ultramar Exploration

Evian, or later in Paris, continued with Mr Meyer after the war and into the early 1950s. He would have three or four of his principal officers from Venezuela, New York and London. In the late 1940s some of the Texaco technicians involved with the Mercedes joint project were also invited to meet Ultramar people in London. It is a style of management which has continued in later years, although on a much larger scale.

During its first year of existence, Ultramar expanded its holdings and began to develop some of these lands using the geological expertise available through the staff of Caracas Petroleum. By this time, Caracas Petroleum had built up a strong team of geologists, many of whom were recruited by Professor Illing from the Royal School of Mines, or from other oil companies with interests in South America. Maurice Kamen-Kaye, previously mentioned, worked with Spens and Greig to produce the first large-scale geological maps of the Caracas and Ultramar concessions in central and eastern Venezuela. Relying at first on plane-table surveying, these geologists were more like explorers, living and working in extremely primitive conditions in terrain that was largely unmapped and frequently hostile. During this period Greig contracted malaria, while Spens and later Bailey were bitten by foxes and spent some time living with the threat of rabies. Events of this kind were not uncommon, and the early geologists certainly understood the meaning of the word 'Exploration' in Ultramar's title.

Roy Brotherhood, who arrived in Venezuela in 1939, has commented in detail on the camp life. 'The interior of Venezuela provided little in support of exploration efforts. The simplest of these operations was that which employed one technical person, either a surveyor or a geologist (who usually doubled as his own surveyor) and a few native labourers and a couple of burros. Shelter was provided by simple tarpaulins strung between trees and bedding was a hammock with its ever-present mosquito net. By and large food was that which was available locally, although a few canned goods were carried. This was particularly the case with milk which was kept in powdered form and mixed with freshly boiled water as required. A taste for the local casabe bread, native cheese (queso llanero) and black coffee sweetened with crude brown sugar (papelón) was soon acquired. Chickens supplied the main meat, but occasionally a shot-gun would provide venison or quail as luxuries.

'A slightly superior type of exploration party was the gravity crew which had several technicians - geologists, geophysicists and sometimes a surveyor - with about 50 natives. These were mainly used for cutting trails through the tropical forests, building crossings of streams and preparing sites for exploration activities and camps. The camps were somewhat better than the one-man variety, but were still rather primitive. Tents with mosquito netting sides were used for sleeping and tarpaulins covered mess and office areas. By placing a 55-gallon oil drum over a simple frame about seven feet high, a shower was improvised with cold water in the morning and, after the day's sunshine, warm water in the afternoon. At first food was poor but after obtaining a kerosene refrigerator, making arrangements to buy and slaughter a rather emaciated cow each week and the hiring of a Chinese cook, the meals improved. Transportation was provided by a number of lorries which were satisfactory in the dry season but a real problem in the rains since they were not fitted with winches. For this reason activities during that season were strictly limited.

'The largest exploration efforts were those connected with seismic work. These were parties with 20 or more technical personnel and up to 200 labourers. They were highly mechanised because of the nature of the work. Living conditions were vastly superior to the other mobile camps and high-quality food was served from refrigerated storage and regularly supplied from Caracas. Electrical energy was obtained from portable generators and the lorries were equipped with adequate winches to keep them moving in all but the worst conditions. Much of this was necessitated by the very nature of the work which called for heavy equipment to drill shot holes and transport recording equipment. The camps themselves needed suitable accommodation for extensive office and laboratory work. Good food and reasonable living conditions were essential to attract and keep the expatriate staff for months at a time on a seven day a week schedule. It was usually found uneconomic to work these parties during the rainy season since productivity became so low due to the adverse conditions.

'Another type of camp had to be organised at a later stage in the exploration process. This was at the drilling phase, when the earlier work, which was only capable of suggesting favourable structural conditions, had to be followed by the actual sampling of the various formations at the indicated locations. To do this it was necessary to import and transport to isolated spots a vast quantity of extremely heavy equipment required for lengthy drilling operations. As with the other exploratory activities, housing for the personnel was a prime responsibility and since these operations were static for a longer

The staple diet. Roy Brotherhood in the field in 1939

George Higgins in the shower, Venezuela, 1939

period of time they could be semi-permanent. Under these circumstances it was practical to use canvas and wooden screened huts with comfortable cots for housing. The mess hall was similarly more attractive and the food comparable with that in the seismic camps.'

During the latter years of the 1930s additional geologists and geophysicists became involved, including Dr Hobson who, after a short spell with Caracas Petroleum, was employed directly by Illing as one of his assistants and partners, and George Higgins, who joined in September 1938. Higgins and Brotherhood were involved in the development of gravity (or torsion balance) surveying in Venezuela. The transition from the comfort of a sea journey to the rigours of Venezuelan camp life was often difficult. 'At that time the only way to travel was by sea', Brotherhood recalls, 'and this involved a two-week voyage crossing the Atlantic from Madeira to Barbados, then to Trinidad and finally Venezuela. After this great luxury, it was a terrific let-down to arrive in a foreign country, not speaking the language and knowing no one. It was even worse when, after a

The field kitchen and the
Chinese cook, 1939

Exploration camp in
the Llanos, 1939

On the road from Caracas,
1939

34

few days in Caracas, I spent two days in an ancient open touring car before finding the small primitive camp to which I was attached.

'We learned many things the hard way and I will always remember the beautiful camp site we chose and where we slept so well, but woke up next morning to find ourselves in the middle of a foot deep lake. On one occasion we had camped too close to a local farmer who kept pigs, but apparently not too well since they started foraging on our rice and bean supplies. Our final resort, to prevent total privation, was bird shot from our shot gun. We had considerable difficulty in persuading the equivalent of the local magistrate that the swine had developed a bad case of worms! But all our learning was not through errors and suffering. By necessity we learned Spanish, not from books, but from the people themselves and certainly we could not blame them if what we learned was not always well received in the polite drawing rooms in Caracas.

'From time to time we spent a few days in Caracas, which was then a delightful colonial type city with many modern amenities. On these occasions we could enjoy excellent French food and wine and social events at the clubs. A favourite Sunday outing was either to the mountains or the beach. It is hard to say which trip was more difficult since the former involved a lot of climbing in the tropical sun and the latter a hazardous ride down the winding hairpin bends on the road to the coast. Half way down there was a famous monument featuring a badly wrecked car to remind everyone of the perils of that road. In order to remain effective the wrecked car was occasionally changed for a more up to date model.'

Ultramar's first Annual General Meeting was held on 9 November 1936 and the Directors' Report summarises Ultramar's activities during its first year of operation. The company held concessions in the States of Monagas, Guárico and Zamora (later known as Barinas). There were also royalty rights over large areas of Anzoátegui and Guárico. Many of the holdings were supported by favourable geological reports and were in regions in which other oil companies had considerable interests.

The pattern of expansion continued during 1937 with increases in concession holdings and royalty rights. Two other developments of interest occurred during the year. Alfred Meyer became a director of Ultramar and his service contract as Venezuelan manager was cancelled, an event that formalised the important role he was playing in the company's growth. At the same time, Meyer was instrumental in widening Ultramar's area of activity by persuading the Board to sanction the purchase of 80% of a Colombian exploration company, Sindicato de Petróleos Bolívar. This interest in Colombia was to develop quite rapidly. Ultramar decided to subscribe at par for the remaining shares. The capital of the company was increased over tenfold, and in due course the name changed to Compañía de Petróleos Bolívar. A consultant geologist, Dr Mueller-Carlson, was appointed to carry out the necessary survey work. It is interesting to note that a policy was taken out to insure Dr Mueller-Carlson's life for $25,000 against the risks of air travel. This would appear to be the first mention of flying in connection with Ultramar's activities, but unfortunately it is not clear whether the flying was for aerial survey work or as a means of transport.

The courtyard in CPSA's office in Caracas

Skidding a drilling rig across the Llanos in the 1940s

A seismic party with a recording truck in central Venezuela in the 1930s. Professor Illing is second from left

# THE EARLY YEARS 1935-40

The most important event for Ultramar in 1938 was the decision to merge Ultramar with Caracas Petroleum. Following a valuation of the assets of both companies, conducted largely by Professor Illing, Ultramar made an offer to the shareholders of Caracas Petroleum for the acquisition of the shares of their company in return for 670,375 Ultramar shares. In the event, 99.7% of Caracas shareholders accepted the offer and the two companies were merged in June 1938. This entirely logical event brought together two companies that had not only worked closely together during the previous three years, but which had common staff and shareholders. The merger also brought together their respective concession holdings, which now totalled 1,139,593 hectares. At the same time Ultramar's authorised capital was increased to £1 million. This paved the way for Ultramar to begin drilling operations in its own name.

Late in 1938, it was decided to form a new subsidiary company in Venezuela, designed to replace Caracas Petroleum Corporation and to take over direct control of Ultramar's interests and activities in South America. It was felt that a company incorporated under Venezuelan laws should oversee Ultramar's future development, and so Caracas Petroleum Sociedad Anónima (CPSA) came into being. The necessary arrangements for the formation of CPSA were handled by Alfred Meyer and Arthur Lawder. Continuity between Caracas Petroleum Corporation and CPSA was ensured by their having staff in common, notably the manager, Ebert Boylan. With respect to the latter, Kamen-Kaye has written: 'Mr Boylan, our manager, was himself a geologist, with rugged field experience, some of it in the mountains and foothills of eastern Venezuela. His personal background may have been as rugged as his experience. I would have classified our manager vaguely as a Texan. Actually this physical giant of a man, large in girth as he was great in height, had come from Joplin, Missouri, and was educated at the University of Oklahoma. Set on his big body was a large head, but boyish with its blue eyes and fair hair. The impression of boyishness above the shoulders, however, was of fleeting importance, no more. My attention was drawn instead to the fact that Boylan wore a broad-brimmed hat and chewed a cud of tobacco while seated enigmatically at his desk.

'After I had sat down, Boylan spat copiously into a brass cuspidor, released thereby for conversation, although not necessarily for a plethora of words. As I think about this greeting, I tend to believe that more may have been at issue for Boylan than a necessity to desalivate to begin communication. I theorize that he wished to signal, if his hat had not already done so for him, that he was a man of the plains. Having established his image he could enjoy the great surprise that ensued when it was discovered that Boylan was much more than a visitor might imagine. I had barely recovered from his external signals when I knew that I was dealing with a competitive intelligence. In fact, no more than a brief conversation was necessary to establish that he was a much better geologist than his disavowals might suggest. Sometimes Illing wrote technical letters to the Caracas office, but Boylan was essentially the chief geologist of the company. With my arrival he had four geologists for whom to lay out work in the field, and for whom to act as director in many other ways. At the same time, at Meyer's insistence, he kept a careful and efficient

37

The well head of Guayabo 2, the first oil discovery in the Mercedes Chain Lots

Seismic rig in the field in 1939

eye on all expenditures. In addition, he studied carefully, and reported to Meyer in great detail, all aspects of Venezuelan banking, the economy and politics.'

Once established, CPSA quickly took over the ownership of all the concessions held by Ultramar, as well as the assets of Caracas Petroleum Corporation. One of the first tasks faced by the new company was to look after Ultramar's interests in the drilling operations now being undertaken by Guárico Oilfields. This company, a wholly-owned subsidiary of Central Mining, was established late in 1937 primarily to undertake drilling operations in central Venezuela. As Central Mining was long established in oil production and owned drilling rigs, it was the logical agent to drill on the CPSA concessions. The first well in the State of Guárico, Guayabo 1, was drilled to a considerable depth, and this was followed by the even deeper Guayabo 2. The first ultimately proved to be dry, but the second found good oil shows at about 4,400 feet before being abandoned due to technical problems. This was the first discovery of light oil in the so-called Mercedes Chain Lots in the State of Guárico and prepared the way for the development of the Mercedes field. The true significance of this discovery was graphically expressed by Maurice Kamen-Kaye: 'Wells drilled in untried areas yield new and valuable data. Meyer, when informed that geologists were talking in this vein, observed wryly that he was not greatly interested in contributions to science. This was a good turn of phrase, but he had been instructed, nonetheless, that something considerably more important than unvarnished data had emerged from the drilling operation... In the privacy of the garden I took out of a jar a small piece of brownish sandstone, a chip of a

38

core sample that had been brought up to the floor of the drilling rig from nearly a mile below the surface. We crumbled the chip in the upturned lid of the jar, then added to it a little ether. As the ether evaporated, a dark brown oil ring appeared on the lid. That ring was oil from central Venezuela, the first known to exist there.'

The importance of the discovery was not lost on the mining shareholders, particularly Central Mining. This company naturally had a considerable interest in these activities, maintained both by their subsidiary Guárico Oilfields and by their long-term plan that any oil discoveries would be directly to the advantage of their refinery in Trinidad. With this in mind, Central Mining secured an option to participate with CPSA in future Guárico operations, and there was considerable interchange of staff between the two companies. It is possible that pressure from Central Mining led to a change in the structure of Ultramar's Board in December of 1938, when Consolidated Gold Fields, the Union Corporation and Central Mining nominated directors. Sir Cecil Rodwell from Consolidated Gold Fields, Rolland Beaumont from Central Mining and Cyrus Pott from the Union Corporation joined the Board, thereby ensuring that all the major mining shareholders were represented. Also in December of 1938 came the official notification that permission to deal in the shares of Ultramar on the London Stock Exchange had been granted, an important event fulfilling one of the initial aims behind Ultramar's foundation.

One of the more interesting events that occurred towards the end of the year was the opening of negotiations with Standard Oil of New Jersey concerning the joint development of certain concessions held by Ultramar. The discussions were instigated by Alfred Meyer with the help of Arthur Lawder in New York, and several preliminary meetings were arranged. The main discussions were held in London in January 1939, attended by Meyer on behalf of Ultramar and Holman and Piesse on behalf of Standard. It appears that, despite initial enthusiasm on both sides, no agreement could be made and there were no further meetings following Meyer's report to the Ultramar Board on 15 March 1939. However, this attempt to involve a larger and more experienced oil company as a partner in the development of the Mercedes field was a new approach for Ultramar, and one that anticipated future events.

During 1939 geological and geophysical survey work continued, both in Venezuela and in Colombia. Work began on the first well drilled in CPSA's own name, El Machete 1, which produced some oil shows but not enough to justify commercial development. The latter part of the year was overshadowed by the outbreak of World War II which event was to have serious and lasting consequences for Ultramar. One immediate effect was that the Annual General Meeting scheduled for 1939 did not take place, and was postponed, with the approval of the Board of Trade, until 1940. It was this 'lost' meeting which has led to Ultramar celebrating its 50th Anniversary at its 49th Annual General Meeting in 1985.

Alfred Meyer now realised that for a time he would have to see Ultramar through without much help from the London end. He looked around for a competent oil man to help and quickly found him. John Assheton (who preferred to be called Jim) joined the

George Higgins listens to the declaration
of war in September 1939 at the Casa Domke,
a German pension in Caracas where many of
the expatriate employees then lived

John Assheton

New York staff in November 1939 and brought a wealth of technical and international experience to the company. A tough, forceful man, Assheton had no time for slow thinkers. Starting as an office boy, he had risen through the ranks to become president of Mexican Eagle, owned jointly by Shell and the Whitehall Group, and one of the largest oil-producing companies in the world prior to the nationalisation of the oil business in Mexico. His contribution to Ultramar was to be immediate and long lasting. Like Meyer, he was fluent in Spanish and liked Latin Americans. It was a perfect fit. Assheton was appointed a director of Ultramar in 1940 and remained on the Board until his retirement in 1955.

The main problem brought on by the war concerned the financing of the company. The British Treasury imposed restrictions on the flow of currency abroad, and so Ultramar was no longer able to raise money and remit it to finance development in South America. Some remittances were permitted to be made to the end of 1939 with temporary finance obtained for this purpose, but further applications to the Treasury for sending funds abroad were refused. An application to increase the capital of the company was also refused. It quickly became clear that the war threatened not only future development plans but also the continued existence of Ultramar in its present form and a number of new avenues had to be explored. At first, Alfred Meyer attempted to negotiate a loan from foreign sources directly to CPSA, but this was not successful.

The most important development was the opening of negotiations between CPSA and the Texas Company (referred to henceforth as Texaco, its future name). Held in New York and Caracas, these talks continued into 1940.

Handled predominantly by Meyer, Assheton, and Morris Henry Frank, who had become Caracas Petroleum's General Counsel in New York, the result was a joint operating agreement for the development of the Mercedes fields in Guárico. Discussions were lengthy and laborious and were not helped when documents confirming Ultramar's legal ownership of many of the concessions were destroyed during one of the early air raids on London. A draft agreement between CPSA and the Tolima Land Company, a subsidiary of Texaco, was shown to the Board on 31 May 1940. However, detailed discussions continued during the summer, and it was not until August that shareholders were fully informed about the agreement.

The extraordinary nature of the partnership and the contrast between the two partners were well understood by Maurice Kamen-Kaye, who also appreciated the important role played by Professor Illing: 'I find now that before we embarked on that boat for New York a momentous agreement had been signed by Meyer and his associates. Under the terms of that agreement Caracas Petroleum entered into the most important partnership of its existence. A deciding factor for our new partner, one of the giants of the oil industry, was its late entry into Venezuela. In most other parts of the world, neighbouring Colombia included, our partner was entrenched, was a producer of oil, and also of vast aggregate profits. Before actual signing of the agreement there were visits to our areas by engineers, geologists and officers of the partner. On one such visit the Chairman himself came, an extraordinarily high officer for an occasion like this. With him came his senior vice president for international geological exploration and several other officers. Illing was the only representative of consequence for Caracas Petroleum. Of the two other members of the company present, I was one, to expedite the examination of core samples and allied subsurface geological data.

'The day belonged to Illing. His flair, his knowledge, his ability to clarify background, to organise and present geological thought, and his accomplished fluency, were absolutely impressive. His effect on the visitors could be felt, and may have played a part in the decision to appoint him adviser to the joint company that would come into being on signing of the agreement. I know of no other case of a giant company taking over the operation of a partnership but accepting the geological adviser of its very small partner as its own geological adviser for the operation. This appointment was a remarkable tribute to Illing, and a notable enhancement of his professional status.'.

The many changes which had occurred during the previous two years had one final effect. At an Extraordinary General Meeting held on 12 April 1940, the name of the company was changed from Ultramar Exploration Company Limited to Ultramar Company Limited, underlining the change to an investment holding company whose activities were carried out by subsidiaries. At the same meeting a proposal to increase the authorised capital to £1.25 million by the creation of 500,000 new shares was also approved. As it was to play a part in the Texaco negotiations, this increase in capital was given Treasury approval.

In the field in the early 1940s. *Left to right:* J. Assheton, A. Meyer, Bill Woodson
(Texaco manager), Ebert Boylan

# THE
# TEXACO
# PARTNERSHIP

3

In August of 1940, the Ultramar shareholders were sent a circular which explained for the first time the details of the agreement reached with Texaco for the joint development of the Mercedes field. As a first step, CPSA purchased the acreage of Guárico Oilfields, the Central Mining subsidiary that had drilled the first exploratory wells in the Mercedes area and which had an option for the joint development of the field. The purchase was financed with Ultramar shares. CPSA also bought Guárico Oilfields' drilling equipment, some of which remained stored in central Venezuela through the war years.

CPSA and Texaco formed two new companies, S.A. Petróleos Las Mercedes and S.A. Petrolera Manapire, to which CPSA and Texaco transferred a large part of their concessions in central Venezuela together with sufficient capital to allow for field work and drilling. Most of the cash was originally provided by Texaco while CPSA contributed more acreage. The concessions at this time owned by the Mercedes company totalled 521,967 acres, while the Manapire company had 1,243,680 acres. Although larger, the Manapire concessions were considered more speculative.

The impact of the agreement with Texaco was immeasurable and changed the character and direction of Ultramar. It ensured development of the central Venezuelan region, an area that had been largely ignored by other oil companies who had concentrated their efforts around Maracaibo in western Venezuela and Oficina in the eastern part of the country. Although the agreement was on a 50/50 basis, it was inevitable that Texaco had to carry much of the cost during the war and to take on the responsibility of operating. The Defence (Finance) Regulations in force from the outbreak of war made it impossible for any funds to be sent to Venezuela from England after the end of 1939, a position that did not change until 1943. Luckily, CPSA was beginning to receive considerable income from its royalty interests, and so it was able to make some contributions. However, Texaco seemed prepared to take on the lion's share and poured money, men and materials into the Venezuelan Llanos.

The development of Mercedes is a fascinating story, underlining the pioneering spirit that was an essential part of the oil business during this period. That part of the State of Guárico in which the Mercedes oil fields lay was for the most part an unpopulated bleak and featureless plain with few trees. In general, it was an uncompromising and

The typical landscape in the Llanos

unmapped landscape. There were few roads or villages, and almost everything required had to be brought into the area. It was a region known as the Llanos, typified by small and sparse chaparro trees, thin grass, lines of moriche palms at streams and broad, gravel-cemented mesas that gave no help to the geologist. To see below the surface of the Llanos, seismography was essential. The first task was the setting up of drilling camps, which have been described by Brotherhood in the previous chapter. The natural difficulties created by the landscape were compounded by the war in Europe, which resulted in shortages of equipment and materials, as well as delays in shipping. The kind of problems faced by the drilling crews are well described by Ed Gorham, a Texaco engineer, who soon became manager with the responsibility for setting up the Mercedes operation: 'Drilling equipment was much in demand and practically impossible for a non-producing company to acquire. Contract seismic parties could be put into the field but drilling rigs were a different story. CPSA had a British-made National Supply rig but there were no back-up spare parts. All its machinery, including the nuts and bolts, had been made to different specifications from those which we were used to in the U.S. After fighting a losing battle with this problem, it was decided to move in a Texaco rig from eastern Venezuela. A study showed that all the access roads and bridges were quite inadequate, and so the rig was brought up the Orinoco River by barges and then dragged across the Llanos by Athey wagons and Caterpillar tractors. This truly gargantuan task was achieved with inadequate transport equipment and by untrained personnel, but the rig arrived and drilled the first successful Mercedes well.'

It was clear from the start that Texaco was prepared to work closely with their much smaller partner, even though they were to all intents and purposes the operator. There was a considerable amount of geological cooperation between the two, with the first task being the evaluation of all the existing data, including the many hundreds of feet of core samples produced by the drilling operations of the past two years. These were stored in an old corrugated iron shed at Roblecito, the central camp for these operations, and, although old, many were found to have oil colouration and odour. At the same time, Texaco brought in the equipment to undertake a more detailed seismographic investigation designed to make the selection of drilling sites more accurate. Texaco went ahead and drilled the first well of the joint venture, Mercedes 1, on a site selected predominantly on the strength of their own seismographic evidence. When the well was found to be dry, the seismographic data was studied again, and more attention was paid to CPSA's geological evidence. New surveys were undertaken, with a close degree of cooperation between the partners. Illing, who had already established a good relationship with Fred Sealey, Texaco's senior geologist, sailed to Venezuela and joined the seismographers in the field. The two teams worked side by side and used all available evidence to select a drilling site for the Mercedes 2 well. This well was drilled during the autumn of 1941, and was successful in proving a series of gas and oil-bearing sands below 4,000 feet. The well was cased and production tested, giving 363 barrels of oil per day through a quarter inch choke and 744 barrels through a three-eighths inch choke. It was a 35 degree gravity good quality oil. These results not only proved, to everyone's relief, that there was a commercial basis to the new partnership, but also indicated a new area for oil production in Guárico, more than 100 miles west of the nearest established oilfield.

Although friendly, the relationship between the two partners remained unbalanced, with Texaco frequently threatening to bury CPSA beneath the weight of its technical expertise. Kamen-Kaye was well aware of CPSA's struggle for survival: 'These were years of intense professional endeavour. Most of this work the partner carried out with commendable thoroughness, to be expected of the local arm of a giant organisation. For a small company like ours, the effort had to be of another kind. Our company, as a financial equal in the partnership, had no alternative but to fashion for itself a distinctive geological initiative, if only for purposes of representation. To do nothing more than accept geological material supplied to us would have been to accept professional hegemony. Conscious of what was at stake, Illing battled against odds to ensure that imaginative and intuitive geological offerings of our side should balance the massive output of the other side. He himself contributed a brilliant general report in which he gathered together, unified, and improved, a number of concepts and insights that had emerged along the way. This, containing as it did some excellent presentations of fundamental geology, did much to keep us from being overpowered by the partner. The information that came from work done on our concession, the interplay of ideas among the geologists who dealt with that information, and the conclusions drawn, broke new ground for most of us. I believe that all who were involved became better geologists as a result.'

Following this initial success, an extensive drilling programme was planned with the aim of developing the Mercedes area as a commercial oil field. At this stage there was, of

Drilling at Mercedes in the 1940s

course, no outlet for the oil and so Mercedes 2 was capped to await future developments. However, the decision was made to make use of the gas, and therefore the well was dually completed, at considerable risk because of the lack of the necessary equipment. Inevitably a blow-out occurred, which ran for three days before the well was brought under control again, and linked to the separators and test tanks. The excitement of the discovery was intensified by its having been achieved in difficult terrain and with inadequate equipment.

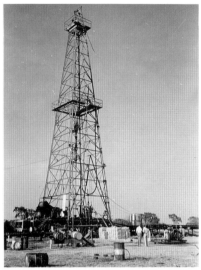

Rigs on the Mercedes field in the late 1940s

During 1942 more wells were drilled. Mercedes 3, located 1.5 miles east of the proven area, went down to 5,706 feet but was dry. Mercedes 4, about one mile west of the successful Mercedes 2 well, was drilled to 5,614 feet, finding oil and gas sands above and below the Cretaceous, and proving the potential of the sub-Cretaceous regions in this part of Venezuela. On test, this well produced 410 barrels per day through a quarter inch choke. A test well was also drilled on the Manapire concessions. This confirmed the existence of oil bearing formations, but the oil itself was heavy and oxidised. The drilling programme continued into 1943, although progress was increasingly hampered by shortages of equipment and materials. Mercedes 5 and Mercedes 6 were successfully production tested. However, in June 1943 the drilling programme came to a halt as the equipment problem had become acute. Although there was an increasing shortage of oil because of the demands of the war, and although fewer fields were being developed, the Mercedes field was still too new and too unproven to have any real muscle in the fight for supplies. The oil was proven, but there was no commercial production.

By the end of 1943 the situation began to improve, partly because additional finance had been raised in London and partly because there was increasing international interest in Guárico with a number of companies acquiring concessions adjacent to those held by the Mercedes company. Also important was Texaco's increasing commitment to the field in terms of both manpower and equipment, underlined by their decision to exercise certain additional options. At first, although the discovery of oil had justified the setting up of the partnership, there had been some doubts, expressed both by Texaco and CPSA technicians, as to whether there would be sufficient oil to justify the massive expenditure necessary for full-scale commercial production. Now these doubts seem to have been put aside, and a drilling programme was drawn up that was designed to ensure sufficient production. This programme was based on new seismographic and geological surveys,

47

Vahan Djalaloff, *right*, in the Texaco office in Caracas

Roughnecks at Mercedes in the 1940s

THE TEXACO PARTNERSHIP

which were in any case made necessary by the passing of a new Venezuelan Petroleum Law in 1943. This legislation increased taxes and royalties payable to the Venezuelan Government on all concessions converted under the new law, but it also gave a new 40-year life to all converted holdings. All the Mercedes and Manapire holdings were reassessed and certain of the less promising areas were discarded. The remaining concessions, which now totalled 974,000 acres, were converted under the new law. During the following months, extensive new concessions were also purchased, both by the joint companies and by CPSA in its own name, bringing the total to nearly 2,000,000 acres.

The drilling programme was intended to expand the proven area, but exploration was not neglected. During the latter part of 1943, Merst 1 was drilled as a wildcat but was abandoned. However, Mercedes 7, four miles west of Mercedes 6, was successful, yielding 370 barrels of oil per day on test. During 1944 two further wells were drilled, Mercedes 8, three miles southwest of Mercedes 7, and Mercedes 9, three-quarters of a mile beyond 8. Both of these were tested as oil producers in commercial quantities, but equally important perhaps in the long term were the gas deposits discovered at the same time. Under test these two wells produced a total of 4,500,000 cubic feet of gas per day. They were both completed as dual oil and gas producers. The string of Mercedes wells indicated the presence of oil in commercial quantities over a seven-mile belt across the Mercedes Chain Lots and a plan was then drawn up to drill fourteen more wells in this region, with the aim of discovering enough reserves to justify the costs of constructing an outlet. During this period a second exploratory well was also drilled in Manapire, about 25 miles southeast of the Mercedes discoveries. This was abandoned, having revealed geological data that caused some of the concessions held in the area to be discarded.

The steady expansion of field activities that took place between 1942 and 1945 inevitably brought about a dramatic increase in the demand for support facilities. The Mercedes region of Guárico was totally undeveloped and virtually uninhabited and so fully self-sufficient camps had to be established. When the war halted drilling in late 1939, CPSA had established a small camp at a quiet spot called Palacio, about ten miles away from what was to become the heart of the Mercedes field. Here, equipment used by Guárico Oilfields and CPSA had been stored, along with some prefabricated huts. A smaller, and far more rudimentary field camp had also been built where the first wells had actually been drilled, and it was here, at Roblecito, that the Mercedes company decided to build the first camp city. This was a massive operation, not, of course, entirely unfamiliar to Texaco who had built other camp cities from scratch, but for CPSA the scale and the expenditure seemed at first overwhelming. A number of CPSA employees observed with varying degrees of enthusiasm the rapid creation of a self-contained community out of nothing.

The complexity of the operation impressed Roy Brotherhood: 'All facilities had to be built for both the expatriate and native personnel. The latter had to be brought from considerable distances and therefore housed at the centre of the operations. Family housing was added to the bachelor quarters and mess hall with which we had started

49

At the Palacio camp in the 1940s          The remains of the Palacio camp,
                                                    photographed in 1958

operations. In turn this meant the establishment of commissaries for the supply of groceries, schools for children and health clinics. Eventually these clinics had to be expanded into complete hospital facilities. The purely operational requirements were staggering. Being so far removed from normal oilfield services, it was necessary to provide these for ourselves. To maintain the heavy drilling equipment, a warehouse with a comprehensive inventory was essential, but in order effectively to use this equipment it was necessary to have a well-equipped machine shop and garage services for the automotive fleet. Without utility services normally found in a town, none of this would have functioned and so electrical power had to be generated on a large scale, sewage and water systems had to be installed, telephone and radio links had to be established and operated, road networks were created through the bush and even an airstrip was required. The physical requirements were staggering and costly and added to this were the day to day problems connected with running the technical, operational and personnel sides of the business.'

Another report concentrated on the social life and the advantages of camp life for children: 'A spontaneous community spirit would spread in the entire area and social committees would be functioning, sports groups would be organised and study groups, music groups and theatre groups would be meeting regularly. Of course, the parties are legendary, and some of the costume balls could have competed anywhere. The ones who derived the greatest enjoyment of all were the children. The camps were like huge parks, but better. All traffic was carefully supervised and the children had an almost unlimited area to roam, trees to climb and games to play. Many complained bitterly when taken on vacation. Even after several years in Caracas, some parents found that their children's idea of a "real" vacation would be to return to the camp in the interior.'

Some of the social activities had a more constructive purpose. There was a large English community in Caracas, a community whose already close ties were strengthened

50

by the war. Feelings of impotence at being so far away from Europe prompted a number of supportive ventures, including a shop for war charities. Called El Rincón Británico (The British Corner), and situated near the heart of the city, this shop was organised by a group of expatriate wives. One of this group was Dorothy Kamen-Kaye who started as a supplier of home-made fudge, and then went on to write and produce, with the help of a Cuban-born American colleague, a bilingual cookbook. Much to Maurice Kamen-Kaye's relief, who had been persuaded in a weak moment to help underwrite any losses, *Buen Provecho* was an immediate success, the first printing selling out in three days. Subsequent editions produced considerable income for the war charities, and later for other Venezuelan causes and charities. The book is still in print today.

However, there were others who viewed the rapid growth of the camp, and the even more rapid growth of expenditure, with a certain amount of alarm. Notable among these was Vahan Djalaloff who had been associated with Alfred Meyer and Caracas Petroleum during the 1930s before bringing his great knowledge and experience to CPSA. Djalaloff's origins were in southern Russia, where as a young petroleum engineer, he had discovered the Grozny oil fields and in about 1910 became a millionaire. Forced to flee after the Russian Revolution, he had worked in oil fields in various parts of the world. Unlike his colleagues, he was able to distance himself from the excitement of the moment and place the Mercedes discovery in its true context. As Kamen-Kaye has written: 'Djalaloff dwelt constantly on the necessity for dispassionate consideration as we sat on our canvas chairs in his camp at night. Compared with flows in Anzoátegui to the east, our flow of oil would have to be called modest. The agony of no oil had passed, but now Djalaloff was to introduce the agony of possibly not enough oil, or of barely enough oil to compensate for the major outlay that lay ahead. He knew that the partnership would have to bear the expense of drilling more than a hundred wells. Expenses on this account were quite clear, but another type of expense went ill with him. As the pace of drilling increased, so the pace of elaboration of the camp increased. At the completion of each house, more costly than its predecessor, Djalaloff would wince as though in pain. Repeatedly he asked whether we knew how many barrels of oil we had to discover to pay for each of these houses.'

While Djalaloff's detached views and his wealth of experience endeared him to many of the younger CPSA staff, he was viewed with rather more caution by the senior managers. This extraordinary man, whose personality was a curious blend of Armenian and French, had effectively been isolated in Venezuela by the war, cut off from his family in Paris to whom he longed to return. He had, at the suggestion of Ebert Boylan, established the camp at Palacio and lived there in order to run it and look after the equipment stored there. He established there a solitary but adequate base, from where he could cast a somewhat jaundiced eye over extravagances at Roblecito. The simplicity of his camp and the frugality of his budget made Roblecito seem palatial and ostentatious. He knew that the drilling superintendents and the senior engineers lived like proconsuls, in houses built from the ground up. His isolation and his independent and sometimes bitter views inevitably kept him apart from his colleagues, who tended to regard

Aerial view of the Roblecito camp under construction

Djalaloff as 'a funny old Russian'. However, as Kamen-Kaye recalls, he did his best in his own way to overcome hostility: 'Djalaloff was aware of the impression he created and attempted to remove it by pragmatic means, the ones he knew best. Gradually the people in the big camp grew to be aware that Djalaloff, behind his barricade of consonants and syntactic inversions, was capable of offering astute views on questions of drilling and engineering. They also grew to admire his prowess at poker. He joined their games diffidently, and took part in them with mannerisms that seemed laughable in a game of such relentless aggression. Yet, at the end of games lasting sometimes until dawn they would find themselves leaner in the pocket a surprising number of times.' As soon as Paris was liberated, Djalaloff was on his way back to France where he rejoined his family. Once free from his period of confinement at Palacio, he was able from time to time to return to Caracas to play a more direct, and ultimately more useful and important role in the future development of Ultramar. He remained a factor in Ultramar's life through the 1950s and a teacher of oil technology to the next generation of Ultramar leaders - Nelson, Lorbeer and Bensen.

The Mercedes camp city expanded at a dramatic rate and eventually included over 200 houses of various types, a fully-staffed 22-bed hospital, a nine-hole golf course and

Aerial view of the Roblecito camp

many miles of roads. At its peak, which was reached in 1947, the camp housed 2,000 employees, including 150 expatriate British and Americans, many with their families. In addition to those directly involved in the company operations, there were the various contractors whose labour forces overflowed into the surrounding countryside and some of whom built their own temporary camps. Over a period of a very few years, a remote and inaccessible region of Venezuela was transformed into a self-contained industrial township, complete with all its support facilities. Today, forty years later, Roblecito is used as an army training centre.

Once the decision had been made to develop the Mercedes field, there followed naturally the problems of storage, distribution and transportation of the oil. Central Venezuela was a long way from any deep-water port and so various ways of transporting the oil to the coast were considered. The shortest distance to the sea was due north, but this route involved the building of a pipeline over the mountains which would have been a formidable and expensive feat of engineering. Another option was a pipeline south to the Orinoco, with a barge terminal for the onward shipment of the oil to existing port facilities in Ciudad Bolívar. The third possibility was to build a 157-mile pipeline northeast towards the Puerto La Cruz area, where a tanker terminal had already been

Typical staff house
at Roblecito

Typical senior staff
house at Roblecito

The original bachelor staff
camp at Roblecito

built to serve the pipelines coming from eastern Venezuela. After much study and agonising, the two partners chose the third option, deciding at the same time not to connect their pipeline to the terminal at Puerto La Cruz but instead to build their own port and tank installation at Pamatacual, a few miles further east. This major decision was made during the early months of 1945 and was induced by the imminent ending of the war in Europe. Materials and equipment were once again becoming more available and so the major constructional work involved in the pipeline and terminal could be undertaken.

During the war years, Venezuela and New York had become the centre of Ultramar's activities. Isolated by the war, the Ultramar Board of Directors in London was inevitably far less involved in the business than it had been before the war. Contact was maintained, partly by monthly progress reports and partly by occasional visits to Venezuela by Professor Illing and other technical people. There were links between London and New York, and at the end of 1943 Hermann Marx went to America on Ultramar business. However, the Board was mostly concerned with finance to support the expansion of the Mercedes field, and the reports at the wartime Annual General Meetings reflect this as well as keeping the shareholders generally informed of developments in the field. No real financing was possible until 1943, when permission was received from the Treasury for the purchase and transmission to Venezuela of $2,500,000. The money was raised by the issue of shares, increasing the capital to £1,500,000. The placement of the shares was underwritten by Morgan Grenfell, who had become Ultramar's merchant bank with their take-over of Cull and Company. Another share issue took place in 1944 and was again underwritten by Morgan Grenfell, designed to raise the finance for the purchase of a further $2,000,000 for transmission to Venezuela. This was followed by a third share issue, in 1945.

There was a reorganisation of the royalty business, with the setting up in 1941 of two separate royalty companies, Venezuelan Royalties and Anzoátegui Royalties, to which a large part of the royalty holdings were transferred. The shares of these royalty companies were used to a limited extent in the 1940s to compensate top staff members of CPSA. Ultramar was finding it difficult to hold good men at the salary levels to which it was reduced because of limited cash available. By giving bonuses in royalty company shares or allowing staff members to buy these shares at par value, an incentive was created. It was decided to wind up the Colombian company which had exhausted its capital. Only one of the concessions held was thought to be of potential value, but this required a high level of expenditure for further development and it was felt that the necessary finance would be impossible to obtain. However, an office was maintained in Bogotá until 1952 and Douglas Hubbard was in charge.

There were a number of directorial changes in London during the war. In 1940, Beaumont resigned, to be replaced by Alfred Brett from Central Mining. In 1943 Richard Thompson resigned to take up military duties and Herbert Oram, formerly of Cull and Company, replaced him. Thompson was to return after the war as an executive on the CPSA staff in Venezuela. In 1944, Brigadier Stokes became a director, replacing

The camp hospital
at Roblecito
under construction

Labourers' apartment
units at Roblecito

The warehouse
at Roblecito

J. O. May who resigned after four years on the Board. Stokes increased Central Mining's representation on Ultramar's Board to two directors which reflected their dominance over the other mining shareholders during this period. A number of CPSA staff were also employed by Central Mining's subsidiaries, and during the early years of the war, when activities in Venezuela were limited, some of these, including Roy Brotherhood and George Higgins, moved to Trinidad. It is perhaps significant that Central Mining's interest in Ultramar increased noticeably after the discovery of the Mercedes field, underlining their determination to ensure that any oil produced commercially would be available to their refinery in Trinidad.

On 15 April 1944, Walter Maclachlan died and Alfred Brett became Chairman of Ultramar. Maclachlan had been Chairman first of Orinoco Oilfields and then of Ultramar and had given the company a solid start during a difficult period. With the appointment of Brett, there came a distinct shift in emphasis for, whereas Maclachlan had been independent, Brett represented the interests of Central Mining, of which he was also a managing director. Central Mining was now in a dominant position on the Ultramar Board and so the stage was set for some of the unfortunate internecine Board squabbles that were to occur during the post-war period.

With Maclachlan's death in 1944, Ultramar made an application to the War Office for the temporary release of Campbell Nelson from the army. The latter had been the liquidator of Orinoco Oilfields and helped in the administration of Ultramar in its early years. Apparently, Ultramar was high priority with the Ministry of Fuel and Power, and the release was quickly granted for six months and subsequently extended. Although Ultramar still had no staff of its own, Nelson now became the manager of the London office.

Maurice Kamen-Kaye and Arnold Lorbeer in the field in 1947

# POST-WAR PROBLEMS 4

In the immediate aftermath of the Second World War, Ultramar had two clear objectives. The first was to bring the proven oil fields in central Venezuela into commercial production as quickly as possible to earn revenue, and the second was to explore and develop the other concessions held by the Mercedes and the Manapire companies. The fulfilment of these objectives demanded an ever-increasing commitment of time, manpower and, above all, money, and so the story of the immediate post-war years is essentially Ultramar's struggle to raise sufficient finance to maintain CPSA's 50% share in the joint venture with Texaco. It must be remembered that, apart from the royalty companies whose revenues were increasing steadily, reaching over $1 million by 1948, Ultramar and its subsidiaries still had no regular income, and only the prospect of one when the oil could be marketed.

The major operational problem was an outlet for the oil. The decision had been made, as related earlier, to build a pipeline 157 miles northeast to the coast near Puerto La Cruz. This choice was no doubt influenced by the so-called Guárico Road which the oil industry had obligated itself to build when it received concession grants in the State of Guárico in 1945 and 1946. Central Venezuela had suddenly become a 'hot' area and Creole (Esso), Shell, Atlantic (Arco), Phillips, Socony (Mobil), Sinclair and others had taken land grants. The concessions were initially serviced largely by the main gravel road between Caracas and Ciudad Bolívar which passed through the towns of El Sombrero, Las Mercedes, Chaguaramas, Valle de la Pascua and El Tigre. A more direct road from central Venezuela to the eastern ports was necessary and the oil industry undertook to build a gravel road from El Sombrero, via Chaguaramas, to a point on the coast near Guanta. All the major oil companies operating in central Venezuela participated in the cost of construction of this road on the basis of a complicated formula involving size of concessions, distance from the road and distance to the port area. The Mercedes company, by reason of its large holdings in the region through which the road ran, was a major participant. Creole was the construction operator. The route traversed by the Guárico Road was underdeveloped and barren. Maurice Kamen-Kaye used it shortly after its completion:

'Early in 1947 I travelled the road, from its beginning, not many miles north of Djalaloff's camp (Palacio), to its end at the coast. The road was gravelled, but in the

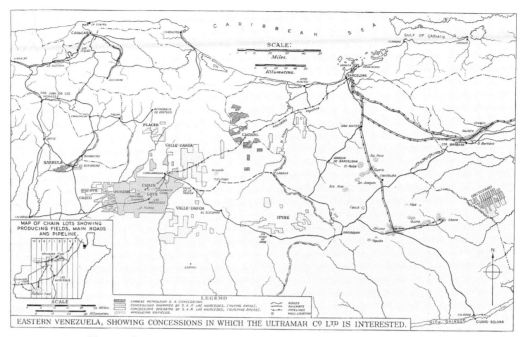

Venezuelan concessions in which Ultramar had an interest in 1949

interests of economy otherwise rudimentary, its engineering accomplished mainly by the bulldozing of trenches along the sides. There were large numbers of corrugated iron culverts to keep the low places dry and two or three important bridges were built over some nearly perennially large streams. The road ran completely in low country, mostly through spiny scrub growing on clay, with here and there some patches of higher gravel and sand, or patches of salt-covered flat. Stores with gasoline pumps had not yet materialised, and the whole route was remarkably lonely. A rare piece of shade, or a clump of some of the taller weeds, especially if in bloom, would be reason enough to stop.'

The material for the pipeline and the Pamatacual terminal was ordered early in 1947 and the contract for construction was awarded to Williams Bros. The line was to have an initial capacity of 64,000 barrels per day, which could be easily increased to 100,000 barrels per day by additional pumping facilities. The pipeline followed the right of way established by the new Guárico Road for a large part of the distance and this eased the construction task. Construction was rapid and generally well carried out and was completed in May 1948. The line was later also used by Atlantic Refining to ship oil from two fields in Guárico and to a lesser extent by two other companies.

Drilling continued in the Mercedes field so that there would be sufficient producing wells to make the pipeline, and the whole operation, economic. By mid 1946, 27 wells had been drilled on the Chain Lots, of which 17 had been completed as oil wells, 5 as gas

60

Pipeline construction in 1947

The start of the
pipeline at Roblecito

Venezuela, 1947. *Top left:* Djalaloff at the Palacio camp, *top right:* road building at Las Mercedes, *centre left, right to left:* Djalaloff, Dorothy Kamen-Kaye, Maurice Kamen-Kaye and Roy Brotherhood at the Palacio camp, *centre right, left to right:* Dan Bailey, Roy Brotherhood, Maurice Kamen-Kaye, Ed Hesketh, *bottom left:* CPSA geologist W. G. Poole at a Mercedes drilling rig wells, and 5 had been abandoned. By 1948 the total number drilled reached 45. Exploration drilling had also taken place in other areas, notably to the west in Punzón-Grico, to the north in Camaz-Placer in partnership with Atlantic Refining, and to the south in Palacio. Of these regions, Palacio was to prove to be the most important field, with 23 producing oil wells drilled by 1948. Elsewhere, detailed exploration was identifying fields that were to be important during the next decade, for example Ipire and Guavinita.

The development of the Mercedes fields and the building of the pipeline inevitably began to bring about changes that affected CPSA in Venezuela and in New York, as well as Ultramar in London. The CPSA office in Caracas in 1946 was an old single storey building with an enclosed courtyard, facing a narrow street in a pleasant part of the town. The Texaco office was nearby, so the two companies naturally lived and worked closely together. In those days, Caracas still had the flavour of an old Spanish colonial city, for the dramatic changes that were to occur with the growth of the economy during the late 1940s and early 1950s were still in the future. Streets were narrow and cobbled, flanked by attractively old-fashioned one or two storey buildings, many of which still echoed the leisurely elegance of an earlier era. All this was to change shortly and both Texaco and CPSA moved into an office building in the centre of Caracas.

As equipment became increasingly available after the war, so too did staff. Richard Thompson was released from the RAF but, instead of returning to London, he now went to Venezuela to take over the job of assistant manager. Roy Brotherhood returned from Trinidad to rejoin the hard core of Boylan, Kamen-Kaye, Jim Marsh and Djalaloff, and a number of new technical staff were recruited. These included John Caston, a 1946 graduate of the Royal School of Mines, who later transferred to Texaco and eventually became head of all their Venezuelan operations, and Ed Hesketh, who eventually succeeded Kamen-Kaye as Ultramar's chief geologist.

CPSA also had the services of John May, formerly chief physicist with Trinidad Leaseholds. Soon after the war John May had joined Professor Illing in a new venture, Petroleum Scientific Services Limited, which had been formed by Illing in London in 1946 as an independent consultancy. The offices at 15 Throgmorton Avenue previously used by Meyer were taken over by Petroleum Scientific Services, along with Miss Marks, who now became Illing's personal assistant. Initially the new company worked almost exclusively for Ultramar, establishing a relationship that was to last for several decades, and when John May joined the partnership he was sent out to Venezuela to monitor the start-up of Mercedes production, arriving in Caracas in 1947. The new company did not alter Illing's close relationship with Ultramar. He was still a significant shareholder, his monthly progress reports were still sent to the Board in London, and in March 1946 he was given a new five-year contract, which included an option to purchase a further 20,000 Ultramar shares.

New blood was also being injected into the New York office, notably in the form of Arnold Lorbeer who joined CPSA in October 1945. Assheton and Lawder were by now in their mid sixties, while Meyer was even older, and so there was an increasing need to create a new generation of younger management. Lorbeer was introduced to CPSA by Morris Henry Frank, who was General Counsel for CPSA and a close friend of Meyer. Following a lunch together, Frank took Lorbeer to meet Meyer, Assheton and Lawder. The meeting led on to dinner, and by the next morning Lorbeer had become a part of Ultramar, a decision that was to play a vital role in the company's subsequent development over the next three decades. Born in London to German-American parents, Lorbeer was educated in Europe and America before joining General Motors in Argentina in 1936. Fluent in German and Spanish, he had travelled extensively in South America and in 1940 he was called into the U.S. Army. In 1943 he was transferred to OSS, the predecessor of the CIA, to train guerilla warfare military units to harass the Germans behind their lines. In 1944 he was parachuted into France and Italy to organise maquis and partisan groups, remaining behind the lines until the German surrender. Having been persuaded to place his talents with Ultramar rather than return to General Motors, Lorbeer then spent much of the next two years in Venezuela, where Djalaloff turned him into an oil man, teaching him all he knew about drilling and production.

Events in Venezuela and New York were echoed in London. Freed from some of the financial and currency restrictions imposed by the war, the Board had to concern itself immediately with the problem of raising sufficient money to enable the development of Mercedes to proceed at full speed. From December 1945 Ultramar was given permission by the Treasury to purchase $500,000 per month for transmission to Venezuela, and so the main problem was raising the necessary finance. At first, money was borrowed from the four mining companies and Morgan Grenfell, who supplied a series of short-term loans between February 1946 and March 1947 that totalled over £1 million. A new issue of 531,773 ten shilling shares at 72 shillings and 6 pence in June 1946 was also quickly swallowed up, but further finance was still required for the continuing drilling and development programme. Marx and Meyer attempted to raise finance in New York, but without much success.

The continuing demands for money made the mining companies increasingly restive about their investment, which was highlighted by the uneven composition of the Ultramar Board. The majority of the directors were representatives of the four shareholding mining companies, who did not hesitate to pass on to their own companies for analysis all the reports and documents circulated to the Ultramar Board. As the mining companies held only about 50% of the stock at this time, it was felt by many that the directors were not always acting in the best interests of Ultramar and all its shareholders. Even the Chairman, Alfred Brett, seemed to see Ultramar only as a potential supplier of crude oil to Central Mining's Pointe à Pierre refinery in Trinidad. Other directors felt that the crude oil should go to the highest bidder, and the most obvious candidate was likely to be Texaco. In the event, negotiations were started in December 1947 and a contract was subsequently signed in April 1948 with Texaco for the sale of all Mercedes production up to 60,000 barrels per day for a minimum period of five years. However, even before this deal was concluded, tensions in London had brought about a number of Board changes. Micklem and Pott resigned, to be replaced by

The Barbula well, one of the two wells drilled
by CPSA in its own name in 1947

The Palacio camp in the late 1940s

R. D. Peters and Lord Harlech, while Walter Maclachlan's son Malcolm was appointed instead of Rodwell. However, the most important change occurred in August 1946 when ill-health forced Brett to give up the chairmanship. At the same time Brigadier Stokes resigned, which left each of the four mining companies with one representative on the Board.

The need for an independent Chairman of Ultramar was now critical, a need that had already been a matter of discussion between Meyer, Assheton, Marx and Illing through the early months of 1946. It is probably no coincidence that at this time Meyer appointed Hermann Marx as his alternate on the Board, presumably to try to create some sort of balance. This move certainly took everyone by surprise for neither Marx, nor his partner Cull, had ever before accepted a directorship in the company.

On 21 August 1946, the Board appointed Sir Edwin Herbert as a director, and the same day he became the new Chairman. Herbert had been suggested by Brendan Bracken, the Chairman of Union Corporation, who had been Minister of Information during the war. Herbert had been Chief Censor at the Ministry for which services he had been knighted. A senior partner of the solicitors Sydney Morse and Company and later President of the Law Society, Herbert was later to serve the Government in many ways and received a life peerage in 1963, taking the title Lord Tangley. For Ultramar, the significance of Sir Edwin Herbert cannot be overstated, for he was a man with important contacts in the City who enjoyed the independence of mind, integrity and the forceful personality required of a good chairman. Above all, he believed in the future of Ultramar and was therefore able to bring his experience and tenacity to help the company through the difficult years that lay ahead.

The Board was further strengthened in January 1947 by the appointment of Campbell Nelson. A partner of Hugh Limebeer and Company since 1935, Nelson had been involved with Ultramar's business from the beginning. This now took up 70% of his time. He had frequently attended Board meetings and, apart from service in the British Army, he had handled Ultramar's administration, accounts and share transfers almost without interruption. This close involvement with Ultramar had brought Nelson into contact with Meyer, Illing, Marx and Assheton as well as with the Board, and so he was a natural choice for appointment as the first executive director based in London. From 1947 he began to travel abroad for Ultramar, visiting Venezuela and New York. It became clear that Lorbeer and Nelson were to form the backbone of a new management generation when they effectively swapped jobs for a six-month period between September 1947 and March 1948. Lorbeer came to London while Nelson went to Venezuela, a process that ensured that both gained experience in field and financial management.

It is important to remember that, despite the scale of its overseas operations, Ultramar still had no U.K. staff of its own. The company had taken over the lease of some offices in Broad Street Place in 1947 but Limebeer's, who had their offices in the same building, still handled all their administrative affairs. In the absence of Nelson, another Limebeer partner, Gilbert Potier, looked after Ultramar's interests. During 1948 this was to change. Ultramar began to develop a more independent existence with the introduction of a company pension scheme along with other aspects of conventional commercial life.

The most urgent problem facing the reconstructed Board was the shortage of finance, a situation that was becoming increasingly desperate as the costs in Venezuela soared while the mining companies were unwilling to increase their loans. Sir Edwin Herbert tackled the problem in his usual forthright manner and in January 1947 he opened negotiations with the Finance Corporation for Industry (FCI). This organisation, a government-sponsored merchant bank, had been set up to help British industry recover in the immediate aftermath of the war. Herbert and a representative of Morgan Grenfell had discussions with the general manager of FCI. At first it did not look too hopeful for it had not been the policy of FCI either to support enterprises based overseas or those which had other means of raising finance, but in the event Herbert and Morgan Grenfell must have made a persuasive team for in March the FCI agreed to advance up to £2 million, provided Morgan Grenfell and the four mining groups guaranteed an equal amount.

Ultramar's finances were soon put on an even keel. The FCI loaned £1.75 million for five years at 3.5% interest rate and a public issue of a new 4.5% unsecured loan stock 1947/57 was made with a total value of £3.5 million, underwritten by Morgan Grenfell and the mining companies. The *Financial Times* commented at the time: '... the loan stock, unsecured, is scarcely a gilt edged investment ... not a common method of raising funds, but appropriate for an oil company still in a comparatively early stage of development.'

The financial arrangements were based upon the Mercedes field being brought

Gas separator in the Mercedes field in the late 1940s

quickly into production, with enough output to give a good return and enable the loans to be repaid. With the dramatic expansion of activity during 1947 and 1948, it seemed likely that the necessary targets could be met. However, it was acknowledged that the production capacity of the completed wells could not be predicted with any real accuracy and a cautionary note was sounded in the Directors' Report of June 1947: 'Las Mercedes has been handicapped by lack of sufficient storage capacity and until the tank farm in the field has been installed, adequate production tests over a considerable period of the various completed wells are not possible. Sufficient oil reserves have been established to justify the expectation of an initial production of at least 25,000 barrels per day by the time the pipeline is ready.' The figure of 25,000 barrels per day, which was to haunt Ultramar in the not so distant future, seemed a reasonable estimate at the time, based on the scientific and production data available.

With the finances under control, and the field development progressing rapidly, Ultramar and its subsidiaries seemed set for success. Confidence had been increased by the new Board and the building of a young management team, and with the completion of the pipeline and the first oil sales in July of 1948, the future looked promising. One of those to respond to the new spirit of confidence was Professor Illing, who had always felt overshadowed by the might of Texaco. He longed to operate independently, partly to prove his own geological theories and partly to establish CPSA as an oil company in its own right. By the terms of the agreement with Texaco, CPSA was free to drill on its own, but only on concessions located outside those included in the partnership. Some suitable locations were available and so, overcoming the reluctance of some of their colleagues, Illing and others pushed for a drilling venture in CPSA's name. Two wells were drilled, but the results were disappointing. As Alfred Meyer so aptly stated, 'we made a contribution to science'.

Work on the Mercedes concessions gathered momentum and during the early months of 1948, wells were being completed at the rate of two per week, and many wells took only three weeks from spudding to completion. By the time the first oil entered the pipeline on 18 June 1948, some 83 wells had been completed, and so it was widely believed that the target of 25,000 barrels per day, rising to 35,000 by mid 1949, could be met. However, it was not to be. Indeed, events over the next year were such, and so unforeseen, that Ultramar very nearly foundered.

The problem concerned the production target, which turned out to have been too optimistic. The actual production during the first year barely exceeded 15,000 barrels per day. By June 1949, 120 wells were in operation, but on average each well was only producing 131 barrels per day. To most technicians the shortfall came as a complete surprise, although there had been one or two warning voices prior to the production start-up. One of the more notable was John May: 'When I first arrived at Mercedes, the field was being prepared for the start of production at a forecast rate of, I think, 25,000 barrels per day. This seemed unduly optimistic to me and, in order to get a feel for the probable sustainable rate, I decided to check the reserve estimates which had not been revised for some time and were based on the results of a handful of scattered wells and poor quality seismic. Not being a geologist, I teamed up with Joe Wilson of Texaco (he, by the way, had once kept more or less tame ocelots as house pets in Caracas). Eventually we reported developed reserves at around half the value of earlier estimates and, although we discussed other classes of probable and possible reserves, the report led to much alarm and despondency in some quarters; so much so that Meyer refused to speak to me the next time we met. This estrangement did not last very long after Illing and Brotherhood had interpreted the small print.'

For the Board, the news was potentially disastrous, for all the loans had been structured on the basis of income at the estimated rate of production. There were a number of rather stormy meetings, and Illing was called back to London to explain to the Board the reasons for the bad performance.

The main reason seemed to have been poor completion techniques. Many of the wells had been drilled and completed long before they could be properly production tested, owing to the lack of storage facilities. When these wells were opened up, in some cases two or three years after completion, it was discovered that the completion techniques had been inadequate. In the Mercedes field there were gas and water sands in very close proximity to the oil-bearing sands and cementation was important. Because of poor equipment, inexperienced personnel and improper technique, the cementation was in many cases inadequate and gas and water soon infiltrated. Some wells had to be shut down altogether, while others, pending recompletion, operated on a reduced choke. At the time, the loss of production due to poor completions was estimated at 4,000 barrels per day.

Roger Ffoulkes-Jones (known as Gogs), who was assistant production foreman with Mercedes at that time, commented on other problems: 'Equipment and material was difficult to obtain. Much of it was army surplus, some of poor quality and not entirely suitable for the use to which it had been put. The gathering lines were of "invasion pipe", very thin walled and clamped together with steel couplings and rubber gaskets. The pipe was quick to lay but gave constant trouble. The main pipeline from Roblecito to Pamatacual, although built with standard pipe, had some early problems and a small plane had to fly the line each day to check for leaks. The flow and gathering lines were walked daily by men on donkeys or on foot. Some storage tanks leaked after a few months' service. It was a continual headache to keep production flowing. The rather primitive airfield had an unsurfaced landing strip and, more often than not, cows and goats had to be driven away before a plane could land. Native labour was completely inexperienced, having been recruited from villages and small holdings in the area. The men had little or no education and were unfamiliar with anything mechanical which made it very hard on the expatriate supervisors who had to be on call 24 hours a day and seven days a week. Native labour could only report trouble, not rectify it. Our best workmen were European immigrants, mainly Italians and Spaniards, of whom fortunately there was a large influx in the late 1940s. There were no telephones, but a fairly efficient radio system connected all pump and gathering stations to the field office which in turn had radio communication with head office in Caracas.'

A second vexing problem was the nature of the reservoirs. The Palacio field lived up to its expectations, producing about 5,000 barrels per day, but in the Mercedes field it was found that some of the sands contained thin laminations of impermeable material that had the effect of splitting the sand into a number of separate reservoirs which greatly reduced the rate of flow. It was generally accepted that the impermeable laminations were an unusual phenomenon that could not easily have been anticipated during drilling.

Matters cannot have been helped by the political situation in Venezuela. The country experienced a period of considerable instability between 1945 and 1948. Many of the expatriate technicians commented on the problems of working against a background of almost continuous social and political upheaval. One of the few direct consequences were the road blocks which the National Guard threw up on the access highways. It could lead to long delays while papers were checked and often compulsory vaccinations were carried out under unsanitary conditions. Those working in the oil fields were often relatively unaware of the various dramas, but for those in Caracas the danger was sometimes more obvious. John May, describing the Avila Hotel where he stayed in 1947, wrote: 'Conveniently near to what was then the centre of the business community, it was still little bothered by the incessant hooting of motorists or the occasional shooting by revolutionaries.' Others were unable to take so detached a view, when they were unwilling spectators to revolution. Roy Brotherhood was thrust by circumstances into one such situation: 'Before long we found ourselves in the midst of a revolution which broke out on October 18, 1945. It was an exciting time, but not particularly dangerous to foreigners who minded their own business. There were a couple of incidents which still stand out in my mind. One concerned the office, which at that time was a typical Spanish-type patio house located near one of the army barracks which was in revolt. A group of "loyal" mounted soldiers came up the street and were ordered to dismount. In doing so in pathetic style, many of the rifles which they were carrying were accidentally fired, some in the direction of our office. Shortly afterwards a plane flew overhead from which hand grenades were being thrown at the barracks. Many landed frighteningly close to our building. The other memory is of a more personal nature and concerned the birth of our first child. The raising of a family had to be timed to fit in with the three-year contracts which were prevalent then so as not to have a babe in arms during the three-month long leave. For different reasons it would appear that this one was not well timed in view of the revolution. We were advised by the obstetrician that the hospitals would probably be full of wounded even if we could get to one and therefore we should have ready a do-it-yourself kit and a white flag to fly on the car. Fortunately the kit was not required since we were able to get into a hospital, although I did have trouble seeing the newborn on October 25th when the new revolutionary President was visiting his hospitalised wounded. One good thing did happen to us because of the revolution; we were able to rent a delightful house in a desirable suburb from a General who was on the losing side and had to stay out of Caracas for quite a while.'

In 1945 the political climate was radically altered when the Acción Democrática (AD) party led by Rómulo Betancourt came to power. This Government, with its broad left-wing stance, was led by men who had witnessed the nationalisation of the Mexican oil industry in 1938 when in exile in that country, and so it was no surprise that the nationalisation of Venezuela's oil resources formed one of the planks in their election manifesto. Under the Minister of Energy, Juan Pablo Pérez Alfonzo, the Government's share of foreign oil profits was raised to 50%. Thus while Betancourt and his successor, Rómulo Gallegos, were in power many of the oil companies reduced their investment or halted development in Venezuela. Central Mining, the only company with oil experience among Ultramar's backers, may well have seen the Acción Democrática Government as another nail in the coffin of their Venezuelan investment. In the event the AD Government was short lived, for in November 1948 the country reverted to a military junta, first led by Major Carlos Delgado Chalbaud and then, following his assassination in 1950, by Major Marcos Pérez Jiménez. The military takeover was not unwelcome to some of the larger international oil companies. Under Jiménez' strict rule, the economy recovered, and overseas companies looked forward again to a period of stability.

The shortfall in Mercedes production in the year following the initial start-up was six million barrels, which effectively reduced the Mercedes company's revenue by about $12 million after the payment of Venezuelan taxes. The immediate consequence was that in the second half of 1948 CPSA was unable to meet its half share of the Mercedes costs, the penalty for which was a reduction of its percentage interest. Despite their reputation

En route to Venezuela in 1948 on board the SS *Santa Rosa. Left to right, standing:*
Harold Dunmore, James Assheton, a Steward, Sir Edwin Herbert, Alfred Meyer
*seated:* Lady Herbert, Mrs Ralph Sandt (the Meyers' daughter), Georgette Meyer

for toughness, Texaco were very cooperative. Funds were provided in advance of the obligations under the oil sales agreement to help CPSA. However, it was agreed that if CPSA could not meet its share of the costs by June 1950, then Texaco would become the majority shareholder in Mercedes. In fact, Ultramar's financial problems were now so serious that the possibility of there still being any holding in Mercedes by that date seemed questionable. In September 1949 the Directors' Report included the following sentence: 'It should be stressed that unless the company is able to obtain adequate readjustments of its existing obligations towards Finance Corporation for Industry and the Loan Stockholders, and is successful in its efforts to raise new finance, there is small prospect of the company being able to continue its business and maintain its investment in Mercedes.'

The drastic shortage of cash was driving the company into a corner. In order to increase its revenue and start paying off the loans, it had to continue drilling to build up the production levels, but in order to drill more wells it needed more finance. The mining companies were extremely disturbed by developments and at Board meetings through the winter of 1948/49 their representative directors were continually asking for more

71

Morris H. Frank, CPSA's General Counsel in New York

Campbell Nelson, photographed in 1952

Sir Edwin Herbert,
photographed in 1956

A drilling rig arrives to aid the Mercedes expansion programme

information about the production problems. During this period two distinct camps began to emerge. On the one side were Central Mining and the Union Corporation, who had begun to lose faith in the whole operation, while on the other were Consolidated Gold Fields and Selection Trust who took a longer view and believed that the company had a future.

Sir Edwin Herbert, Campbell Nelson and the overseas management clearly believed that the company could and should be saved and were confident that it could be reasonably successful in the long term, given adequate support at this critical juncture. The stage was set for a dramatic showdown.

Matters came to a head during the summer of 1949. From 1 July the directors agreed to waive their fees. Later in the same month, Board committees were set up to study the finance problem and the relationship with Texaco. In August a refinancing scheme prepared by a Board committee was rejected by Morgan Grenfell. At the same time it was reported that there was little hope of meeting the interest payment due on the FCI loan and that there was no finance available to buy forward the dollars required for transmission to Venezuela. As the situation worsened, so the number of Board meetings steadily increased. Between 22 July and 27 September of 1949, a total of 21 meetings were held, most of which were attended by all the directors or their alternates. Even Meyer was present for some of the August and September meetings. At a meeting on 14 September, the Chairman laid out in a concise manner the options facing the company. There were three choices: one, that exploration and development should continue and the necessary funds raised; two, that the company's business be limited to the Mercedes and Palacio fields and that work should effectively come to a standstill until money was raised; and three, that the company should be liquidated and its assets sold. Matters were delayed until a full Board could meet on 16 September when the Chairman made it clear

The expanded Roblecito camp

that he backed the first option, but the directors representing Central Mining and the Union Corporation stated that '...the provision of further finance is not justified except for such sums as the creditors of the company may consider necessary to conserve the value of the security for their loans.' An impasse had been reached and so the Chairman called for a vote. The resolution that the company should pursue the first option was carried 6-2, the dissenting directors withdrew from the meeting and a few days later Lord Harlech and Alfred Brett resigned from the Board. Immediately Central Mining and the Union Corporation began to dump their Ultramar shares onto an already depressed market, and Cazenoves were faced with the difficult task of placing their shares at around three shillings per share. Consolidated Gold Fields and Morgan Grenfell came to the rescue and bought a large block, while both Illing and Meyer also greatly increased their personal shareholdings. This board room row compounded the difficulties facing Ultramar, but at least it cleared the air. The Chairman was now able to concentrate on the problem of raising the necessary finance knowing that he had the full support of his Board members.

In late October, a postponement of the interest due on the FCI loan was negotiated, and a week later a Board committee of Herbert, Nelson and Peters was formed to study ways of raising additional finance. Meyer returned to New York and opened

74

negotiations with Texaco, the bankers J. P. Morgan and Company and others to explore the possibility of forming a new group that would buy a one-third interest in the Mercedes company. This came to nothing for on 29 November the Board was able to inform the stockholders of a scheme to raise the £1 million required to restore the position of equality between CPSA and Texaco and it was approved by all interested parties in January 1950.

The new scheme drew its finance from three sources. First, the FCI, whose Chairman Lord Bruce of Melbourne proved to be a loyal and powerful friend to Ultramar, advanced a further £250,000, bringing their total loan to £2 million. Interest of 3.5% was to be payable by the end of September 1951 although a contingency plan allowed for a postponement of three years and a delay of five years on the redemption date of September 1952. Second, £750,000 of Convertible Debenture Stock 1960 was issued and third, the £3.5 million Unsecured Loan Stock was renegotiated and made redeemable not later than 1962, with the interest from June 1949 to May 1954 waived. With this finance, Ultramar was able to remit funds to CPSA and effectively restore CPSA's equality with its partner in the Mercedes company. The crisis was over, but the cost had been considerable. Ultramar was to be saddled with a heavy burden of debt for the next ten years, and the row with the mining companies had badly damaged the reputation of the company. However, the feeling was one of relief that the company had survived. In his report to the Annual General Meeting held in July 1950 the Chairman underlined this feeling: 'After our last Annual Meeting in September 1949, there were some pessimists who predicted that we should never meet at an Annual General Meeting again. They took the view that when you next came to this room you would find in the Chair the grim figure of a liquidator. This has not happened ...'

The view from the CPSA guest house at Pamatacual

# THE 1950s: CONSOLIDATION AND EXPANSION 5

The Chairman, Sir Edwin Herbert, could now tell the Ultramar shareholders that the company had 'turned the corner'. The decade of the fifties was to be a period of consolidation. The financial condition of Ultramar gradually improved as oil production began to meet its targets, new fields were discovered or extended in Venezuela and, encouraged by a young management team supported by a stable Board, the company began to diversify into other oil-producing countries, notably Canada and the United States.

In the early 1950s, efforts were concentrated on paying off short-term loans, the heavy burden of debt that was a legacy from the upheavals and problems of the late 1940s. The revenue from the sales of crude oil was now sufficient to enable the Mercedes company to repay CPSA and Texaco the considerable advances it had received over the years. For example, in 1950 the income from oil sales totalled $18,000,000, an increase of $5,500,000 over the previous year. CPSA sent most of its share of the revenue back to Ultramar, who in turn began to repay the Finance Corporation for Industry loan and the holders of the Convertible Debenture and Loan Stocks. At its peak in January of 1950, Ultramar's debt totalled £6,250,000, but by June of the following year this had already been reduced by over £1,250,000. By the due date of 30 September 1952, the entire FCI loan had been repaid.

In 1956 Ultramar was able to celebrate its 21st birthday, secure in the knowledge that all the short-term debts had been repaid. The holders of the Convertible Debenture and Loan Stock had all been paid off and the company was able to face the future with a degree of equanimity. The royalty companies had played their part in the turnaround and were a lucrative source of income that increased year by year. For example, in 1954 the income from this source was $1,273,000, after payment of heavy Venezuelan taxes. Stability had also been helped by CPSA itself being able to raise finance. At the end of 1955 the greatly improved trading position had enabled CPSA to negotiate independently a loan of $3,600,000 from the First National City Bank and J. P. Morgan in New York, to be repaid over the following four years.

One of the effects of CPSA's repayments to Ultramar was the creation of an exchange surplus. When Ultramar had made the advances to CPSA, the currency exchange rate had averaged about $3.90 to the pound, but the repayments were made at a rate of about

Tank farm at Oritupano

$2.80 to the pound. This meant that each repayment of $1,000,000 created an exchange surplus of about £100,000 on the Ultramar books. By 1956 the Capital Reserve formed from the exchange surplus was considerable and so in that year Ultramar made its first Capital Surplus Distribution to shareholders of one shilling per ten shilling share. A number of similar distributions followed. These effectively took the place of dividends. The unexpected bonus of the exchange surplus caused tax problems and so, on the advice of the eminent tax counsel Millard Tucker, Ultramar changed its Memorandum of Association in 1953. This made it clear that Ultramar was an investment company, and therefore the exchange surpluses did not count as taxable profits.

Thus, after a little over twenty years, Ultramar had finally repaid the optimism of its original backers. Alfred Meyer and those mining companies who had stood by Ultramar through thick and thin were able to enjoy, at last, the fruits of their investment. It had been a long and hard struggle.

During the 1950s there was steady expansion of Ultramar's oil and gas interests in

# THE 1950s: CONSOLIDATION AND EXPANSION

Venezuela. The existing Mercedes fields were further developed, the Vengref refinery at Puerto La Cruz was tied into the Mercedes pipeline, and new field tank batteries were completed. In 1951 the M-210 field was discovered, and this soon proved to be the most prolific of the Mercedes fields, compensating for the decline of the older areas. In what Sir Edwin Herbert referred to as 'one of life's little ironies', the M-210 field was discovered under the airstrip in the Mercedes camp area. During the building of the camp, the geologists had been asked to select a suitable site for the airfield that they could guarantee would be as far as possible from any actual or potential producing area. They were wrong, but Herbert did not seem particularly surprised. He said: 'It is perhaps a sound role for a layman to regard both the hopes and fears of the experts with a certain stoical scepticism until they have been tested by the only instrument that can give a final answer, I mean the drill.' Fortunately a commercial air service was now available at a nearby village, and so the loss of the airstrip did not pose a serious problem. The discovery naturally caused some wry comments at the camp, and there were fears, fortunately unfounded, that the golf course, built also over a so-called 'non-productive' area, might be threatened.

By the mid 1950s, Mercedes was becoming a conventional oilfield operation. Existing wells were produced to their best advantage, whether by natural flow, by gas lift, water drive, pumping or by other artificial forms of lifting. Extension wells were drilled to exploit known reservoirs and at the same time there was a continuous pattern of exploration drilling to find new reservoirs. In 1952 the original target figure of 25,000 barrels per day was finally reached and production then stayed at about this level until 1958 when an all-time high of over 28,500 barrels per day was attained.

Record production figures were made possible by a new series of joint ventures. In 1954 a pooling agreement was made between Mercedes and the Atlantic Refining Company over the Oritupano area in eastern Venezuela. Each company contributed equal acreage, shared expenses and split the proceeds, with Atlantic acting as the operator. Output was limited until 1957 when a major field with multiple sands was discovered in the southwest part of the region. This field, Oritu 14, was rapidly developed and within two years 54 wells were producing over 7,000 barrels per day. The same year, the Oritupano pipeline was built, an 18.5 mile 14 inch line linking the field with the eastern Venezuelan pipeline system that ran into the terminal at Puerto La Cruz.

In 1956 Mercedes negotiated a three-year farmout option with Shell, covering 514,378 acres in the Unare-Zurón area to the northeast of the Chain Lots. This was potentially attractive to the Mercedes company because the area could be operated from the camp at Roblecito, and the oil pipeline to Pamatacual crossed the Unare-Zurón concession area.

Apart from producing and selling crude oil, CPSA also began to obtain a considerable income from the sale of natural gas. From the earliest days of field exploration many wells had been completed as dual oil and gas producers. This foresighted decision enabled the Mercedes company to conclude two gas sale agreements with the Venezuelan Atlantic Refining Company in 1952 and 1954. In the first year, income from gas sales

Gas compressor in the Mercedes field

Drilling at Oritupano in the 1950s

Tankers at Puerto La Cruz, where the pipeline from the Oritupano field
joined the existing network

totalled $29,000, a figure that increased dramatically over the next few years, reaching $2,375,000 by 1958. This income reflected a sale of over 80 million cubic feet of gas per day. The gas was stripped of some liquids at the Mercedes field tank batteries and then pipelined to compressors. At the main station, there were seven large compressors and two smaller ones. This station, the largest in Venezuela at the time, fed the gas, compressed to 1,000 psi, into a main transmission pipeline which in turn piped the gas to power stations in Caracas and other industrial centres. During this period demand for gas from both domestic and commercial users was increasing dramatically, thanks in part to the booming economy that had been built up by the Pérez Jiménez Government. By the terms of the 1954 gas agreement, Mercedes had ownership of the gas gathering lines and the compressor station, with a half interest in the pipeline from the station to an ancillary plant at Lechoso. However the main transmission line from Lechoso to Caracas and the other centres remained under the control of the Atlantic Refining Company. Mercedes paid Atlantic $2,000,000 for the equipment they purchased but in return they earned more for the gas. The investment was clearly worthwhile for, in addition to the increased revenue it created, it gave Mercedes more flexibility in the field.

Conditions in the central Venezuelan fields could still be somewhat hazardous. Frank Kay, a British petroleum engineer, moved to the Roblecito camp with his family in 1954. His job was to keep the Caracas office informed about how field operations were progressing, a task that involved him in frequent trips by car over all kinds of roads and tracks. He wrote:

'Within and near the camp quite smooth, durable roads had been made by mixing in heavy oil with the sandy soil and letting the graded mixture dry out in the sun - the so-called "black top" roads. Elsewhere it was gravel, anything from pea size to large rocks. During the dry season, roughly November to March, reddish dust was the common hazard in driving and one soon became adept in winding up car windows as soon as you saw another vehicle, with its cloud of dust, approaching and even then a fair amount seeped into the car. Meeting a bus or truck increased the hazard as you always had to bargain on something following it. Gravel road travel was punishing to the underside of vehicles and to minimise the risk of petrol tanks being holed by flying stones it was the practice to fit a light metal sheeting around them. Even so accidents could happen so it was quite a good idea to carry chewing gum with you so a temporary repair could be made - useful on radiators too. A blow from a large boulder could bend your track rod, so it was not silly at all to follow the old timer's practice of carrying a length of rope in the boot. Tie one end to the bend, the other to a convenient tree (if you could find one) and back away therefrom in jerks in attempts to effect straightening. The wet season settled the dust situation all right but brought other problems as the matrix of the gravel was often red clay, very slippery and prone to being the base of mud holes in low spots. One soon learnt to avoid slipping off the crest of a graded road for you might have to wait a long long time before anyone came by to pull you out of the roadside ditch. I well remember being rescued one night by a local cattle truck in such circumstances - I was towed out of trouble (my lights had failed) and then some forty kilometres to the local

Venezuelan concessions in which Ultramar had an interest in 1956

Gas pumping station in the Mercedes field

town and round about it until a garage was found that was open. I had the utmost difficulty in getting my benefactor to accept the local equivalent of £2 for his trouble! All Roblecitonians carried wire tow ropes as a matter of course.'

Apart from these 'natural' hazards, travellers had also to contend with problems that were essentially man-made. The Pérez Jiménez Government encouraged investment in Venezuela by overseas companies but the harsh nature of the regime inevitably produced a degree of internal unrest which increased steadily through the 1950s. Oil companies were usually able to keep themselves well away from the political arena, but those employees working in the field could not fail to come across the somewhat repressive methods of political and social control practised by the police and the militia. Frank Kay again: 'Everybody within the country had to carry an identity document (cédula) at all times and that had to be produced on demand from anyone in authority. In the case of foreigners, that document was an internal passport, a small booklet of eight pages containing such details as an official head and shoulders photograph of you holding your cédula number, your thumb print, basic physical characteristics, profession and address. When a foreign visitor wished to make a field visit from Caracas, he was well advised to carry this cédula with him as a safety precaution against any identity and/or arms check he might encounter on his trip into the interior. Such checks could occur anywhere, especially in times of political tension, but most frequently on the road that crossed the jungle-covered mountains south of Caracas on its way to the Mercedes camp. The mountains were a hot bed for anti-government guerilla activity, so from a number of strong points therein the military conducted operations against the guerillas. Thus cédula, personal baggage and vehicle checks at barrier points were commonplace, whilst similar requests (the Venezuelan soldier appearing to be far more polite than his brother in the Guardia Nacional) could be made at any place where a patrol might decide to slide out of the jungle and halt your progress.'

The Mercedes camp at Roblecito was by this time fully operational, and there were many facilities to make life bearable for the expatriate families based there. The centre of social life was the club with tennis courts, bowling alley and golf course. Films were shown three evenings a week, and there was a steady stream of barbecues and parties, with a number of well-established annual events, including the children's Christmas party, the New Year's party and the Western party - the last-named being remembered by many for its fancy dress and beard-growing competitions. Until 1953 the one vital facility that was missing was a swimming pool.

The pool had been promised by management if production reached 25,000 barrels per day, a figure which always seemed out of reach. Finally, one day when CPSA/Texaco 'brass' were visiting Roblecito, the production target was pinned down to a specific week and, lo and behold, it was met. The pool was built. Dr Dao, the highly respected chief medical officer, was not very pleased, but he decided that it was preferable to have a swimming pool over which he would have some control than for the staff to continue to swim in nearby water holes. The pool was a great success.

The schools at the camp catered for children up to the age of ten, but after that they were usually sent away to schools in the United States or Barbados, or even England. The most difficult period was the long summer vacation when all the children returned to the camp, testing to the limit their mothers' organisational powers. A change from camp life could be obtained either by a visit to Caracas, or by a weekend stay at the camp at the Pamatacual loading facility. This was a somewhat epic trip, involving hours of driving along the Guárico Road that was built along the pipeline, but for Frank Kay and many others it provided a welcome treat. 'The setting of the camp was magnificent, the housing set on the hillside above a land-locked bay in which there was a small island rising out of the deep blue sea. Bathing from the island was excellent and the port captain was most accommodating in arranging for his tanker loading tug to take parties to and from the island in the course of the vessel's more essential duties. It was a tiring business (eight hours) to get to this paradise from the Mercedes camp, but the added bonus of real shops in nearby Puerto La Cruz made it well worthwhile.'

Far from the camp, Ultramar began to develop problems of a different and potentially more damaging type. The ripples caused by the crisis of 1948/9 had not entirely died down, and these now took a new shape. There was an increasing divergence of opinion between Professor Illing and the geologists of the Mercedes company over the best method of exploration in central Venezuela. The close relationship that Illing had established with Texaco through his friendship with Fred Sealey had begun to fade. A hint of the brewing storm was given in Illing's report, printed in the Ultramar Annual Report in May 1952. 'So far exploration has been largely guided by seismic work and in the early stages this tool gave excellent results in the exploration and development of the Mercedes field. However, the prospects brought to light by seismic work are gradually

84

A tanker at Pamatacual, the Mercedes port terminal

being exhausted, and if exploration is to proceed other methods of survey must be applied. Opinion is by no means unanimous at this stage on this difficult problem, or on the new type of survey that could most usefully be introduced. However, the writer considers that the core hole surveys represent a promising avenue.'

In fact, Illing had come to be a firm and uncompromising advocate of core drilling and he finally persuaded the Mercedes partners to support an expensive core drilling programme in the Chain Lots and the Valle Dakoa area to prove his point. Illing's son Leslie, a geologist who had worked for Trinidad Leaseholds in the Bahamas and for Shell in Mexico before joining CPSA in 1952, summed up the results: 'Techniques involving extensive shallow drilling to identifiable geological markers were developed and applied to the area between the Mercedes fields and Palacio to the south. However, lack of early success led Texaco to abandon the method. Illing believed that the new approach had not been given fair trial. He continued to monitor the development of the fields that had been discovered, but distanced himself from the exploration policies adopted by Texaco.'

As the dispute developed, most of the top management of Ultramar and CPSA took Texaco's side. In his Chairman's statement in July 1953 Herbert said: '... it was thought better for a consistent policy to be followed, based on the views of one group rather than to follow a policy based upon a compromise between their views and those of Professor Illing.' The relationship between Illing and the Chairman had been deteriorating since 1950 and in the end they were barely on speaking terms. There were a number of factors

85

The golf course at the Roblecito camp

that influenced this, including a degree of personal rivalry. However, more important had been the initial shortfall in production from the Mercedes field which had done little to increase Illing's standing in the Chairman's eyes. In addition, Illing's consultancy work for Shell in Mexico and his close association with Central Mining, whose abrupt withdrawal had caused so many difficulties, may have coloured Herbert's judgment. Assheton firmly endorsed Herbert's views, with the result that Professor Illing's active involvement with the exploration and development of Mercedes ceased in 1953.

The swimming pool at the Roblecito camp

Roger Ffoulkes-Jones (Gogs), Margaret Thompson, Richard Thompson, and
Mildred Forrester, British Vice-Consul, by the Caracas-Valencia train

However, Illing's company, now renamed V. C. Illing & Partners (the partners then being Drs May and Hobson) was to continue to work for Ultramar in a consultative capacity for many years to come.

The geological controversy had its lighter side. At one point, in an attempt to resolve the problem, Texaco and CPSA agreed on an arbitrator, an elderly renowned American geologist. After studying the data in New York, this gentleman proceeded to London to talk to Illing and inspect his records. Unfortunately, in those days London was subject to prolonged periods of smog, a dense yellowish vapour which hugged the ground and often made vision and travel impossible. The arbitrator was marooned at the Hyde Park Hotel in London for five days and then returned home in disgust. Each morning he started out in a limousine for Illing's offices in Surrey but got fog-bound each day and never saw the Professor. His conclusion was that 'the Lord obviously did not intend for him to give a verdict'.

Many careers were affected by this geological feud. Maurice Kamen-Kaye, CPSA's chief geologist, faced with an irreconcilable difference of geological opinion between himself and his erstwhile mentor, Professor Illing, resigned. Boylan left his job as manager of the Caracas office, a job he had held since the earliest days of Ultramar, and was replaced by Richard Thompson, while Leslie Illing left CPSA after less than a year and took a job with Shell in Calgary. Another to be affected, but in a different way, was

Three Ultramar Chairmen in Uniform
in World War II
*Top left:* Arnold Lorbeer, U.S. Army,
*top right:* Campbell Nelson, British
Army, *left:* Lloyd Bensen, U.S. Navy

Lloyd Bensen who had joined CPSA in New York as, to use his own phrase, 'a high class office boy'. After three years in the U.S. Navy during World War II, Bensen had studied a variety of subjects at Tulane University in New Orleans and New York University, finishing up with a degree in geology. In 1950 he was sent by the university placement bureau to an interview with the Caracas Vaseline (sic) Company, where he was hired, largely on the basis of instinct, by the office manager, Hazel Lee. Attached to Jim Assheton, Bensen spent the early part of his business life with CPSA making a fully detailed record of all Illing's comments before, during and after each well was drilled. Assheton was assembling the evidence with which he was later to convict Illing, at least in his own mind, and Bensen was his reluctant apprentice. He was rescued from this thankless task by Lorbeer who, recognising his potential, sent him to Venezuela to be trained by Djalaloff. As he recalls, this training was highly valuable, and covered both predictable and unexpected areas of expertise: 'While I was in Venezuela I was really being trained. I learned how to drill wells, and worked with the geologists, went on field trips, argued with the land owners to get the rights to drill on their property, I even went out and laid pipeline. It was a marvellous experience for a young fellow with a small company. I guess even Djalaloff was impressed because he gave me a strong recommendation. He said, "well, he seems to work hard and besides he's got one real strong point, he's one hell of a poker player".' From this base, Bensen was quickly able to take his place in the new management team.

The view of Caracas from the CPSA office in the 1950s

The Illing story should not be closed without a positive word. Professor Illing was undoubtedly a prime factor in the early history of Ultramar. Along with Alfred Meyer and Hermann Marx, he must be regarded as one of its founders. Lorbeer remembers him as a 'well-read, charming, very intelligent man and also an indefatigable worker'.

The Ultramar staff changes were part of a broader pattern of development that was beginning to determine Ultramar's future. The old guard was phasing out from day to day management, replaced by a new and younger generation led by Nelson in London, Lorbeer, Brotherhood and Bensen in New York and Thompson, Ffoulkes-Jones and Hesketh in Caracas. There were Board changes as well. Malcolm Maclachlan resigned, to be replaced by R. H. A. Neuschild from Consolidated Gold Fields. Sir Kenneth Mealing from Morgan Grenfell joined the Board in 1950 and when Assheton retired in 1955, he was replaced by Arnold Lorbeer, who had taken over from Meyer as chief executive of operations in 1954. In 1957, R. D. Peters died, following a long illness, and with his death came the withdrawal from Ultramar of Selection Trust, the mining group he had represented. From this date onwards only Consolidated Gold Fields remained from the original four mining sponsors of Ultramar, and they have continued to support the company to the present day. Herbert Oram, another director who had stood by Ultramar during its most difficult period, died in 1959. His death severed a link with another of the company's founders, the merchant bankers Cull and Company.

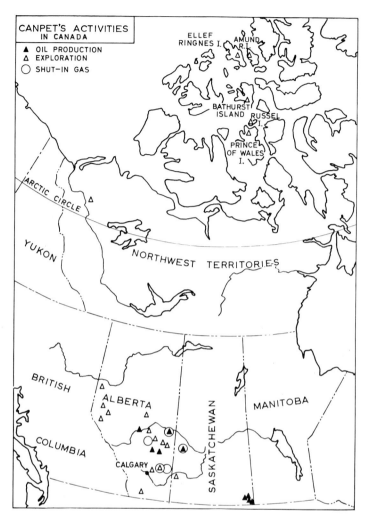

Ultramar's interests in Canada in 1959

The Board was now firmly committed to Ultramar's interests, and so was at least partly responsive to the idea put forward by some of the younger managers that the company should begin to diversify into areas outside Venezuela. Forecasts of future production and potential reserves in areas held by CPSA and the Mercedes company in Venezuela seemed to indicate a profitable future, and so there were some who thought that to look elsewhere was both unnecessary and extravagant. Management, on the other hand, felt that there were a number of clouds hanging over the future of Venezuela, and so in the long term it would be a good idea to start building up producing companies elsewhere. In the end it was the new management that carried the day, with an ambition to turn Ultramar from a reasonably secure but unexciting Venezuelan oil producer into a lively and adventurous company.

90

David Gilbert, Frank Prebble and Frank Kay in Calgary during the early 1950s

In 1952, Ultramar began to investigate western Canada, where recent reef oil discoveries had aroused great interest. Keith Cullingham, a British geologist and a graduate of the Royal School of Mines, was hired by CPSA to work in Venezuela in May of 1952. At the last minute he was asked to detour through Calgary, to report on the local situation before continuing his journey to Venezuela. The early days in Canada are best described by Cullingham himself.

'I arrived in Calgary towards the end of May 1952 as a visitor but Calgary remained home until January 1973. The city in 1952 had a population of less than 150,000 people. The mountain ranges were at your back door and it was very much a cattle and meat packing centre, but there was no mistaking there was an oil boom. The fever was everywhere with stories of fresh discoveries, some apocryphal, every day. Office accommodation was very tight as was a place to live. There was enthusiasm and a desire to share the excitement, a confidence in the future, a great deal of help available and a land position that gave opportunity to start small and grow big. New companies and new mergers were announced every day, and joint operations and joint interests were the general rule. It did not take long to write a report of recommendation. Presumably this helped to clarify the position and firm any inclination already there, as instructions came that I should remain in Calgary and we would begin operations. Douglas Hubbard, a banker and entrepreneur in Colombia, had come to Calgary, from Bogotá, to arrange the formalities of company organisation and financing. We opened our first office with Doug, myself and a part-time secretary in the Burns Building, not really in the centre of activity but the only space available at all suitable. I started to obtain reports, maps and any information that would be useful in acquiring a sound basic knowledge on which to evaluate proposals and eventually build our own plays. Doug arranged lawyers, bankers, financing, organisational and company formation agreements and regulations. We both

Exploration and production
sites in western Canada
during the 1950s, including *top
left* Eagle Lake (with Hank
Laska) and *top right* Mannville
(with Frank Prebble)

visited, made contacts, lunched and it seems frequently partied, including our first Calgary Stampede. The liquor laws in Alberta at that time were archaic. Bars were separate for men and women, and then only served beer or a very popular mixture of beer and tomato juice called Redeye. However, clubs flourished and most companies had their own bars or at least bottles. Despite difficulties and distractions, we progressed and by August 1952 Canpet Exploration Limited was incorporated, a wholly owned subsidiary of CPSA with 50,000 shares of stock and with equity capital of Can.$500,000. The object of the company was to participate in a limited way in oil and gas exploration and development in western Canada. With the company formed, work could concentrate on the main objective, evaluating the potential and eventually entering into oil and gas plays. This meant regional mapping over horizons from the Devonian to upper Cretaceous, evaluating techniques, keeping abreast of the very active drilling programme and the results, and continual meetings. In the spring of 1953, Roy Brotherhood came to direct operations, but he returned to Venezuela in June 1954, and I was left as manager.' Douglas Hubbard had retired earlier, his job done.

Exploration in Canada was just as difficult as in Venezuela. The terrain was equally inhospitable, with the additional problem of the cold. With his considerable experience in the field in Venezuela, Roy Brotherhood was well able to appreciate both the similarities and differences: 'In Venezuela when you were driving anywhere you always carried a rope but in Canada you always had a sleeping bag in the car because if you went off the road you weren't going to walk anywhere. You couldn't sit in your car and run the engine as you would probably kill yourself. The only thing to do was to sit tight until someone came along, and then hope to find a gas station that could thaw you out with a cup of coffee.' Negotiations with farmers over drilling leases could also be both complex and, at times, dramatic, owing to the nature of Canadian mineral rights legislation. Frank Prebble, who joined in 1954 as land and office manager, had to develop a rapid familiarity with the techniques involved: 'In the early days most mineral rights were freehold, at least until the Provinces were formed when they were generally reserved for the Crown. So if you wanted to carry out exploratory drilling you had to get hold of the leases. If they were held by the government it was straightforward but often they were owned by the farmer. He wouldn't come to you so you had to get a lawyer and go out to him to negotiate. It was a slow process while you gained his confidence but the negotiating was often enjoyable. There were various types of lease. Sometimes the farmer would get a royalty of about 12.5% of any revenue produced, sometimes he would sell the rights outright on a block by block basis, and sometimes, if he didn't actually own the rights, all he would get would be Can.$2,000 to cover a month's disturbance on his land. There were always occasions when the farmer was reluctant but they usually came round because $2,000 was still quite a sum out on the Prairies. I do remember one time when we were trying to negotiate with two brothers who wouldn't talk at all, so we went out there and were met by this farmer who took out his rifle and started shooting. We had to call the Mounties but it was all sorted out in the end.'

Canpet Exploration operated in Canada on a limited scale until the end of 1956. By

93

Keith Cullingham, Manager in Calgary

that time it had participated in 21 wells, thirteen of which were completed as oil producers and two as gas. It had interests in 433,601 acres, and had just started oil production with a total of 4,108 barrels at the end of 1956. In most of the wells Canpet had only a small interest, the largest percentage being in two gas wells at Sheerness, Alberta. Canpet had also begun to look for development prospects in Saskatchewan. After four years it was safe to say that the Canadian venture had been moderately successful. The level of activity had increased year by year, supported by CPSA out of its own resources, and the future looked quite promising. However, it was apparent that Canpet would not be able to undertake any significant expansion or development without a large increase in investment.

In order to raise the necessary capital, Gold Fields American Development Company Limited, a subsidiary of Consolidated Gold Fields, and Apex Trinidad Oilfields Limited, a company originally formed by Walter Maclachlan, each agreed to take a 25% interest in Canpet in return for an investment of Can.$500,000 each. The result of this cash injection was immediate. Canpet acquired proven acreage in Alberta and exploratory lands in Saskatchewan and the drilling activity increased, along with the success ratio. The company moved to new offices in Calgary's main business area, and new staff were recruited, including Hans Garde-Hansen, Phil Clarke, Dennis Russell, and Hank Laska, all of whom later played roles in other Ultramar operations. By the end of 1957, Canpet had an interest in 36 producing oil wells and seven gas wells. The pattern of progress was continued during 1958 and 1959, with the high point being the exploratory success in the Eureka-Dodsland area of Saskatchewan, a region that was later to become the backbone of Ultramar's oil production in western Canada. At the beginning, this concession was held by another company, but with the help of Morris Henry Frank, General Counsel in New York, Canpet was able to buy out this company. Lloyd Bensen

94

Drilling in Orange Grove, Texas, in 1959

has remarked that 'the field was discovered by litigation rather than drilling'. At the end of 1958 a new company, Ultramar Canada Limited, was formed, and CPSA's interest in Canpet was transferred to it. This new wholly owned holding company was a reflection of Ultramar's increasing involvement in all aspects of oil production and marketing in Canada.

Events in Canada encouraged further diversification, and so in September 1957 another wholly owned Ultramar subsidiary was formed, Caracas Petroleum U.S. Limited (CPUS), with an office in the Southland Center in Dallas, Texas. Lloyd Bensen who, following his stint in Venezuela with Djalaloff, had worked in New York under the wing of Lorbeer and Frank and in Canada with Cullingham, was initially given the task of managing the American operation. Bensen was by now a well rounded oilman, with plenty of field experience and an excellent poker player to boot, thanks largely to his time with Djalaloff. In Dallas he was joined by William Robinson, an English graduate of Imperial College with the degree of Doctor of Geology. Robinson had originally been recruited by Professor Illing to help him with his consultancy work for the Mexican Government by acting as his representative. When Illing's contact lost political power there was less call for a representative, and so Robinson was easily persuaded to cross the border to Dallas. The Texas venture was initially quite small, and it was operated from the start jointly with the Texkan Oil Company, a privately owned enterprise. In the first year, seventeen wells were drilled, of which three were completed as gas producers and two as oil. The first year's output totalled 6,430 barrels of oil, a figure that rose rapidly in succeeding years. Most of the wells were drilled in Brooks County and Hidalgo

95

*Above and below:* A workover rig drilling in Matagorda County, Texas, in 1959 in partnership
with Texkan. The drilling crews were from Princeton University on vacation employment

County, near the Mexican border, while others were further north in Matagorda
County. Bensen was in a good position to observe the contrast between the drilling
methods used by the Texkan/CPUS operation and those of the nationalised oil industry
in Mexico: 'We were punching down and completing holes every 28 days, using a small
rig and small crew, while across the border I could see a huge rig with masses of people
making no real progress. Once I saw they had all gone off to have a party with

politicians, musicians and their camp followers, leaving the drill running. It got firmly stuck involving months of delay.'

At the same time, another venture was started in Louisiana. This was a farmout in which CPUS was to be the operator on lands held by two mining companies, St. Joseph's Lead and Cerro de Pasco. Bensen was again the manager and five deep wells were drilled, all of which turned out to be dry. After about a year the Louisiana acreage was abandoned.

The push to diversify had largely come from Lorbeer and, although the results were not spectacular, it had been justified by events in Venezuela and elsewhere. By the mid 1950s there had been a serious danger of complacency overtaking Ultramar's original pioneering spirit, with too great a reliance on one producing area and one marketing system. Lorbeer was worried about all the eggs being in one basket, and so he worked hard to change the attitude, supported by Nelson in London and increasingly by Bensen and Brotherhood in New York. From 1956 support came from a number of directions, some not welcome. The political situation in Venezuela was proving to be increasingly unstable as popular discontent grew with the Pérez Jiménez Government. Disturbances and riots were fairly common from 1956 onwards and, although these rarely had any direct effect on oil company Caracas offices or production areas, they were often witnessed by the local staff and visitors from New York or London.

Francisco Reyes, who at that time was chief accountant in the Caracas office, wrote: 'Caracas Petroleum occupied part of the fourth floor of the Karam Building situated approximately five blocks away from Palacio Miraflores, where the Venezuelan President and his Cabinet officers were located. We, therefore, had a good view of all the political turmoils which took place on a regular basis. Towards the latter part of the year 1956, the strikes and manifestations intensified and on one particular day things really got out of hand. The crowd was furious and were turning over and burning cars on the streets and destroying display windows of the stores in the Avenida Urdaneta. At approximately 11:00 a.m. they invaded a restaurant located on the ground floor in our building and set it afire. This restaurant was owned by one of Pérez Jiménez' ministers. Everyone in the building was, of course, very scared and I approached our general manager suggesting that our employees be sent home to avoid any problems. He immediately agreed with this recommendation. I suggested that he as well as the remaining foreign personnel should also do likewise because one never knows how a furious crowd may react against foreigners. He looked at me straight for a few seconds and stated, "Mr Reyes, we Englishmen die with our boots on." I replied, "Well, sir, not being an Englishman and since I am not wearing boots, I shall join the local staff and also go home."

'I returned to my office and started to clear my desk and made certain that our valuable documents were placed in the safe. Having done this, I dashed down the stairs to the basement garage to use the rear exit because the front door was still blocked by the angry mob destroying the restaurant. As I was dashing towards the exit, someone in the crowd caught my eye. I turned back to get a better look and to my surprise it was our general manager. He had beaten me to the basement parking lot. I walked over to him and asked: "What happened, sir, no boots either?" He didn't answer me and from the look he gave me I understood that I had better not say anything further, so I left.'

The fairly constant atmosphere of upheaval was disquieting but it inevitably had its more amusing moments, one of which was recorded by Ffoulkes-Jones, assistant manager in Caracas from 1956: 'There was a large house near our apartment in Los Palos Grandes in which lived a family believed by the authorities to be anti-government and communist. It was thought illegal meetings were being held there and it was being carefully watched by the Guardia Nacional. Between our flat and the house was a vacant lot with very tall grass and scrub. One night the Guardia heard something moving in the grass and, believing it to be the communists, they let fire with their automatic machine guns, hitting the walls of our building. There was great excitement, with army trucks and jeeps arriving with reinforcements. After about an hour all was quiet again and we went to bed. Next morning we saw the Guardia Nacional removing a dead horse from the vacant lot.'

The situation continued to deteriorate and then in January 1958 the Government of Pérez Jiménez was overthrown. For some days mobs roamed the streets, burning cars and looting the shops. Tear gas was freely used and those not directly involved stayed at home, while normal commercial life ground to a halt, hindered in any case by the general strike which had been called. Early one morning, Pérez Jiménez fled the country, flying from La Carlota airport in his private plane and taking with him a personal fortune alleged to total several hundred million dollars. Admiral Larazabal took control of the country until Betancourt could return from exile and take up the reins of government again in the name of Acción Democrática. Arnold Lorbeer witnessed the revolution as he was visiting the Caracas office at the time with John Owers, and subsequently sent a graphic report of the events to the Chairman in London: 'The general strike was scheduled for noon, 21 January. In Caracas, the strike was an instantaneous success. Thompson, Owers and I were about to sit down to lunch at the Athletic Club, a few doors from our office, when promptly at noon bedlam broke loose. It seemed that every automobile horn in Caracas began to sound off (it is against the law to blow your horn in Caracas). The entire affair had the aspects of a carnival for about ten to fifteen minutes, but then it began to get rough. Street gangs stopped buses and used them to block traffic. The rebels used Molotoff cocktails to burn buses and cars.

'The police used machetes and tear gas bombs as well as firing directly into the crowds. Street gangs fought back with bricks, bottles and small arms. A tear gas bomb exploded in the lobby of our office building and stopped work for that day. A curfew was decreed from 6 p.m. to 5 a.m. and army units replaced the police that evening. Owers, Kay (who had come in from the field) and I were staying at the Avila Hotel and there was considerable shooting around there, probably because the house of one of Pérez Jiménez' chief collaborators was within a few hundred yards of the hotel. It was my first experience sitting on a hotel veranda sipping martinis while people were sniping at each other on the streets around us. Pérez Jiménez and a half dozen or so of his closest collaborators fled. The news spread through Caracas during the morning hours and the city went wild with joy.'

John Owers, a partner of Limebeer and Company, had gone to New York and Caracas on Ultramar's behalf to revise the accounting system. It was Owers' first overseas trip for Ultramar, and was probably his most exciting, although there were to be many more as he became increasingly involved with the company. He worked closely in London with Campbell Nelson and Gilbert Potier, having risen rapidly to an important position in Limebeer, a company he had first joined as an office boy in 1937, prior to distinguished service in the Royal Air Force during the war.

Despite fears to the contrary, life in Venezuela returned quickly to normal after the revolution. Within a few months democratic elections were held which confirmed Betancourt as President. It was a different style of government which he introduced, and it was quickly clear that the days of the booming oil economy were over. Income taxes were virtually doubled, and the oil companies were singled out. In February 1958 Ultramar's shareholders received a circular stating that 'recent political events in Venezuela have not caused any interruption in oil production'. Nonetheless the writing was on the wall. Many took the view that Venezuela could no longer be considered a secure long-term investment, particularly as nationalisation was one of the planks of the Betancourt Government. The process of diversification that Ultramar had started somewhat reluctantly now became increasingly urgent.

The need for a change in direction was underlined by other events outside Venezuela. Since the end of the Suez crisis in 1956, there had been an oversupply of crude oil with world supply outstripping demand, a situation accentuated by discoveries of major reserves throughout the world. Ultramar's marketing agreement with Texaco had run out in 1956, but had been renegotiated for a further three-year period at a somewhat lower selling price for the crude. In July 1958 Texaco gave notice that this new agreement would not be renewed when it expired in July 1959. The oil glut had already caused Ultramar to reduce production. The same circular of February 1958 that was designed to calm fears about the Venezuelan political situation also informed shareholders that production had been cut back to 27,000 barrels per day and that 40 wells had been temporarily shut down. The cut back affected all areas of production. Suddenly, after a decade of relative stability, Ultramar had an uncertain future yet again. The final blow fell in March 1959 when Eisenhower's Government announced mandatory oil import quotas, a measure designed to protect the United States domestic oil industry. Texaco reduced its purchases under the oil sales agreement, which in any case was to expire in three months' time.

Ultramar was now faced with a crucial decision. There were three options, first to continue to produce crude oil and hope to find new buyers, despite the world oil crisis and their lack of marketing experience, second to sell most of its Venezuelan oil and gas holdings and become a royalty company, and third to create its own market outlets through a refining and marketing operation.

The *Atlantic Marchioness* was the first tanker at the Holyrood dock in Newfoundland, arriving on 4 February 1961

100

# AN
# INTEGRATED
# OIL
# BUSINESS

# 6

The early months of 1959 were a testing time for Ultramar. With the end of the crude oil sales agreement with Texaco looming on the horizon, the company was forced to come to grips with the fact that there was more to the oil business than just drilling and producing gas and crude oil. The various options were considered in rapid succession. The first, to sell the gas and oil reserves in Venezuela and retain only the royalty companies and the small but growing interests in western Canada and the United States, was examined thoroughly. Negotiations were conducted with Standard of Indiana and a number of other larger oil companies and the idea was actively pursued, even though the sale would have meant a partial liquidation of Ultramar. In the end, it was not carried out. At the same time, in the short term, attempts were made to find buyers for the Venezuelan crude. Some success was achieved but the combination of an oil glut and the imposition of United States import quotas made this difficult and the prices being obtained left little profit. Ultramar had no marketing organisation and little experience, even though the senior managers were learning fast. The third route, and perhaps the riskiest, was for the company to integrate with an existing organisation and diversify into its own refining and marketing operations. For a small company with no refinery, no ships and no outlets and whose staff were all reared in exploration and production, this third choice seemed distinctly unpromising. It is therefore to the Board's eternal credit that it allowed its younger managers, Lorbeer, Nelson, Bensen and others, to convince it that this was the course to follow. This was in every way a critical decision, and one which was to transform Ultramar and determine its pattern of growth into the future.

Efforts at first concentrated on the marketing of Ultramar's oil as crude with Lloyd Bensen being put in charge of building an organisation and converting a small oil producer into a selling entity that could hold its own in an unfavourable marketplace dominated by experienced giants. The crude simply had to be sold, by one means or another, and so sales techniques had to be adventurous, flexible and occasionally heroic. Bensen remembers this exciting time: 'I had to find out what happens after the oil leaves the field. Texaco was very helpful and one of their very nice professionals said, "Well from the Vengref refinery you have so much gasoline and so much kerosene but it's not enough to make a cargo". So he exchanged it for me into one saleable cargo and introduced me to some of the brokers. I was a babe in the woods. The company went out

Aerial view of the Los Angeles refinery in 1959

and hired a few management trainees, and then we accidentally found a fellow by the name of Charles Quigley. He was a brilliant and very able man. When the crude oil purchase contract finally ended with Texaco, we had already been weaned into this new game although Assheton still said at the time that we should sell out the company as we would need a staff of a thousand, or we would never get to move all the oil. Quigley and I actually moved all the company's oil on our own. We sold the products throughout the world and when we added it all up, we did better than break even. It was just the two of us, selling bulk cargoes to the toughest buyers and traders in the world. We were doing pretty well.' Dr Charles Quigley was a former consultant oil refinery engineer, who had worked in Cuba before the Castro revolution and who was used to the machinations and manoeuverings of the larger oil companies. He describes one incident which underlines the lengths to which Ultramar had to go to conclude a sale:

'We had sold a cargo of Oritupano crude to Raffinerie Belge de Petroles in Antwerp, which we had represented as having low salt content (under 10 pounds per 1,000 barrels). When Gulf delivered the crude oil to the ship at the Mene Grande Terminal in Venezuela it was over 75 pounds per 1,000 barrels. Gulf would only guarantee to deliver the specified gravity of the crude oil, and so they blended crudes from different sources. The excellent crude which we had delivered to their pipeline was not the same crude they delivered at the port. The buyer offered one dollar less per barrel, but this we

102

Golden Eagle service station in Los Angeles in 1960

couldn't accept, so we had the cargo shipped to Antwerp and there we desalted it in a new refinery tank with heat additives and river water. George Melamid, the owner and president of the Belgian company, was impressed by our performance and gave us a contract for sale of our heavy crude for one year in return for a small desalter installed at our cost. Everybody was happy.' On another occasion, a sale of crude to a Chilean customer came to an abrupt end when a Chilean gunboat appeared in the Venezuelan port to load the cargo.

During this period, an agreement was made with Sinclair Oil at their Puerto La Cruz refinery to process a part of the Mercedes crude oil into products, because the latter produced a greater return than crude and were in some cases more saleable. Some products were already coming from the Vengref refinery in which Ultramar had years before bought a small interest. By these means Ultramar was able to trade extensively in bunker fuel oil, building up regular contacts with companies such as Metropolitan Petroleum of New York. However, the uncertainties of the market quickly made it clear that Ultramar could not continue for long to operate in this manner.

Stability was dependent upon a more controlled market and that could only be achieved by the company having its own refinery and market. Having made the decision to integrate and diversify, the purchase of a refinery was the next logical step and it did not take long for Ultramar, with the help of consultants, to begin the search for a suitable candidate.

Early in 1959, Ultramar was introduced to John Shaheen, an entrepreneur with

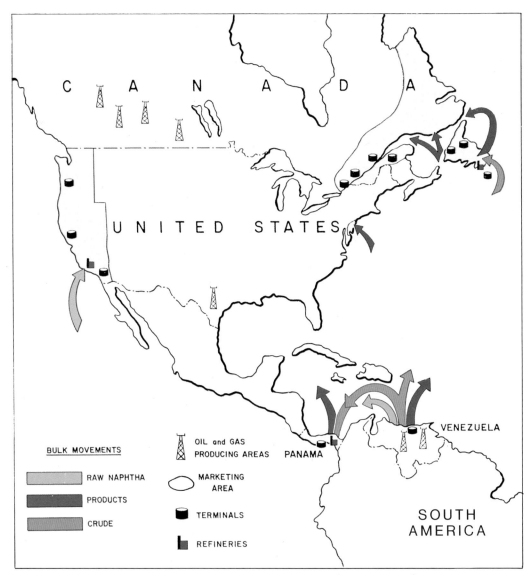

Map of the Americas showing the proposed upstream and downstream relationship in 1964

extensive West Coast oil interests. The introduction was effected by White Weld, an investment banking company led by Jean Cattier, who was related by marriage to Alfred Meyer. The initial meeting was in Alfred Meyer's New York office with Morris Frank and Arnold Lorbeer present. At this time, although already in his early eighties, Alfred Meyer was still coming to the office every day and was mentally very alert.

An energetic and brilliant man, John Shaheen was born in 1915 in Tampico, Illinois, a small town also renowned as the birthplace of Ronald Reagan. Following a university education, he served in the U.S. Navy during the Second World War, was attached to

104

John Shaheen

Golden Eagle's Los Angeles
terminal in 1960

OSS, and had an illustrious war record. By the 1950s he had established a considerable reputation as a business entrepreneur and oil man, particularly in California, and was constantly looking for opportunities for expansion. One of his more significant companies was the Golden Eagle Refining Company, incorporated in Delaware in October 1957. In April 1958 Golden Eagle had acquired the marketing and refining interests of a long established California oil company, Sunset International Petroleum. Sunset could trace its origins back to 1922 when a famous Los Angeles oil entrepreneur, Chauncy C. Julian, founded the Julian Petroleum Company. This company grew rapidly but not without problems. There were cash shortages and then in 1927 a stock manipulation scandal ruined Julian and his company. The assets were bought by the Sunset Pacific Oil Company, which in turn sold out to the Sunset Oil Company in 1934. In 1950 Sunset was merged with the Eagle Oil Company, retaining Sunset as the company name, but using the Golden Eagle symbol for the first time on their gasoline stations. Four years later the Sunset International Oil Company was formed from a merger between Sunset and the International Mining Company, paving the way for the refining and marketing acquisition by John Shaheen's Golden Eagle Refining Company. By this means Shaheen obtained an oil business whose assets included a 9,000 barrels per day refinery in Torrance, Los Angeles, along with a 77-acre freehold site, leased deep-water marine terminals in Los Angeles and San Francisco, with related storage facilities, a crude oil storage station at Signal Hill, Los Angeles, a 50-mile pipeline system and eighteen gasoline stations.

Following this acquisition of Sunset, Shaheen transferred its assets to another company which he owned, the Panama Refining and Petrochemical Company. The

105

Julian Petroleum and Sunset Pacific drum labels
These companies were forerunners of Golden Eagle

latter had been incorporated in Panama in April 1956, with a view to building a new refinery complex in Panama using a concession granted by the Panamanian Government. The terms of the concession were generous and included exoneration from income taxes for 25 years and duty free imports of equipment. Despite these impressive assets, Shaheen was short of cash and his companies were heavily in debt.

Following the initial meetings in New York, John Shaheen was introduced to Herbert and Nelson. In Ultramar's eyes at that time Shaheen seemed to offer almost everything the company needed, and negotiations were started. These proved to be lengthy and tortuous. The Board in London first considered the possibility of a link with the Panama Refining and Petrochemical Company in March of 1959. At the Annual General Meeting held in July the same year, the Chairman reported that 'negotiations were in progress to give Ultramar a controlling interest in a refinery project and a rapidly growing marketing organisation'. In March 1960 shareholders received a letter detailing the assets to be acquired and explaining the purchase agreement which was dependent upon Ultramar's authorised capital being increased from £3 million to £4.5 million by the creation of 3,000,000 new ten shilling shares. This was agreed at an Extraordinary General Meeting, leaving the way clear for Ultramar to purchase the Panama company and all its assets from Shaheen for 1,500,000 Ultramar Shares, payable over a number of years. At the Annual General Meeting held in June 1960, the Chairman was able to announce that the deal had been completed, and that John Shaheen had been made an Ultramar director.

At the time the marriage seemed to suit both parties. Ultramar had acquired a refining and marketing organisation, along with the concession for the Panama refinery which, when built, would be able to look after much of the Venezuelan crude output. The scheme was a simple one. The new Panama refinery, a fairly basic plant, would produce naphtha from the crude which in turn would be shipped to California for refining into gasoline for the West Coast market. The heavy ends of the barrel remaining in Panama would be sold as bunker fuel. For Shaheen, Ultramar was effectively a saviour. Following Eisenhower's imposition of import quotas in 1959, his company had suffered

The Payardi refinery, Panama, photographed in 1975

increasingly from adverse market conditions. The negotiations he had opened, first with Phillips and then with Ultramar, were designed to extract Golden Eagle of California and the Panama company from its financial straits. Thus, despite the rather convoluted courtship, both parties were actually desperate for the marriage to take place, and it is a matter of debate as to who needed who the most.

Ultramar now seemed in a position to make the transition from an oil and gas producer to a fully integrated oil company. Ultramar, however, was still a small company and so it could be flexible in its attitudes and operations. Although somewhat stretched by the purchase of the Panama company, the cost was largely in stock and Ultramar's finances were in good shape. There had been several profitable years during the late 1950s, and by judicious and often creative accounting backed by new loans, notably one for $4.5 million negotiated in September 1959 by CPSA from the First National City Bank of New York, the company seemed well placed to enter a broader sphere of activity. However, the next few years were to bring a new and unexpected series of problems.

The first disappointment, and this came almost immediately, was on the organisation side. Although Ultramar had acquired a fine marketing organisation, the staff was experienced in product sales mostly in the U.S. market, and not in crude oil sales at the

Premier Smallwood of Newfoundland and Sir Kenneth Mealing, a director of Ultramar, sign the agreement to build the Holyrood refinery on 4 May 1960. Among those standing are Campbell Nelson, Arnold Lorbeer and John Shaheen

Jack Polk at the site selected for the Holyrood refinery

The Holyrood refinery under construction during the summer of 1960

international level. Bensen and Quigley were soon back handling that division. However, with this acquisition Ultramar did gain a group of experienced and talented oil people which served the company well over the years and provided the nucleus for the emerging refining, marketing and financial divisions. These included Dale Austin, Bertram Ault, Harvey Fifer, Jack Polk, Paul Boyd, Chick Fraser, David Oreck, William Theisen and Ruth Brenner.

Ultramar's net profit for 1959 totalled £1,845,000, a figure three times the size of the previous year's profit, and reflecting the increasingly significant contributions made by Mercedes, Oritupano and the royalty companies. Yet, within a year the pattern had been dramatically reversed, with the company declaring in 1960 a consolidated loss of £300,000. There were a number of factors that influenced this reversal, the most important of which were related to external conditions over which Ultramar had no control. Import restrictions and quotas imposed by the United States Government combined with a worldwide oil glut and fierce price cutting affected all areas of the oil industry, but their effect was particularly damaging in California. Plans to expand and develop the Los Angeles refinery, which had been an essential element in the purchase of Shaheen's company, had to be put off. The basic concept, to link a topping plant in Panama with a finishing operation in California, was rendered impractical by the import restrictions. Shipping naphtha to Los Angeles would not be allowed under the 1960

Premier Smallwood of Newfoundland speaking at the Opening
Ceremony of the Holyrood refinery on 1 December 1961

The completed Holyrood refinery in 1961. In the foreground is the spruce tree carefully
preserved during construction at the request of Jack Carroll, the farmer
who sold his home to make way for the refinery

The menu and booklet produced for the opening of the Holyrood refinery

regulations. The Golden Eagle operation began to lose money and at the same time was still no help in solving the problem of selling Venezuelan crude.

The proposed Panama refinery project, which was the other basic plank in the Shaheen deal, was also beginning to come apart. A new subsidiary, Ultramar Panama, had been formed in April of 1960, and preliminary work, such as site clearance and road building, was under way. In September 1961 the Chairman reported that the 55,000 barrels per day Panama refinery was under construction, and that total costs were estimated at $45 million. In order to help finance the cost of construction, Shaheen had entered into supply agreements with five major oil companies for the purchase of 42,000 barrels per day of crude oil for the refinery. This, of course, did not fit in well with Ultramar's needs and plans to utilise its own Venezuelan oil. There were those in Ultramar who began to think that the Panama project might have to be abandoned, especially since it was beginning to drain cash. Continuing activities in Canada and the United States also required increasing investment, without as yet any clear sign of either Canpet or CPUS making significant contributions to income.

Faced with these problems, Ultramar inevitably sought for other solutions. Arnold Lorbeer was directly involved in this period of rather frenetic and occasionally disjointed activity: 'We made a number of false starts during the early 1960s. We signed a letter of intent with Kuwait National Petroleum for a joint operation, but somewhere along the way it got buried in the desert. We entered into an agreement with Sinclair for a

111

Canadian staff members in Newfoundland in the early 1960s. *Left to right:*
Jack Polk, Chick Fraser, James Allan, Steve Legan, Paul Boyd

Golden Eagle service station in eastern Canada in 1963

partnership in eastern Canada and even had Premier Smallwood of Newfoundland come to New York to bless it, but something happened inside Sinclair and the agreement was not carried out. We negotiated an agreement with Humble Oil for a joint refinery in Los Angeles, but it was never ratified. We spent months negotiating a deal with Fina for joint operations in various spheres and then turned it down ourselves. We sent delegations to St. Helena and the Cape Verde Islands to study possible refineries and bunkering stations but could not put it together.'

Marketing continued to cause problems. The marketing organisation that had been bought from Shaheen was being slowly, and sometimes painfully, integrated into Ultramar. There were a number of experienced employees who had been around since the Sunset, pre-Shaheen days, but they had no expertise in the international crude business and so at first could contribute little to New York. With the price wars raging in California, they had their own battles to fight. The West Coast losses continued to mount, reaching a peak of £594,000 in 1961, but they were somewhat offset by the creation of new finance from a number of sources. In July 1960 a new 7% Convertible Loan Stock 1975/8 was offered to Ultramar shareholders to raise £3.25 million, and a loan of $1.5 million was negotiated with the Canadian Imperial Bank of Commerce.

This loan, and that from the First National City Bank of New York, marked the start of banking relationships that were to be increasingly vital to Ultramar in the years ahead, with these banks joining the Morgan banks as Ultramar's core bankers. Despite the cash shortage, the Capital Surplus distribution to shareholders, based on the exchange surplus, was still being made, with a sixth payment in 1960. A stock option plan for the benefit of the staff was introduced with the aim of attracting and holding top-class executives, and a plan was prepared for the purchase by Ultramar of all the outside shares in the Venezuelan royalty companies.

The degree of financial stability maintained in London and New York, plus the inherent flexibility of what was still a small and young company, enabled Ultramar to come to grips with the various problems. The Panama situation which had at first threatened to swamp the company was solved in a forthright manner. After much discussion and considerable expenditure, the concession to build a refinery at Portobelo was turned over to Refineria Panama S.A., a company jointly owned by Continental Oil Company and National Bulk Carriers, as part of a larger deal whereby Ultramar acquired at cost a one-third interest in another Panama refinery owned by the same partnership, with processing rights equal to one-third of the capacity of the refinery. This latter refinery had been designed with a capacity of 36,000 barrels per day at Payardi Island, 5.5 miles east of the Atlantic entrance to the Panama Canal, but operated at a higher throughput. In effect, the existence of this refinery had always undermined the validity of the Shaheen/Ultramar scheme, which had looked good in theory but not so exciting in practice. With the completion of the Payardi refinery in 1962, it brought finally to a close any idea Ultramar may still have entertained of having their own refinery in Panama and the decision was made to join forces. The terms were favourable, with payment for the one-third interest deferred until the years 1964-8, and so, for a far smaller investment than originally envisaged, Ultramar obtained part of their crude oil marketing requirements outside the United States. The situation in Panama quickly settled down and within a year of the agreement the Payardi refinery was working well. Ultramar sold crude oil to the refinery and in turn purchased products for its growing markets. The reasons why the original two owners built the Payardi refinery is a story in itself, since National Bulk Carriers had no crude supply of its own or marketing organisation and Conoco also at that time had very little presence in the Caribbean. Ultramar was much better equipped to handle the importation of crude oil and the sale and export of the refined products.

Flexibility also brought California under control. After a couple of years of heavy losses incurred fighting the gasoline war against the majors, it was decided to reduce the sales of gasoline. The Los Angeles refinery was revamped and thereafter concentrated on the production of JP-4 aviation fuel and low sulphur fuel oil. This was a shrewd move for within a year Golden Eagle had become the largest independent supplier of jet fuel to the U.S. military in California. This, and a general improvement in market conditions, helped to turn the California operation back to profit.

A most significant decision of this period was to develop a market for products in eastern Canada. The background to this decision was the loss of the United States market because of the import restrictions, which gave Ultramar an urgent need for a market outside the United States for the light products coming from the Panama refinery. After rapid consideration of a number of possible solutions, Ultramar turned its attention towards the provinces of Quebec and Newfoundland.

In 1960, despite its historical and contemporary importance as a transatlantic communications base, Newfoundland was still a comparatively undeveloped region. One reason for this was the weather. Newfoundland has a harsh climate, dominated by a damp cold and fog. Another of course was the poor agricultural land. Newfoundland cannot produce adequate food to feed its people. Conditions of snow and ice can be extreme, and it was not unusual to see icebergs along the east coast in late June. In these inhospitable conditions travel overland was at first particularly hard. Roads were primitive and until 1958 there was no continuous road across the island. Even that was a dusty and uneven gravel road, destructive to tyres and vehicles, and uncomfortable for passengers. During dry weather the dust could penetrate everything, even closed suitcases, while no long journey could be completed without at least one puncture. These conditions did not alter until the early 1960s when the all-weather Trans-Canada Highway was opened.

The initial impetus to develop a refining and marketing complex in Newfoundland seems to have been made by John Shaheen. In March 1960, when negotiations between Shaheen and Ultramar were still in progress, a Letter of Intent concerning the building of a refinery and its related facilities in Newfoundland was signed by Lundrigan's Construction Limited and the Panama company. This letter made it clear that the project was dependent upon certain action by the Newfoundland Government. Once this was forthcoming, an agreement was signed between Premier Smallwood of

114

Well manifolds and gas separators at Oritupano in 1959

Group at the Oritupano field in the 1960s, standing below the Texaco and Ultramar signs

Newfoundland and Sir Kenneth Mealing on behalf of Ultramar to bring into existence the Holyrood refinery. By this time, John Shaheen was an Ultramar director, and Ultramar had taken over the Newfoundland scheme along with the other assets of the Panama company. The agreement with the Newfoundland Government provided for a refinery on an 80-acre site in Holyrood, twenty miles from St. John's on Conception Bay, with an initial capacity of 5,000 barrels per day, with related production and storage facilities for a wide range of products, including asphalt, bunker fuels, furnace oil, diesel and gasoline. The Newfoundland Government agreed to purchase all of its petroleum requirements from the company for twenty years. The aim from the start was to create a complete refining and marketing operation for Newfoundland.

The construction of the refinery itself was made simpler by Charles Quigley and Chick Fraser finding in a Los Angeles yard the material and equipment for a 7,000 barrels per day refinery. This had been designed and made for Thailand, but the financial arrangements had failed and the equipment was for sale. Despite certain initial problems, such as the absence of a process design, the equipment was purchased and transported to Holyrood. Once on site, other units were added such as tankage, pipelines and dock facilities, and construction was quickly begun under the direction of Jack Polk.

The latter was at the time already in his sixties but quite a legendary oil industry character. A great great grandson of President Polk of the United States, he was a U.S. Naval Academy graduate who had gone into oil and supervised the building of the large

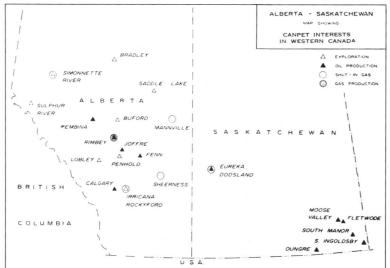

Ultramar's interests
in western Canada
in 1962
Exploration in western
Canada during the
early 1960s:

The rig and camp at
Ronde Lake

A Beaver floatplane at
Norman Wells on the
Mackenzie River

Amuay refinery for Esso in Venezuela. He was a tough man who won over the Newfoundland labour force by laying pipe alongside of them in the coldest of weather. The story has been told that in the Second World War, having abandoned the navy for the army, he was colonel of an engineer unit that found itself short of rations on one of the islands in the Pacific. He got a small motor launch and approached one of the big U.S. battleships with the greeting 'Ahoy! Jack Polk - class of '23 - I need rations.' He got them.

At an early stage the refining capacity of the Holyrood refinery was increased to 8,500 barrels per day, the first of a number of planned expansions that ultimately took the capacity to 15,000 barrels per day. Despite the inhospitable surroundings, construction of the unit proceeded at a good pace and by February 1961 sufficient storage and docking facilities had been built for a shipment to arrive. On 4 February the first tanker, *Atlantic Marchioness,* arrived at Holyrood with a cargo of refined products from Venezuela, and Golden Eagle's marketing operation was launched.

By October the refinery was ready to receive its first shipment of crude oil and 193,000 barrels were unloaded from one of the largest tankers ever to come to Newfoundland. Charles Quigley was there to receive the ship, and was concerned that because of its size, it might not be able to dock: 'Two weeks before startup I was on the site. The refinery was ready for operation. We had a cargo of crude coming up from Venezuela but the bay was chock full of ice. In addition, there was a large iceberg sitting out at the entrance to the bay. I couldn't see how any ship could ever make port in that ice, and it was supposed to be an ice-free port. Jack Polk allayed my fears and assured me the wind would blow the bay free of ice before the ship arrived. Sure enough, it did.' On 1 December 1961 the Holyrood refinery was officially opened by Premier Smallwood, with Sir Edwin Herbert speaking on a trans-Canada radio broadcast. The opening was a festive occasion - the kind of affair Ultramar has always done well. A chef was brought in from Montreal, 'to provide' as Lorbeer remembers, 'our more squeamish guests with something more than the traditional Newfoundland delicacies of codfish tongues and seal flippers'.

The refinery itself was a major investment for Ultramar, but additional finance was also required to build the network of storage tanks and deep-water terminal facilities across the Province and to establish service stations and other retail outlets. Some of this was raised by short-term loans and lease-back arrangements, but the greater part came from a mortgage given by Esso on the Holyrood refinery backed by a crude oil purchase agreement. This financing arrangement was channelled through the Canadian and Caribbean Oil Company, a company created for this purpose, which was granted a 50% interest in the refinery. Later, Ultramar repurchased the 50% equity interest granted to Can-Carib and refinanced the mortgage loan on the refinery.

The burden of debt during this period was onerous, and Ultramar had to renegotiate some of its long-term loans and to arrange bridging loans to refund short-term debts. The refinery itself, although built relatively quickly and on stream by the target date, operated at a loss for some time, while the establishing of the marketing network in eastern Canada also proved to be both slower and more expensive than anticipated. The net result was three years of losses for Ultramar, 1960, 1961 and 1962, totalling over £1 million. The new investments were the direct cause of the losses, but the situation was aggravated by the teething troubles inevitable in a company that was trying to grow too fast.

Simultaneous with the beginning of operations in Newfoundland was Ultramar's entry into the Quebec market. Paul Boyd was put in charge of this division and headquarters were established in Montreal. Boyd was an experienced marketing man who had worked for a number of major companies and was thoroughly familiar with gasoline selling techniques. Considerable use was made here of the system of sale and lease back. Gasoline stations and terminals were financed in this way. For example, in 1961 the Montreal terminal facility was sold to the Futterman Corporation for $1.5 million, the cost of its construction, and leased back for $145,000 per annum. The Canadian company also took advantage of buying into existing marketing organisations such as Cornwall Petroleum in Ontario through whose twelve service stations Golden Eagle products were sold. Some of the acquisitions, like Gauthier in Chicoutimi, were made for Ultramar stock. Golden Eagle of Canada, which eventually branched out to all the Provinces of eastern Canada, became Ultramar's largest investment, a position it has continued to hold to this day.

The complex and expensive process of integration dominated Ultramar's activities during the early 1960s but should not be allowed to overshadow developments in the established areas of production. In Venezuela increased taxation and reduced capital expenditures combined to lower the annual rate of production. Little new exploration drilling was being carried out and some of the older wells were starting to dry up. There was still an oversupply of crude on the world market and so some of the more marginal concessions were given up as the costs of oil production were no longer matched by potential income. The farmout arrangement with Shell covering Unare-Zurón was not renewed when it ran out in 1959, and by 1963 over 500,000 acres had been surrendered. The concessions retained totalled 477,000 acres, of which 407,000 were held by the Mercedes company, and 70,000 wholly owned by Ultramar. The most important of the wholly owned properties were in the State of Barinas where an exploratory dry hole was drilled in 1963.

At that time, Venezuela was still a profitable operation. There were however endless disputes and discussions about levels of taxation with Venezuelan Government officials, some significant, and some trivial. It was Venezuelan policy to use U.S. posted prices as a basis for income taxes even though the world market price for crude oil was lower.

By 1960 production from the new Oritupano field was well ahead of Mercedes, 21,600 barrels as opposed to 16,900 barrels per day, a position that was not to change because of minimal investment in Mercedes. Gas sales from Mercedes, on the other hand, were buoyant, reaching a peak of 74 million cubic feet per day in 1961. As the Mercedes company was now selling crude oil to the parent companies at cost, the net profit of Mercedes was derived from gas sales. The success of Oritupano encouraged Texaco and Ultramar each to buy half of the share held by Atlantic Refining in 1963,

118

and so the field became a straightforward joint operation similar to Mercedes. In 1964 there was a major effort to increase production of this field with investment of $2 million to complete twelve development wells. The royalty companies continued as a major source of income, encouraging Ultramar in its attempts to buy shares from outside stockholders.

In western Canada, Canpet maintained the steady process of exploration and development established during the late 1950s, supported by re-investment of the receipts from oil sales, by loans and by Ultramar's own resources. Drilling continued in the proven areas, with Canpet having an interest in over 150 wells in the Eureka-Dodsland region by 1963, and in exploration and test drilling carried out at Ronde Lake in the Northwest Territories and in British Columbia, as well as in Saskatchewan and Alberta. At this time, interest was being shown in the Arctic Islands, and in 1961 Canpet had a small percentage in the first test well to be drilled in this region. The inhospitable nature of the terrain and the climate meant that exploration parties had to rely extensively on air transport. The universal aircraft was the Beaver, which could be fitted with floats to operate from lakes, or with large low-pressure tyres which enabled it to fly from ice or rough terrain. The exploration of a block in British Columbia was marred by a fatal crash in 1960 in which David Bell, a consultant geologist, two student assistants and the pilot were killed when their aircraft hit a mountain-side on take-off from Lorna Lake. Despite the weather and the harsh and unpredictable conditions, this accident was the only Ultramar fatality during exploration work in Canada.

By 1962 Canpet was in quite a healthy position. Oil production had reached 1,315 barrels per day. For the first time the company made a small operating profit, celebrated by a move to a new office in the prime part of Calgary. This pattern continued in 1963, prompting Ultramar at the end of the year to buy back the 50% interest in Canpet held by Gold Fields and Triad (a subsidiary of BP who had bought Apex in 1962). The Triad share was bought for Can.$1 million, while Gold Fields received 400,000 Ultramar shares. At the same time, Canpet's name was changed to Golden Eagle Oil and Gas Limited to bring it in line with other Ultramar companies.

Operations also continued in the United States, but on a lesser scale. At the end of 1962, a total of £785,000 had been invested in CPUS's activities in Texas, and a small amount of oil and gas was being produced commercially. Within a year this had risen to 120 barrels per day and 1.25 million cubic feet of gas per day, but the company still operated at a loss until 1964.

There were also some changes in the New York headquarters. The first of these concerned the name of the company. In 1959 the old title, Caracas Petroleum Corporation of New York, was changed to American Ultramar. The offices themselves were still unchanged, despite the steady increase in staff, particularly after the purchase of the Panama company. They were located in the Lincoln Building, a rather old building, with no air conditioning. Instead there was a house rule that when the summer temperature reached 90 degrees, ice cream would be bought for the entire staff. There were regular visits by London directors, including Sir Edwin Herbert, who generally

Senior executive staff in New York in 1966. *Left to right:* Arnold Lorbeer, Dale Austin, Roy Brotherhood, Richard Thompson, Lloyd Bensen, Bertram Ault

came over twice a year, but communications were still fairly primitive. The international telephone system was erratic, the telex was in its infancy and so coordination between offices was based on letters and cables, and of course personal visits. This suited the Meyer method of business management which had been continued by Lorbeer and others but it sometimes caused misunderstandings between London and New York. Inevitably, Ultramar's rapid growth during the early 1960s greatly increased the significance of the New York office at the expense of London. The loans negotiated with American banks also shifted some element of financial control away from London. The London office was effectively run by Campbell Nelson. Nelson, who had been Ultramar's Managing Director since 1960, was involved in all spheres of operation, and was the main link between London and New York. On one occasion William Spencer, later to become President of Citibank, visited the Ultramar offices in London which were not very smart. Nelson describes the occasion: 'Though the building in Broad Street Place had a certain charm looking out over the gardens of Finsbury Circus it was old and not very well kept. It is believed to have started life as a lunatic asylum which caused us some merriment over the years. The lifts were somewhat antique and Alfred Meyer had always been reluctant to use them, preferring to walk to the 4th floor. I had a pleasant meeting with

120

Operations management team in New York in 1968. *Left to right:* Lloyd Bensen, Frank Sisti, Joseph Ament, Ralph Capozzi, Dale Austin, Edward Robbins, John Tivnan

Bill Spencer and as I escorted him to the lift he put his arm round me and said, "Campbell, I am pleased to see that you are not wasting your shareholders' money on the office".'

A number of other important changes took place in 1963. Two subsidiary companies were formed, Ultramar Liberia Limited and Ultramar Golden Eagle Limited (U.K.), which indicated a direction of future development. Alfred Meyer retired as a director, at the age of 87, and was made Honorary President. The Chairman was awarded a life peerage in recognition of his services as Chairman of a Royal Commission on Local Government in London, and took the title of Lord Tangley. Richard Thompson was made an Ultramar director on 14 May 1963, and later that year moved to the New York office from Venezuela to be executive vice president under Lorbeer. Thompson had been an Ultramar director before, from 1935 to 1943, as a representative of Cull and Company.

Thompson's move to New York was not unconnected with the increasingly uneasy relationship between John Shaheen and the other Ultramar directors. Shaheen was a man of great ambition and business ability, but his entrepreneurial ideas were out of step with Ultramar's resources and organisation. He was often at odds with the main Board in London, and his operational methods were taxing in the extreme. Personally motivated only by business, he would often call meetings late at night at his New York club, unaware that his fellow executives had lives outside Ultramar. In 1960 both Shaheen and Ultramar had been greatly in need of what the other had to offer, but by 1963 they had grown apart. Shaheen had other interests and was disenchanted with the way Ultramar operated. It was too conservative for him, and his favourite expression was that 'It's run like a bank'. At the end of 1963, divorce proceedings were started, which proved to be as long lasting and as complicated as the courtship in 1959-60. Lorbeer and Nelson handled most of the negotiations, aided by Orin Knudsen, the company General Counsel, who had succeeded Morris Frank after his premature death in 1959, and Charles Wishaw, a top lawyer, was brought over from Freshfields. The issue was complicated by a loan that American Ultramar had made to a company controlled by Shaheen and which was guaranteed by him.

In January 1965 a series of strongly worded cables and letters were exchanged between Shaheen and the Chairman, which ended when Shaheen resigned from the Board on 15 February. A few days later a settlement was reached. The debt was written off and Shaheen received certain small payments, but Ultramar retained all the assets in Panama, California and Canada, and the existing crude oil contracts. Equally important, most of the Golden Eagle staff who had come with Shaheen elected to stay with Ultramar. Shaheen's large Ultramar shareholding later passed to Mobil when they foreclosed on the collateral for a loan and Mobil in turn asked Ultramar to help dispose of the shares, apparently fearful that U.S. anti-trust legislation would not allow them to remain an Ultramar shareholder.

About the time of Shaheen's departure there were a number of managerial changes. Hans Garde-Hansen took over in Venezuela, replacing Thompson, and William Robinson became manager in Panama. These two maintained the Imperial College association first started by Professor Illing. David Oreck, Paul Boyd and Jack Polk, all formerly with the Shaheen organisation, were the managers in Los Angeles, Montreal and Newfoundland, while Keith Cullingham continued as manager in Calgary. Dale Austin moved from the West Coast to New York to work with Lloyd Bensen on developing marketing and refining. Bensen was in charge of marketing, refining and shipping, while Brotherhood headed the exploration and production department. Bertram Ault, a financial wizard who had been Shaheen's right-hand man, became vice president of finance in New York. Ault was also a poet of some originality, specialising in pastiches of English 17th-century poetry, and he and Dick Thompson were in the habit of communicating with each other in verse. This management team led by Lorbeer and Nelson was to carry the company forward into the 1970s.

In 1964 Ultramar made a profit of £455,000. More important, for the first time all the subsidiary companies, now structured as three divisions, Caribbean, Canadian and U.S.A., were independently profitable that year. The early 1960s had been a testing time but the company had succeeded in integrating and diversifying during a period marked by shortage of cash and over-supply of oil. Ultramar in 1964 was effectively a totally

New York office administration staff in January 1959. *Left to right:* Jean Kane, John Tivnan, Edna Perri (later Mrs Lloyd Bensen) and Nina Perri (later Mrs Joseph Ament)

different company from that which had seen the end of the Texaco crude oil purchase agreement in 1959. The transition had been painful but fast, and the new company was a much stronger one. The association with John Shaheen no doubt had facilitated the transition. In the short term, the Shaheen marriage had been beneficial for Ultramar, but it ended in divorce when the two parties developed different aims. The Chairman made no reference to it in his statement at the Annual General Meeting held on 1 July 1965.

In these years there developed two peculiar management philosophies which distinguished Ultramar from other companies of its size and which helped to keep it alive when others failed or were taken over. First, Ultramar did not generally disturb the major companies but was content to be a large fish in a small pond. Activities such as a refinery in Newfoundland and later a refinery in Quebec City, a self-propelled barge bunkering business in Panama, aviation jet fuel in California, gas transmission in central Venezuela and drilling on the Port-au-Port Peninsula in Newfoundland were all unique to Ultramar and at the time not in competition with other companies. In fact, in its early history Ultramar, perhaps unwittingly, always seems to have maintained a special relationship with one major oil company or another, a relationship that sometimes even included financial help.

The second rather unusual situation was the close personal friendship that existed among the top management. Following the schisms of the late 1940s, Nelson, Lorbeer, Thompson, Bensen and a few others built up close ties which helped their business relations and for years kept Ultramar singularly free of corporate politics. A number of the executives married within the company, or to girls met through business contacts. Arnold Lorbeer recalls: 'It started in the late 1940s when Alfred Meyer's daughter, Nene, married Ralph Sandt out of the New York office. The wedding was at Notre Dame Cathedral in Paris. Everyone was invited but me. They needed someone to mind the store. In the late 1950s and early 1960s we had some gala corporate weddings, Dick Thompson to a girl he had met at the British Embassy in Caracas, Lloyd Bensen to Edna, whom he met in the New York office, Bob Walter to Gina also from the New York office and Roger Nunns to Joan in the London office. The Bensen wedding in New York in 1961 was attended by Meyer, Nelson, Shaheen and virtually the entire corporate staff. I was best man.'

The bunker barge *Golden Owl* on her maiden voyage from the Texas shipyard in 1969

# CARIBBEAN CONCLUSION 7

The late 1960s and early 1970s were to witness a steady decline in Ultramar's fortunes in Venezuela. Reduced oil output was matched by reduced investment, and Ultramar's primary interests moved to other parts of the world. The main reason for this was the political and taxation situation in Venezuela. At the same time, Venezuela also began to decline as one of the world's major oil producing countries. The reduction of oil exports to the United States due to restrictions, the emergence of many new highly competitive producing countries in the Middle East, Africa and elsewhere, and the general reduction in transportation costs, resulting from the great increase in the size of tankers, all contributed to slow the growth of the Venezuelan oil industry. In 1958 Venezuela produced 142 million tons, equivalent to 17% of the world's output. In 1972 the output was 182 million tons, but this now represented only 7% of the total. During the same period, the annual growth rate in Venezuela's oil production was 3%, a sharp decline from the 10% that had been the norm during the previous fifteen years. A reduction in the country's economic dependence upon oil had also been a deliberate policy of the Acción Democrática Government since it came to power in 1958. This government also felt that it could control oil prices by regulating the amount of production. The more oil it allowed to be produced, the less control it had over the revenue earned. This attitude inspired Venezuela to play a major role in the founding of OPEC.

The Venezuelan bureaucracy greatly increased its involvement in the international oil business. From the early 1960s the Ministry of Mines and Hydrocarbons established for income tax purposes a price per barrel of oil that had little relation to the actual market selling price and was inevitably higher. As a result Venezuelan revenues increased to $1 per barrel by 1970, over double the rate in 1958. The leader of this philosophy was Juan Pablo Perez Alfonzo, Minister of Hydrocarbons during the early 1960s, who believed that Venezuela could justify a tax rate of $10 per barrel, a rate that was in those days a dream, but which was to become reality ten years later.

Throughout this period Ultramar maintained its presence in Venezuela, but there was little new development or investment. The only additional acreage acquired was at Jobal, north of Mercedes near the pipeline. A few shallow producing wells were drilled here in 1964 and 1965. The Ipire field was also brought into production, but this was an outlying area from which the crude oil had to be hauled 58 miles overland to the nearest

Management team in Venezuela in 1967.
*Left to right:* Frank Kay, William Robinson, Francisco Reyes, Gorgias Garriga

pipeline station. Output from Ipire was never more than 750 barrels per day, and was in any case short lived as the concessions in Ipire and Barinas were relinquished in 1965. In the central Mercedes area there was a steady reduction of output with no new wells being drilled to replace those that were exhausted. By 1966 production was down to 5,000 barrels per day, and the camp at Roblecito was being cut back. Gas sales and royalty income were also reduced as a result of taxation. Oritupano was now the most rewarding of Ultramar's Venezuelan interests, with some exploration and drilling still taking place. In 1965 this resulted in a 33% increase in output, but the burden of excessive taxation was a major disincentive there.

Aware that their policies were effectively bringing overseas investment to an end, the Venezuelan Government tried to ease the situation in 1967 by making overall tax settlements with all the oil companies on claims going back for several years. This led to several months of hard bargaining with Ultramar reaching a settlement in a rather unconventional manner, as described by Francisco Reyes: 'The final meeting took place as arranged and, since the President of CPSA (Arnold Lorbeer) was fluent in Spanish, it was agreed that he would present Ultramar's case and explain why the tax authority's claims were unreasonable. After all the usual preliminaries, we sat round a conference

126

Golden Eagle bulk plant and service station on the Trans-Isthmian Highway in Panama in 1970

One of the British-built Scammell tank trucks bought to expand marketing operations in Panama in 1967

table in the Tax Administrator's office, and the President began his exposition. He was doing beautifully, even excelling his usual best, when the chair in which he was seated suddenly collapsed, and he fell to the floor. There was long silence, broken at last by the Tax Administrator who jumped up and helped our President to his feet, saying with great solemnity, "Mr President, the weight of your argument broke the chair." Needless to say, after this the discussions proceeded smoothly, and we reached a fair settlement.'

The position in Venezuela improved a little in 1967. Government restrictions on gas sales were removed and the impact of the Six Day War in the Middle East brought about an increase in production and royalty revenue, thanks to the closure of the Suez Canal and the resulting increased demand for Venezuelan oil. However, the overall

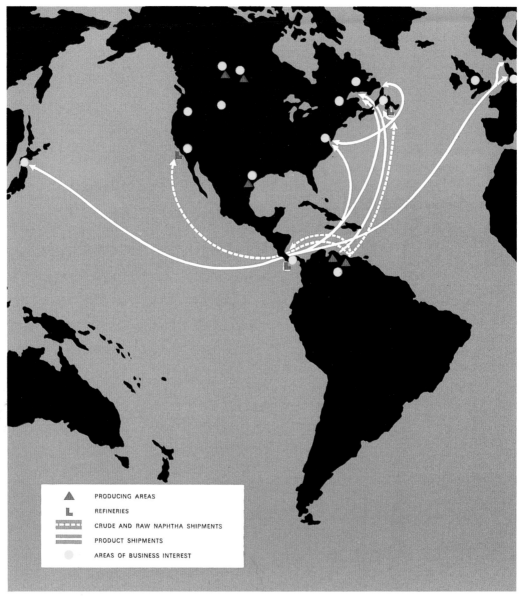

The worldwide activities of Ultramar in 1966

Squid jigging in Newfoundland; for a short period dried fish was
sent to Panama in the dry-cargo holds of tankers

trend was still downward. In 1970 and 1971, Mercedes operated at a loss, gas sales declined again and even Oritupano was shut down for a period. In the end there seemed little point in holding on to Mercedes. The terminal at Pamatacual had already been sold, the Ultramar directors having declined the suggestion that it be turned into a holiday resort, and in August 1971 negotiations were opened to sell Mercedes to local Venezuelan interests. Within a few months Mercedes had been sold. Without the burden of carrying Mercedes, Venezuelan operations began to look healthier. New wells were drilled in Oritupano, bringing an increase in oil and gas production. By now William Robinson was in charge in Caracas, and he was a more dynamic manager than his predecessor. The early 1970s saw a return to profitability partly because income from Venezuela, particularly the royalty payments, was increased by the oil crisis of 1973-4.

However, the oil crisis also brought a new series of problems. Encouraged by the results of its show of force as one of the leaders of OPEC, the Venezuelan Government was now talking openly about nationalisation, the spectre that had been lurking in the background since 1958. A state oil company, CVP, had been in existence since the early 1960s, and had operated a number of concessions jointly with overseas companies, a pattern that looked quite promising for the future. Ultramar themselves had worked with CVP on a joint well in the Oritupano area. However, this all became irrelevant in 1975 when a commission appointed by the Venezuelan Government to review the position of

The tanker *Eagle* in the Panama Canal in 1965, the start of the
bunkering business in Panama

The tanker *Falcon* bunkering a ship in Panamanian waters in 1966

the country's oil business reported in favour of immediate nationalisation. The basis for this was that, as many of the concessions held by overseas companies would run out in 1983 and 1984, there was no incentive for new major investment. It was felt that most companies would simply extract what profits they could from investment made in the past. This was of no use to Venezuela, and so nationalisation was introduced with effect from 1 January 1976. Compensation was offered, but it was based on the depreciated book value of the companies' assets. On the auditor's advice, Ultramar had written down its Venezuelan assets to nominal amounts and this now proved to have been a sad mistake.

Ultramar received very little compensation for its assets and no compensation was given for royalty holdings. Thus, on the one hand the Chairman could state: 'the loss of the Venezuelan business is having no material effect on company finances', while on the other Ultramar could say farewell to a regular source of income that was producing at that stage over £3 million per year. It is a reflection of the success of Ultramar's policy of integration that the company could absorb a loss of this scale without undue consequences. With nationalisation, over 40 years of close association between Venezuela and Ultramar effectively came to a close, a period that, despite its slow beginnings, had seen the production of over 250 million barrels of oil. It was probably as well that the three men who had been largely responsible in bringing Ultramar's Venezuelan dream into reality were not around to witness the end. Professor Illing had died in 1969, Alfred Meyer in November 1965 and Vahan Djalaloff in January 1973.

In April 1976 a new company, Ultramar de Venezuela S.A., was incorporated in Caracas. This was an agency company that took over the remaining interests and staff of CPSA and was under the management of Gorgias Garriga. The company continues in existence and gives help in arranging crude purchase contracts from Venezuela by companies of the Ultramar Group.

Panama was the other main element in the newly designated Caribbean Division. Now Ultramar's largest investment in the Caribbean was the one-third interest in Refineria Panama which was being paid for in the five instalments agreed as part of the original purchase contract. The refinery itself was operating at capacity, running at an average of over 46,000 barrels per day in 1965, and there were plans for expansion. There was also considerable interest in a projected petrochemical plant at Portobelo, a scheme that had originally been part of Ultramar's own refinery plan. This was revived regularly over the next few years, and some development work was undertaken. For instance, in September 1967, an agreement to develop the petrochemical plant was signed between Ultramar, Conoco and National Bulk Carriers and in July 1970 plans to build the plant were announced. These did not come to anything. Plans to enlarge the refinery, however, took a more concrete shape and there were several expansion programmes aimed towards an eventual capacity of 100,000 barrels per day. Although this target was not reached, throughput had increased to 79,000 barrels by 1971.

Ultramar Panama, the company incorporated in 1960, was also active in marketing, transporting products to Canada and developing its own outlets both locally in Panama

Dale Austin, Joseph Ament and Bertram Ault attending a bunker barge launching
ceremony in Beaumont, Texas, in May 1968

and in various parts of the world. For example, a market for marine diesel oil was
established in Japan.

In the later 1960s the emphasis switched more to local markets, as consumer accounts
in the Canal Zone and Panama itself were built up. The first Golden Eagle gasoline
station in Panama was opened in the Province of Chiriquí in March 1969. However,
Panama's main function was to supply the Canadian and Californian markets with a
wide variety of products, and it was this constant movement of tankers between Panama
and Newfoundland that inspired the idea of backhauling more exotic cargoes. During
1965 studies were made to determine whether the dry-cargo holds of tankers could be
profitably used to carry fruit and vegetables from Panama to Newfoundland and dried
fish on the return voyage. This idea was tested and abandoned, but Bart Murray, who
was then manager in Panama, describes how some unexpected cargoes got through:
'Panama has the finest shrimp in the world. When a ship that was destined for
Newfoundland came to the refinery, we often put a few hundred pounds of shrimp on
board for our people at the Holyrood refinery. One year they reciprocated by sending us
a few hundred Christmas trees, which we sold at bargain prices with a gasoline fillup.
They were the finest Christmas trees Panama had ever seen and were remembered for

132

The launching of a bunker barge in Beaumont, Texas, in 1968

years. As a matter of fact, Christmas trees were also shipped to Venezuela in our dry-cargo holds where we gave them away in the loading ports and won a lot of goodwill. Another arrangement we had was for shipments of prime ribs of beef to be delivered by vessels calling at the refinery, as most food in Panama was poor and particularly the beef. Every time my beef arrived at the refinery there was some kind of upheaval. The first shipment arrived two days after a revolution. We lived in Panama City, about 50 miles from the refinery at Colón, and all the roads were set up with machine-gun posts to check traffic and look for enemies of the State. My contraband beef was 50 miles away and I needed it before it could thaw. So my wife and I dressed our small children, aged six and seven, in their Sunday best and we drove to Colón. We loaded the meat and headed back to Panama City. The National Guard, seeing we were "gringos" with our fair-haired children just waved us through the check points. Another time I was with Leo Berger, the owner of the ship that had brought in my contraband meat. There was trouble at the refinery and all car trunks were being opened and searched. So we put the meat on the passenger seat and sat Captain Leo on top of it until we were safely through.'

The most important Panamanian Ultramar marketing development during this period was the bunkering of ships. It had been noticed that ships waiting to pass through the

The barge *Golden Petrel* ready to deliver fuel in Panamanian waters in 1968

Panama Canal had to leave their position in line and go to a jetty for bunkering, a process that cost both time and money. Ultramar came up with the idea of self-propelled bunkering barges or ships that met and fuelled ships as they waited for their canal passage. Fresh water and provisions were also supplied. It was a bright idea but, in typical Ultramar style, it was started in a rather basic manner. A small old tanker, the *Eagle,* was purchased at the end of 1964 and, with a minimum of refitting, it was put to work. Conditions were primitive, to say the least. Joseph Ament was sent down from New York and put in charge. 'We had no ship-to-shore communications so we would go down to the shore, wave a blanket, and a seaman would row ashore from the *Eagle* for instructions. After a while, we made arrangments to share an office in Colón where we could use a radio. We borrowed a desk and a pine box for a chair. This arrangement cost us nothing and lasted for about six months until we finally moved into our own office.' Despite these rather simple beginnings, the bunkering operation prospered and grew to become an important element in Ultramar's Panamanian business. In 1966 another small tanker was purchased, the *Falcon,* which proved to be even more decrepit. Even the captain thought that the best thing would be to take the ship out to sea and sink it. However, reason prevailed, and the *Falcon* survived to give sterling service until the arrival of two custom-built bunkering barges, the *Golden Petrel* and the *Golden Condor,* in 1968.

These two new barges were built for Ultramar in Texas at the Beaumont yard of Bethlehem Steel at a total cost of $1.5 million. Each could carry 30,000 barrels of bunker fuel oil and was powered by two huge outboard motors. Their design was the result of a feasibility study which had shown that this type of barge was highly manoeuvrable and

134

Campbell Nelson and Arnold Lorbeer visiting a bunker barge at Taboga Island off Panama in the late 1960s. On the return voyage, the motor boat lost its propeller and the group was adrift in the open sea until they were rescued by the Coast Guard

Dorothy Tom, vice president and resident manager, Ultramar Panama in the 1970s and early 1980s

required no tug assistance. More important, a self-propelled barge had a different classification from a tanker and so could be operated by a four-man crew while the old *Eagle,* though smaller, required a crew of fourteen. These self-propelled barges were a considerable investment but the economics of the bunkering operation were such that, within a year, a third barge, the *Golden Owl,* was ordered. This meant that two barges could always be in operation, one at either end of the Canal Zone. By 1970 the three barges were bunkering 45 ships per month at a rate of 12,400 barrels a day and 4.5 million barrels a year. When not involved in bunkering, the barges were used for transport business at the refinery, taking products to various terminals in the Canal Zone. The success of this operation encouraged Ultramar to open a bunkering station at Portobelo, on the Atlantic coast. It was a remote and inaccessible spot, unapproachable by road, and was short lived as few ships took advantage of it. Apart from greatly expanding Ultramar's marketing operations in Panama, the bunkering fleet also represented the company's first experience of ship ownership. The success of the venture perhaps paved the way for the more dramatic maritime activities that were to occur in the near future.

Despite the success of the refinery investment and the marketing interests in Panama, circumstances caused Ultramar to sell the business to Texaco in February 1973. In 1971 Texaco had bought the interest of National Bulk Carriers, which previously had bought out Conoco. So Texaco now owned two-thirds of the refinery and they were eager to acquire Ultramar's one-third. During this period the sale of the Mercedes interests in

135

Group at a Golden Eagle function in Panama in 1962.
*Left to right:* John Owers, Basil Goodfellow, Lloyd Bensen, William Robinson

Venezuela was being concluded, and so the Caribbean Division was effectively being cut down. Also important, Ultramar was financially stretched by the building of the Quebec refinery, and the good price received for the Panama interests was useful. The Quebec refinery was also seen as a replacement for Panama, its completion overcoming the need to spend more by expanding the Panama refinery to a capacity of 100,000 barrels per day. However the sale did not completely close Ultramar's Panama chapter. The office was put under the direction of Dorothy Tom, whose involvement with the Panama company dated back to 1959 and the pre-Ultramar days. Throughout the rest of the 1970s, the Panama office was staffed by specialists who ran the business of Ultramar's trading and shipping companies, and in 1980 it came to life in a number of new ways. Exploration surveys were begun in Panama to search for oil and gas. Similar surveys, but on a smaller scale, had been mounted in 1965, but were discontinued because of lack of legislation governing oil exploration. This is still a handicap. At the same time, a new company, Ultramar Istmica S.A. was launched to undertake property development, and a condominium complex known as Ultramar Plaza was completed in 1982. A number of other subsidiaries, involved in transportation and exploration, have also been registered in Panama.

The terms of the sale of Ultramar's Panama refining and marketing interests to Texaco had some interesting sidelights. Texaco insisted that part of the sales price be in

136

the form of crude oil and induced Ultramar to sign a three-year crude oil contract. This contract was for 25,000 barrels per day of Arabian light crude oil at posted prices. At the time of the sale, it was anticipated that Ultramar would lose a few cents a barrel on the resale or use of the crude oil, but the overall agreement was still satisfactory. As luck would have it, the refinery sale was concluded in the first quarter 1973 just prior to the world oil crisis, and thus Ultramar had available substantial volumes of crude oil for an extended period of time which it was able to place in the market at a considerable profit. It just shows that the wheel of fortune takes strange turns.

Panama today is still part of the Ultramar network, even though it is at this time no longer directly associated with the process of oil production and refining. However, there are many employees who can look back to the golden era of the late 1960s when Panama was not only a major part of Ultramar, but also an important stop on the Caribbean Professional Golf Tour. There was always a Pro-Am round in which Bill Robinson regularly played. 'Bill was always a wreck before the tournament,' Bart Murray recalls, 'because he swore that Arnold Lorbeer would wait until he was playing in the Pro-Am and then telephone. And he usually did.'

It is possible that Panama, and perhaps other areas of Latin America, will figure more prominently in Ultramar's future. It was the scene of the company's beginning and there are still a number of active staff members who served tours of duty in Venezuela or Panama. In January 1984, the Ultramar Board held its monthly meeting in Panama City and combined it with meetings to consider future corporate strategy, including expansion in Panama and elsewhere in central America.

The phasing out of Venezuela and Panama coincided with the ending of several Ultramar careers and considerable shifting around of the top executives. Lord Tangley retired as Chairman of Ultramar in 1970, but continued as a director until his death in 1973. Campbell Nelson became Chairman. Other directors appointed during this period included Basil Goodfellow, Donald McCall, Lloyd Bensen, John Owers, Dale Austin, Sir Kenneth Barrington and Lord Remnant. On the operational side, Arnold Lorbeer decided in 1974 to give up the position of chief executive after twenty years at the helm. However, he continued as a director of Ultramar and an officer of the operating companies. He was succeeded by Lloyd Bensen. Lorbeer came back into full view in 1980 when he succeeded Nelson as Chairman of Ultramar, a position he held until 1985 when Bensen took over and Dale Austin became operational head. Richard Thompson resigned from the Board in 1969. Eugene O'Shea succeeded Knudsen as General Counsel. Ultramar suffered grave losses by the premature deaths of Bertram Ault and William Robinson, who had performed brilliantly in finance and Caribbean operations respectively.

Aerial view of the Quebec refinery at St. Romuald after the
expansion programme in 1983

# THE
# QUEBEC
# REFINERY 8

In 1960 Ultramar established the Golden Eagle Refining Company of Canada and constructed the 7,500 barrels per day refinery near St. John's, Newfoundland. A marketing organisation was built up to sell the products of the Newfoundland and Caribbean refining operations, and terminals were located in Newfoundland and Quebec. A programme of service station building was launched, and many branded independent dealers were appointed. Funds for the building programme were provided by selling the outlets to investors and leasing them back. Home heating fuel volume was built up by a series of acquisitions of independent dealers, and Golden Eagle also became a major supplier to independent sellers of both gasoline and furnace fuel. By 1967, Ultramar had become one of the largest importers of petroleum products in Canada. This, however, left the company very vulnerable should the Canadian Government decide to follow the American example, from which Ultramar had suffered in the early 1960s, of imposing restrictions on the import of refined petroleum products in order to protect its own oil industry. It did not seem likely that imports of crude oil into eastern Canada would be restricted, because it was federal policy to use foreign crude in refineries east of the Ottawa valley. It therefore made sense for Ultramar to have its own refinery on the mainland of Canada, to overcome the possible restrictions on product imports and thus protect its investment and market position.

These pressures persuaded Ultramar by the late 1960s to embark on feasibility studies for a refinery in its marketing area of eastern Canada. Another influential factor was the changing position of the Panama refinery which was now selling most of its products locally while the Canadian market was being supplied by purchases from other Caribbean refineries. The fluctuations between the product prices charged by these refineries and the retail price obtainable in Canada meant that a profit could not always be guaranteed. A team composed of Dale Austin, James Allan and Charles Quigley was appointed in 1968 to make a detailed study. Vital and urgent questions had to be answered as to location, financing and construction.

The location of the refinery was crucial. As the largest market for the company's products was in the Montreal area, it would have seemed logical to locate the refinery there, especially as there was a large, well-established pipeline from Portland, Maine, which carried offshore crude oil to the six existing Montreal refineries. This pipeline

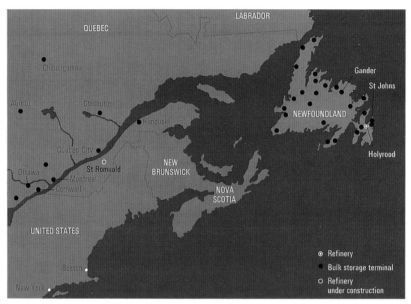

Golden Eagle's bulk storage in eastern Canada in 1969

The Quebec refinery planning team, Dr Charles Quigley (*far left*), James Allan (*centre*),
Dale Austin (*second from right*) with Campbell Nelson (*second from left*) and
John Owers (*far right*) who spearheaded the financing for the refinery

was necessary because the St. Lawrence River between Quebec City and Montreal is not consistently open to tanker navigation during winter months. Ultramar, however, had never been content just to follow where others had led without careful consideration and so other locations were examined. The ultimate decision not to build in Montreal proved fortunate as in later years there has been refining over-capacity in Montreal.

After examination of all possible sites, it was decided by the team to recommend that a refinery be built in the vicinity of Quebec City. The reasons were persuasive. Quebec City lies at the head of year-round deep-water navigation on the St. Lawrence. In addition both the Provincial and Federal Governments, keen to develop Quebec City as a major deep-water port, promised to dredge the channel to allow fully loaded tankers up to 100,000 tons to reach Quebec. The refinery would be the only one in the Quebec City area. This would enable the company to provide its own requirements in the area at minimal transportation cost in addition to meeting the needs of the other oil companies in the area. In return they would supply Ultramar's requirements in the Montreal area, thus saving transport costs all round. Quebec City was also seeing an increase in population greater than anywhere else in Quebec Province thereby providing a growing market for the company's products as well as a pool of labour for construction of the refinery and for operator trainees. Thirdly, the Federal Government had designated Quebec City as a distress unemployment area, which qualified the refinery project for a $5 million grant. The Federal Government also gave Ultramar accelerated capital cost allowances. The Federal, Provincial and Municipal Governments were in addition prepared to co-operate in the provision of the necessary permits for the construction of a refinery.

Austin's team considered concurrently the type of refinery required. The major priority was a refinery which could meet the company's market requirements in the Province of Quebec and in Newfoundland where demand now exceeded refinery production. At this time these were, for the most part, gasolines and middle distillates. Residual fuel oil, used for power plants, pulp and paper mills, the Labrador iron industry and ships' bunkers, was a big business in eastern Canada but was complicated by low-priced supplies from the Caribbean. The existing marketing needs of the company could have been met by the construction of a complex 30,000 barrels per day refinery with hydrocracking and other facilities producing gasolines and middle distillates. Most refineries built in North America at that time were of this type. They were, however, expensive to build and run and the construction cost was estimated at the time to be $100 million. Charles Quigley with Ultramar's market analysts made studies of the crude inputs, the different types of process units, the product yields and the market criteria and came up with a 100,000 barrel per day hydroskimming refinery as ideal for Ultramar's circumstances. This was really a fuel oil refinery, which would provide 50,000 barrels per day of heavy fuel oil and also produce the necessary gasolines and middle distillates. Contributing factors to the decision to go ahead and build this type of refinery were, first, that the cost per barrel was much less than for a more sophisticated refinery, second, that a hydroskimming refinery was more reliable and simpler to

Paul Boyd and Jean Jacques Bertrand, Prime Minister of the Province of Quebec,
digging the first sod to mark the start of construction of the Quebec refinery
at St. Romuald on 14 May 1969

operate, especially in the cold winter weather, and third that, in the opinion of the
marketing staff, the heavy fuel oil would have a long-term profitable market both in
Canada and the northeastern United States. For environmental reasons it was difficult at
this time to obtain permits to build plants in the American northeast. Thus the Quebec
refinery was one of three built in Canada with the part intention of exporting products to
the northeastern United States. Ultramar's plan was to buy low-sulphur crude from
north Africa and export low-sulphur heavy fuel to the U.S. East Coast using backhaul by
crude tankers. Canada did not have such strict sulphur restrictions and so eastern
Canada was a suitable outlet for high-sulphur heavy fuel refined from Venezuelan
crude.

The refinery scheme was approved in the early autumn of 1968. Underlying the
refinery project was a contract with Esso (Exxon), who agreed to supply the refinery
with the necessary crude oil on reasonable terms. Exxon in these years was well disposed
towards Ultramar and had previously helped to get the Newfoundland refinery started.
The basic plan was to bring in light Libyan crude oil and heavy Venezuelan crude oil.

Lord Tangley visits St. Romuald

The products would be gasoline, middle distillates, low and high sulphur fuel oil, liquid petroleum gas and asphalt.

Having decided on the general location and type of refinery, a specific site had to be acquired, a contractor engaged and, most important, the necessary finance raised. The refinery would be the largest single investment Ultramar had ever undertaken and for the most part would have to be financed through loans. Instead of following the normal industry practice of employing a construction firm to design and build the refinery while the finance was raised separately, it was decided to depart from this practice in two ways. Inspired perhaps by the way the Holyrood refinery had been so rapidly built from existing equipment, contractors were approached who could provide off-the-shelf design for processing units already installed at other refineries and thus reduce the total design and building time. Also, all contracts had to be on a turnkey, fixed price basis with a suitable financing package. The number of contractors who were interested in the project on this basis was small and, as Dale Austin recalls, 'By early 1969 the engineering/construction companies were narrowed to Snam Progetti in Milan, Italy, and Procon

143

G.B. in London. A short period was spent flying between these two cities negotiating both the price and financing terms. We had effectively concluded an arrangement with Snam Progetti when out of the blue they telephoned and withdrew their offer. This occurred at the time of an Ultramar Board Meeting in London and, through the persuasive tactics of some members of Ultramar's Board, a financing arrangement was reached with ECGD (Export Credits Guarantee Department), the U.K. Government finance guarantee arm, and a letter of intent was negotiated with Procon G.B. which included all the desirable elements. This all transpired in a 48-hour period and was a most remarkable achievement.'

Sir Kenneth Barrington, Managing Director of Morgan Grenfell, and a member of the Ultramar Board, gave invaluable assistance in arranging the necessary finance. Morgan Grenfell raised 85% of the money needed for the refinery. This was a combination of loans from British clearing banks guaranteed, as outlined above, by the Government's ECGD, plus Eurodollar loans from a consortium of banks led by Morgan Grenfell, National Provincial and Rothschild (International) Ltd. The remaining 15% of the cost had to be found from within Ultramar and was largely supplied by a rights issue to shareholders in October 1968.

In effect, the financing was made possible through ECGD and was made available through a most creative application of that programme's benefits. The programme had been instituted to promote the sale of U.K. supplies and services overseas by backing U.K. bids with financing that was internationally competitive. Ultramar, a British

Group on the dock during construction. *Left to right:* James Allan, Arnold Lorbeer, Campbell Nelson, Dale Austin, Blake Stewart

Arnold Lorbeer, Jean Marchand, Federal Regional Economic Development Minister,
Paul Boyd, Lord Tangley, Lloyd Bensen and James Allan at the Quebec
refinery opening 1 October 1971

Campbell Nelson who spoke in French
at the opening ceremony for the
Quebec refinery

company, presented a bid from a Canadian company, whose shares were also owned by a U.K. company. The construction company was a U.K. company whose shares were owned by a U.S. company. The Ultramar representatives' powers of persuasive argument were stretched to their limits to convince the Government that our arrangement was in compliance with the regulations. Indeed, at the end the Treasury's representative was heard to remark 'The Department's sacred cows lay strewn about our hallways'.

A site of 250 acres was acquired at St. Romuald, on the St. Lawrence River, opposite Quebec City. Most of the land was obtained from the Provincial Government but there were four or five parcels of land adjoining the principal site which were in private hands. John Pepper of the legal firm Campbell, Pepper and Laffoley in Montreal recalls the lengths to which they had to go to obtain the final parcel. 'In winding up we came to the last plot of land which appeared to be necessary to complete the entire parcel. This was a small piece of property no greater than 200 feet by 200 feet in size, on which was constructed a shack of sorts that could not have been valued at more than $5,000. We descended upon the owner with an offer of $10,000, which was immediately refused. Further negotiations resulted in the owner demanding payment of $30,000, which in our minds was a preposterous price considering that we were contemplating nothing more than a shack which was to be demolished upon completion of the sale. Because of the "hold up" by the owner who insisted on his price, and because of our refusal to overpay grossly (this was a studied decision and in keeping with the economics of the time), we did not purchase. We decided that the refinery would always have a corner of 200 feet by 200 feet which would be eliminated from its normal symmetry, but that this did not necessarily matter. With the passing of time it became obvious that that decision made no sense whatsoever and that an effort should be made to acquire the last plot of land, which would complete the refinery property, regardless of price. Needless to say, the owner of the shack was now more encouraged from the construction around his shack which he was experiencing and consequently increased his price. The deal was finally closed by Ultramar being required to pay in excess of $100,000 for the shack and the property of 200 feet by 200 feet which it occupied.'

The contract with Procon (G.B.) was signed in February 1969 and work soon started on clearing the site. Completion was originally scheduled for early 1971 at a cost of Can.$70 million. However, before long both the timetable and the budget had to be adjusted. Much of the equipment was British, and labour disputes at the manufacturers together with a dock strike delayed the arrival of materials and thus construction. At extra cost, equipment had to be added for air and water pollution control as well as additional safety measures in excess of the normal industry requirements on the instruction of the insurance underwriters. Inflation was rampant at that time which increased the cost of the labour and the company also had to make incentive payments for winter work. By December of 1970 Procon was experiencing severe productivity problems, a combination of extremely cold weather and union activity. It was agreed with Procon that Ultramar would take over project management, and to give a clean

146

The Quebec refinery under construction in 1971

The Quebec refinery during construction March 1971

start, all 600 workers were laid off one Friday. A riot ensued, and time-clock huts were set on fire, but it was quickly subdued by the very cooperative Provincial Police who had been forewarned and were standing by. After a couple of weeks under the able management of Blake Stewart, small crews were taken on and gradually the work force built up. There were no more productivity problems, and the job ran smoothly to completion. By the time the refinery came on stream in September 1971, the total cost had risen to Can.$109 million, the additional cost financed out of Ultramar's own cash resources and short-term borrowing. This, however, did nothing to dampen the celebrations when the refinery was officially opened on 1 October 1971. Fourteen hundred guests attended, arriving from all over the world, by many modes of transport, including chartered planes from Toronto, New York and London, and even a chartered train from Montreal.

The first few months were difficult and many experienced people were brought in to help. One of these was Malcolm Haigh, by training a chemist, and at that time manager of Ultramar's Holyrood refinery. 'In early 1972 it was all hands to the pumps at Quebec due to a late startup and the severe winter. I was transferred on two days' notice for a period of two months. I ended up spending six months at Quebec, focusing on offsites, unit train facilities and truck rack expansion.'

Quebec City is 97% French-speaking, and while all of the senior managers and supervisors on our refinery staff were bilingual, the majority of employees had a limited

148

A tanker docking at the Quebec refinery during the early months of 1972

or non-existent facility in English. With rising French-Canadian nationalism, it became both logical and reasonable for Ultramar to operate the refinery in French. All operating, training and technical manuals then had to be in the French language. Having French-Canadian bilingual management, one would think that this would be an easy task. Not so. The managers had never operated in anything but English and had to write the manuals in English for eventual translation into French. The whole exercise was much greater than ever anticipated, involving exchange visits with refiners in France and some excellent cooperation from the Quebec Government which did much of the translation. A useful by-product was a lexicon of refining industry terms now used by all the Montreal refiners which until the early 1970s had operated in English.

Blake Stewart, who had managed BP's refinery in Montreal, joined us in 1970 as refinery manager, and under his leadership the plant was organised on a non-union basis. Contributory to this was the multi-disciplinary approach under which all operators were also skilled tradesmen. Their shifts rotated through both operations and maintenance, and while on the operations shift they were expected to perform routine

149

View over the dock at the Quebec refinery with an Ultramar flag tanker in the background

and emergency maintenance. This system was well received as it added some interest and activity to an otherwise routine operator's job. Employee relations continue to be excellent, and there has never been a strike in the fourteen years of operation. Blake Stewart attracted a number of engineers and operators who contributed to the success of the operation, many of whom were to remain with Ultramar through the years; to cite a few - Gaston Rivet, Raynald Archambault, Jean Gaulin, and Dan McLean from BP, Blaine Beal from Exxon, John Rogers from Gulf, and Ray Langevin from Petrofina.

One of the unusual features of the project was the special dock facility. The proposed dock was elaborately modelled in the Hydraulic Laboratory at the University of Laval. Currents were set up and plastic objects floated to assess the affects of severe winter ice and tidal conditions. As a result of that study, the angle of the dock to the river was changed slightly. When it came time to build it, a widow with eel fishing rights prevented the start of construction for five days. Having rapidly assessed that her annual earnings would be $6,000, Glen Muir and Jim Airth went with a cheque for $6,000 in one pocket and a $2,000 cheque in the other. However, on arrival, they found that her lawyer was demanding $100,000. On the fifth day, it was determined that she had already been refunded the relevant portion of her annual permit costs by the Canadian National Railway. The dock construction foreman, a 'no-nonsense' Dutchman, promptly

150

Aerial view of one
of the collapsed
storage tanks at
the Quebec refinery
in late 1972

The unit train
supplying Ontario
Hydro loading at
St. Romuald in 1974
attended by Malcolm Haigh,
G. Bedford, R. Langevin,
R. Brouillette

The unit train
unloading at the
Lennox power station
of Ontario Hydro

removed her nets and carefully placed them in her front yard. In the event, she received nothing! The dock cost $6 million nonetheless.

From the start there were some difficulties with the refinery and with the supply of crude which meant that it could not run at its planned 100,000 barrels per day. A major set-back was the failure at the end of 1972 of the 500,000 barrel conical roof storage tanks. The roofs of two tanks collapsed altogether and the other seven experienced partial failure. Each in turn had to be taken out of service and it was only in October 1973 that they were all fully repaired. The loss of these tanks meant that for a time there was considerably reduced flexibility in the storage and blending of different grades of fuel oil and it also affected the scheduling of tanker deliveries of crude oil.

In locating the refinery at Quebec City, a commitment had been made by the Federal Government to dredge, by an additional eleven feet in depth, the North Traverse, the eleven-mile stretch of channel in the St. Lawrence on the approaches to the refinery, so as to allow full use of the 55-foot draft at the dock face. It proved to be a more difficult and expensive project than originally contemplated, and the dredging was stretched out over six years, finishing finally in October 1977. The fact that the major Canadian dredging contractors had been accused of collusion and were not available certainly contributed to the delay. While the original dredging was completed in 1974, some of the earlier-dredged portions had silted in, and it took three more years to clean out the entire channel. Further difficulties were caused when the pilots' association went on strike in 1971 and again in 1972, preventing deliveries for up to two weeks. In recent years, however, reason has prevailed with a recognition of the economic importance of the refinery to the Quebec area, and there have been no further problems.

During these years, the delivery economics suffered due to the use of smaller tankers. Since 1977, however, a 41-foot channel has been available which along with 13 to 21 foot tides has given full use of the 55-foot draft wharf. Tankers up to 160,000 tons have serviced the refinery, and 80,000-120,000 tonners call regularly.

The initial problems were matched by some positive developments. In November 1972 the company entered into a five-year fuel supply contract with Ontario Hydro, the Hydro-Electric Power Commission of Ontario, for the supply of high sulphur fuel oil for the generating facilities at Lennox on the north shore of Lake Ontario. At the time this was the largest supply contract ever entered into by the company, with sales in the region of Can.$75 million. The oil under this contract was to be delivered by rail in an entire train dedicated to oil transportation. The 65-car unit known as a unit train was the first of its type in the world and carried 30,000 barrels. It completed the 720-mile round-trip in 48 hours, loading and unloading included. The train's punctuality was such that it was claimed you could set your watch anywhere along the line. Another useful contract involved the processing of crude oil for a major oil company at an initial rate of 10,000 barrels per day for an eight-year period commencing in July 1973.

The Arab-Israeli War of 1973 and the subsequent increase in the price of oil was to have a lasting effect on both the supply of and demand for crude oil and its products. As a result the Canadian Federal Government became increasingly involved in the oil

152

Quebec refinery expansion: the regeneration unit being transported along
the St. Lawrence River, and entering the refinery

industry and began to influence the future of companies such as Ultramar. A decision was taken by the Canadian Government to institute a 'made in Canada' oil price. This involved control of western Canadian crude postings at levels below the OPEC rates and a subsidy paid by the Government to importers of foreign crudes. The subsidies were designed to equalise the costs of foreign and domestic crude. However, they were tied to the official postings of foreign crude. At this time many foreign crudes were unavailable at official postings and the premiums required to purchase some spot crudes, being unsupported by subsidy and unrecoverable in the market, made them uneconomic in Canada. Refineries, unlike Ultramar's, which were connected by pipeline to western Canadian crude were naturally in a more favourable position, as western Canadian crude was purchased at Canadian posted prices.

From 1973 onwards the company was able at times to obtain a limited amount of the more economically priced western Canadian crude oil. This involved on occasion having to take crude from Vancouver down the West Coast of the United States through the Panama Canal and up to Quebec.

The same import subsidy programme provided a further blow when it was applied to the import of heavy fuel oil. This reduced the price at which domestically refined material could be sold in Canada. The Quebec refinery yielded about 50% heavy fuel at this time. Ultramar was, however, fortunate in that it had made a three million barrels per year heavy fuel oil contract to deliver to Ontario Hydro.

A 1974 Canadian Government decision to restrict the export of refined products created a crisis in Ultramar's refinery operations because a considerable amount of low-sulphur heavy fuel oil had been contracted to utilities in the northeastern United States. Winter was approaching and several large New England cities were affected. Ultramar scrambled frantically, at considerable cost, to find substitute supplies. Production was also affected in August 1975 by a fire which shut the refinery for seven weeks.

These developments put Ultramar's staff through a hard test of resourcefulness, resilience, flexibility and inventiveness. As a result of the loss of the American market for low sulphur heavy fuel oil, the company looked for ways of expanding its domestic market and this led to the acquisition of Canadian Fuel Marketers (CFM) from Shell in early 1979. CFM, along with Ultramar, was a very large domestic marketer of heavy fuel oil in eastern Canada and together the two companies had about 50% of the market. Demand for heavy fuel oil in fact remained buoyant until the 1979 political crisis in Iran when the world crude oil again rose in price. Although cushioned to some extent by the Government's subsidy policy, consumers in Canada, particularly commercial consumers, then began to move away from the use of heavy fuel oil and turned to gas. The acquisition of CFM protected the refinery's fuel oil outlets in a declining market.

The oil market veered towards transportation fuels and other fuels. Transportation fuels, gasoline and diesel, filled an increasing share of the total petroleum products market. As early as 1976 the company started to look at a way of improving the economics of the refinery by doing studies for a 20,000 barrels per day fluid catalytic cracking unit. This could convert low value residual fuel oil to higher value gasoline and

The regeneration unit being installed at the Quebec refinery

distillates. It would also mean that lower gravity and cheaper crude oils could be used. Design and engineering studies for this sophistication of the refinery continued until 1980 without any decision being made to go ahead. As the project was expensive, the company had to be sure that the financing and market conditions were such that a good enough return would be achieved.

An important factor in holding up the decision was the lack of a secure supply of crude oil, since Ultramar lost access to more than 40,000 barrels per day in 1979 as a consequence of the international supply crisis following the Iranian revolution. A renewed effort was made to gain access to western Canadian crude oil, but it was only when the Federal Government agreed that Ultramar would have access to Canadian crude on an equal basis with the competition in Montreal that, in 1980, the company went ahead with the up-grading project as a quid pro quo. Some modifications were made to the original design to reduce costs and the capacity of the cracking unit was

155

The Quebec refinery in 1983 with the catalytic cracking unit installed

increased to 30,000 barrels per day. The cost of the refinery sophistication was estimated to be Can.$200 million excluding interest and the funds were provided by three Canadian banks, Canadian Imperial Bank of Commerce, Royal Bank of Canada and Bank of Montreal.

The engineering and construction contracts were awarded to Fluor Canada of Calgary. It was to be an almost entirely Canadian operation because, as well as being engineered and constructed by Canadians, most of the equipment was to be Canadian. Supervision was put in the hands of Blaine Beal. By December 1980 engineering had progressed sufficiently to allow Fluor to make a definitive estimate of costs. Including start-up and financing costs, this now stood at over Can.$300 million, a figure that forced Ultramar management to have some second thoughts. Ultramar decided to slow the pace of the project while it reviewed alternatives, and Fluor was instructed to freeze equipment orders and to cut staff to a level sufficient to complete engineering packages for lump-sum bidding. Equipment orders already issued for major units were left in place. The size and scope of the new units were studied, and several modifications were made and the new vacuum and visbreaking units eliminated. Simultaneously, a search was made for a Canadian partner and even for outside processing capacity which would eliminate the need for the project. By November 1981, having exhausted the options and reduced the size of the project, Fluor was instructed to accelerate work.

Field work started in the spring of 1982. The reactor, regenerator and fractionator were to be some of the largest vessels ever shop fabricated in Canada. Weighing 320, 250 and 250 tons respectively, the transportation of these pieces of equipment was to prove far from easy. They were brought by barge down the St. Lawrence River from Montreal, where they were built, to a specially constructed dock at Quebec. Each enormous vessel was then moved through St. Romuald on a crawler transporter with telephone and power lines raised to let them pass. When they arrived at the refinery a ringer crane brought over specially from the U.K. lifted the vessels onto the structure. The catalytic cracking unit was officially dedicated and a reception held to celebrate the opening on 19 September 1983. In spite of the fact that it was a well-run project, the total cost now amounted to Can.$310 million including interest and start-up work.

The building of the cat cracker has doubled the refinery's capacity to produce gasoline and increased its flexibility to produce a wide range of petroleum products. This upgrading was complemented by the acquisition of a number of marketing companies. Spur Oil in Quebec Province, formerly owned by Murphy Oil, gave Ultramar an additional 100 company-operated gasoline stations and 50 dealer stations. One of the largest acquisitions was Pittston Petroleum which provided additional outlets in the northeastern United States and eastern Canada for the products from the Quebec refinery. The Government of Canada controls exports of products, and while generally export permits for finished products are granted, there are times of tight supply when they are not. To ensure an uninterrupted flow of products to the Pittston locations, these controls had to be overcome. A processing agreement was signed with Pittston, and a special application to the Canadian National Energy Board for a five-year term was approved. Ultramar Petroleum (the new name for Pittston) supplies crude to the Quebec refinery and picks up the refined products produced. This new phase of operation at the Quebec refinery commenced on 31 January 1984, when the *Bermuda Bianca* loaded 200,000 barrels of gasoline for shipment to New York.

Cowley Ultraserve near Oxford, formally opened in 1973 by Campbell Nelson's
wife Pauline, aided by Eva Rueber-Staier, a former Miss World

# MARKETING 9

Ultramar's first exposure to marketing came in the late 1950s when the company could not sell all its Venezuelan crude oil production to Texaco under existing long-term contracts. As described in earlier chapters, some of the production was sold as crude oil while the remainder was refined at a number of local refineries and the products sold. A considerable amount of heavy fuel oil was marketed in New York harbour. Ships were needed and that began our entry into ship chartering. Bensen and Quigley handled these early marketing ventures while Al Marino, Joe Ament and John Tivnan did the ship chartering.

Following the merger with Golden Eagle, during the early 1960s Ultramar struggled to obtain footholds in both the Californian and the eastern Canadian markets, relying on the blend of management initiative, expansion by acquisition and sheer hard work that was to become the characteristic marketing policy for the company. By 1964 Ultramar was established in both North American markets, selling a wide range of products that included gasoline, aviation fuel, heating oil, asphalt and bunker fuel. The three refineries in Newfoundland, Los Angeles and Panama were taking crude from Venezuela and from the open market and supplying finished products to markets in North America. Additional product supplies were being bought, and a number of subsidiary markets were also being developed. These included Panama, where the refinery's output was increasingly absorbed locally, and the ship bunkering business, which was to become one of the mainstays of the Caribbean Division. A third strand was cargo trading, an increasingly important feature of Ultramar's business that was soon to lead to the development of important shipping and transportation interests within the company.

By the end of 1964, Ultramar marketing was structured in three divisions, covering the Caribbean, Canada and the United States, all of which were profitable. In addition, the groundwork had been laid for the formation of a fourth division, covering Europe, but this was not to be active for some years. Each of the first three divisions was relatively autonomous, with its own refinery, its own marketing operations under the Golden Eagle brand and its own crude supplies. In the late 1960s and early 1970s there were a number of plans to expand the Caribbean Division, but most came to nought. These included the opening of negotiations to establish a bunkering station on St. Helena, and the plan to join a Swiss-Italian group in building a refinery in the

159

Promotional map of Newfoundland marking the Golden Eagle service stations and restaurants

Bay Roberts, a Newfoundland terminal

A Newfoundland service station in wintry conditions

## MARKETING

Dominican Republic, a project based on the availability of a suitable deep-water site and a long-term crude supply contract. Of these, the former was rather fanciful, but the latter was an important scheme that became a victim of the political events of 1973. Of course, at this stage only the Caribbean Division could really be considered self-sufficient in crude, but Canada and the United States were supported by long-term crude supply contracts.

The Canadian Division, by now Ultramar's largest investment, was effectively divided into two markets, Newfoundland and eastern Canada. The nature of its geography made Newfoundland fairly independent, a feature that was echoed by the marketing policy. The refinery at Holyrood, a relatively unsophisticated plant, was gradually expanded during the mid 1960s to cater to the increasing demands for fuel oil and asphalt. At the same time, the marine terminals and the branded gasoline stations were steadily expanded. By 1965 there were seven marine terminals and seven satellite terminals in Newfoundland, and 90 branded gasoline stations. The expansion of the market was closely linked to the development of Newfoundland's road system, the most important feature of which was the Trans-Canada Highway, completely paved by 1965. Golden Eagle benefited in two ways, first by supplying all the asphalt for the Newfoundland road programme, and secondly from the increased demand for gasoline and heating oil that resulted from the new roads. As the Province's economy developed, more marine terminals and storage facilities were built, and this in turn led to an expansion of the bunkering market. In 1964, for example, over 190 ships were bunkered through the marine terminals.

The pattern of growth continued in Newfoundland during the late 1960s. In 1966 a part of the storage facilities at Harmon Air Base in Stephenville was taken over from the United States Airforce for use as a terminal, while each year saw an increase in the number of gasoline stations, industrial consumers and the amount of product sold. In 1969 a propane unit was added to Holyrood, capable of producing one million gallons per year.

Ultramar's managers in Newfoundland have been very competent and flexible and the operations in that Province have usually been profitable. Reference has already been made to Jack Polk, Ultramar's first manager. He was followed in succession by James Allan, John Aitken and Roy Myers. The latter is a true son of Newfoundland who came up through Ultramar's ranks on the refinery side.

In mainland Canada market growth followed a similar pattern, although there was a greater concentration on gasoline and heating oil. By 1965 there were 159 branded gasoline stations in Quebec Province, 117 of which had been built by the company. Terminals had been established in Montreal, Quebec, Rimouski, Chicoutimi and Toronto, and customers now included major users such as the Labrador iron ore industry and power companies in the Maritime Provinces. Smaller customers were supplied by a fleet of over 300 Golden Eagle branded trucks. In addition, customer relationships were improved by the introduction of a credit card system and a financing programme to cover heating equipment purchases. By 1969 the total product sales for the Canadian Division

*Top left:* Home heating services in Newfoundland, *top right:* the tanker *Golden Falcon* making a winter delivery to Seven Islands terminal in Quebec Province in 1968, *centre left:* John Aitken, territory manager, Newfoundland, 1965-76, *below left:* Doug Pemberton, refinery manager at Holyrood, 1963-9, *below right:* laying asphalt on the Trans-Canada Highway in 1975

The 20th anniversary celebrations at the Holyrood refinery. *Left to right:* Roy Myers, Walter Nelson, John Hawco, Malcolm Haigh (all former managers of the refinery)

had reached 29,000 barrels per day. The decision to build the Quebec refinery brought about a dramatic review of the Canadian market. It was clear by 1969 that a new approach to marketing would be required if Canada was to absorb the output from the new refinery and so a policy of expansion by acquisition was launched.

The policy was not entirely new, as various small distribution companies, for example Cornwall Petroleum in Ontario, had been purchased in the past, but acquisition activity during 1969 was on a far grander scale. The first company to be bought was A. E. Gauthier the largest independent marketer of home heating oils in the Chicoutimi area of Quebec Province. This was followed by International Fuels, a company selling 30 million gallons of heating oil a year in the greater Montreal area, Gerard Hebert, operating in St. Hyacinthe, and the Wilson Company, a western Quebec business that had been formed in 1928 as the Canadian Ice Company and then entered the home heating fuel market during the 1940s. However, perhaps the most significant purchase was a 50% interest in Neal Petroleum in Toronto because this represented a major effort to expand in the Ontario market.

Neal Petroleum had been formed a few years earlier by George Mottershead, formerly an employee of Liquifuels which in 1967 had been bought by Royal Dutch Shell. This

Golden Eagle home delivery service in eastern Canada in 1971

Arrow service station and car wash, London, Ontario, 1972

Joe McManus,
founder of Arrow Petroleum

George Mottershead,
founder of Neal Petroleum

purchase had left no independent fuel oil company operating as a wholesaler in the Province of Ontario, and so Mottershead decided to fill the gap. The company's beginnings were somewhat primitive. As Mottershead remembers: 'Neal's first office consisted of a card table, four chairs, one broken-down desk and a rented typewriter. My family pledged their entire net worth to finance the company. As products had to be purchased for resale, accounts receivable financed and storage leased, it soon became apparent that considerable additional finance was needed.' Somehow Mottershead survived and three cargoes were imported from the Caribbean and sold during the first few months. 'I remember the first 20,000 ton tanker coming to Toronto in the fall of 1969. It had to be light loaded at Montreal to meet the draught requirements of the St. Lawrence River. It was such a big event that a party was held on board when the ship docked at Toronto. Nearly all our customers and the staff of four attended.'

A chance meeting in 1969 between Mottershead and Bensen at a conference in Houston resulted in Ultramar buying 50% of Neal. With its finance now guaranteed, Neal was able to expand rapidly. Mottershead, as president of Neal Petroleum, was made responsible for the Ontario business. A number of small distribution companies were bought to increase penetration of the Ontario market. Efforts were at first concentrated on the wholesale market, but interests in distribution and retailing were soon added. The major market breakthrough came in 1971 when Ultramar purchased

# A GOLDEN ADVENTURE

Arrow Petroleum, a London, Ontario, based company with over 150 retail gasoline stations trading under the Arrow brand, with a marine terminal on Lake Erie and bulk storage facilities. The relations with Arrow both during the acquisition negotiations and in the later management of the enterprise were difficult because of the strong personality of Joe McManus, Arrow's owner. A giant of a man in every sense of the word, McManus had built Arrow up from nothing and was used to doing things his own way. His paternalistic approach was often in conflict with Neal and Ultramar, and he forgot that he no longer owned the business but continued to try to run it in his own particular style. As Mottershead recalls, confrontation was by no means unusual: 'Joe would pound his desk, shouting, "In spite of all you say, this is the way things are going to be done." Sometimes it would take anything from a day to three weeks to convince Joe that he just couldn't do things his way any longer. Life was certainly never dull when Joe was around.' However, McManus was both a prominent Canadian and a vital component in the development of Ultramar's Ontario operations. McManus later retired from the organisation to concentrate on his other business interests. When he was killed, with his wife, in a car crash at the end of 1975, it was a sad day for all and he was universally mourned, particularly by those who had worked closely with him. Writing in the Ultramar house magazine, *Eagle Eye*, George Mottershead said: 'When they created Joe they threw away the mold.' The purchase of Arrow Petroleum was followed by the acquisition by Ultramar of the remaining 50% of Neal Petroleum, a logical step in developing the market.

The acquisition and development policy had pushed total product sales, mostly light ends, i.e. gasoline and distillate, to 37,000 barrels per day. This volume when added to the programmed low sulphur fuel exports to the northeast United States gave the Quebec refinery the outlet required for initial operation. The storage facilities at the refinery totalled in excess of eight million barrels and gave the operation the flexibility necessary for winter delivery conditions and market requirements. Branded or controlled gasoline stations had not only greatly increased in number but had also been improved by a development policy that had added car washes, restaurants and trailer (caravan) parks to some of the prime sites. The heating oil and asphalt businesses had also grown, and new markets had been established in regions that hitherto had never seen the Golden Eagle name, for example Goose Bay, Labrador. Despite being overshadowed now by Quebec, Newfoundland was still holding its own and also retaining its hold on one-third of the Newfoundland market.

In the United States, Golden Eagle's marketing strategy was very different. Early in the 1960s the small and rather old-fashioned refinery, unable to produce gasoline that could be sold competitively in the price-war dominated Californian market, had been converted to the manufacture of jet aviation fuel. For many years Golden Eagle retained its position as one of the largest independent West Coast producers of aviation fuel while at the same time retaining its interest in the wholesale gasoline market by buying refined products from other oil companies. Between 1964 and 1969, total product sales expanded from 18,000 to 26,000 barrels per day. The late 1960s were marked in California by the

The Thunder Bay truck stop on the Trans-Canada Highway in northern Ontario in 1980

Delivery truck promoting Ultramar diesel in the early 1980s

Golden Eagle truck servicing a Canadian National Railways locomotive in Newfoundland

Marketing and promotion in eastern
Canada:

*Above:* Mobile Mike, a mechanical
salesman posted outside service stations
in 1976
*Left:* The Ultramar blimp and the
related smokey glass promotion of
1978 and a delivery tanker disguised as
a bee for Christmas 1978

Cecil Squire, David Oreck and William
Theisen at the Los Angeles refinery
in 1968

A ship bunkering at the Ultramar fuelling station at Windsor on the Detroit River

fluctuating fortunes of the refinery, whose output was continually at the mercy of government imposed quotas and price wars. From year to year there were dramatic changes in Ultramar's attitude towards the old refinery, and so stability was hard to achieve. Although the production of jet fuels continued to predominate, there was a regularly recurring temptation to rebuild the refinery and re-introduce gasoline production. At the same time, there were plans to overcome the quota problems by making the refinery more dependent upon local supplies, reflected by the absorption of Caracas Petroleum (U.S.) by Golden Eagle in 1965 and the purchase of some producing properties. However, the lack of significant exploration success meant that most of the feedstock had to be bought locally on the open market. Despite the uncertainty, wholesale gasoline sales steadily increased, and new markets were achieved by the introduction of a bunkering operation that included the U.S. Navy among its clients.

In 1970 the Los Angeles refinery, along with the marine terminal and its related facilities, and most of the Golden Eagle staff, was leased for five years to Carson Petroleum, a new company led by David Oreck and William Theisen, formerly Golden Eagle's top executives in California. This decision was influenced by a number of factors. In 1969 the aviation fuel market had shown signs of declining, while the continual problems posed by quotas and price wars made the plan to re-enter the gasoline market rather unattractive. In addition, in 1969 the refinery had experienced its first strike.

169

Service station redevelopment: Repentigny in eastern Canada before and after rebuilding in 1983

The Pipeline fully automated self service system designed for credit card operation, introduced in Canada from September 1983

Ultramar's shares were first listed on the Toronto Stock Exchange on 12 December 1972. *Left to right:* D. N. Stoker of Nesbitt, Thomson & Co., Campbell Nelson, J. R. Kimber, President of the Toronto Stock Exchange, Arnold Lorbeer, George Mottershead

Lasting ten days, during which the refinery was run by its managers, the strike was part of a national campaign by refinery workers who were concerned about the uncertain future facing their industry. The decision to lease the refinery seemed well timed and the thinking behind the decision was carefully explained in the Annual Report: 'This arrangement is attractive to the Group since we do not have a source of United States crude oil for support of the Californian operation. The uncertainty of future crude oil import quotas along with the reduced prices available for jet fuel make the net lease agreement more profitable than the alternative of continuing to run the refinery on our own account.' However, it should be added that Ultramar held on to the wholesale gasoline business in southern California and by this time, Golden Eagle had become the largest independent gasoline distributor on the West Coast and was maintaining profit levels despite the continuing instability of prices.

The opening of the Quebec refinery influenced U.S. marketing in the east, and in 1971 a new subsidiary, Golden Eagle Oil, was formed to sell low sulphur fuel oil from Quebec along the East Coast of the United States. Unfortunately the price fluctuations of the United States products' market that had characterised the 1960s were to continue through the 1970s. The scene was set for a switch in emphasis between the upstream and the downstream divisions of Ultramar's activities. During the 1960s the growth of refining and marketing had overshadowed exploration, giving crude production a secondary role. These positions were now to be reversed as increasing emphasis was placed on the search for new sources of supply.

In Canada, the early 1970s were a period of consolidation. Management and markets inherited as a result of the purchase of Neal, Arrow and the many smaller distribution companies had to be integrated into the existing Ultramar system. Inevitably the first two

171

A Gillies-Guy coal truck in Hamilton, Ontario, in 1918. Gillies-Guy was one of the companies acquired as part of the CFM purchase

Spur service station in Quebec, 1983

Document signing for the purchase of Spur Oil in December 1983. *Left to right:* John Robertson, *Ultramar Canada,* Nick Di Tomaso, *Spur,* Bob Farquharson, *Murphy Oil,* Laurie Woodruff, *Ultramar Canada*

MARKETING

years were fairly confused before duplications and rivalries were sorted out and a co-ordinated marketing policy was formulated and applied. There was considerable debate, for example, about the continued use of Arrow and other brand names. In 1972 there were still over 250 Arrow branded stations despite early plans to unify all Golden Eagle activities under one brand name. Local problems caused Ultramar to send senior management from New York and London to mastermind the process of unification. The most important of these was David Elton, who together with Peter Raven had his baptism of fire in sorting out the fledgling U.K. marketing organisation. He came to Ontario in 1974 to take over from George Mottershead. During the next two years Elton, helped by Peter Maitland, forged the various Ontario marketing companies into one cohesive unit and turned the losses into profit. Rivalries and duplication between the Quebec and Ontario organisations were eliminated.

Consolidation was accompanied by growth. The Canadian gasoline station network was steadily expanded and improved, reaching a total of 1,100 stations in eastern Canada by 1975. At the same time, the nature of the gasoline station was changing with the development of the self-service principle. Although first developed during the early 1950s, the self-service idea had not really been taken seriously until the early 1970s. European and particularly British companies were the first to apply the principle widely. Gradually the idea spread to Canada, and from 1975 prime outlets were being turned over to self-service operation. In addition to the self-service concept there were other ideas of merchandising. In 1974 an adventurous Golden Eagle lessee who operated a gasoline station in Jonquière, Quebec, had shown that gasoline sales could be boosted by 40% with the addition of a small display area selling dry goods, canned foods and novelties. From this came the convenience store concept, a blend of gasoline station and general retail outlet, backed by restaurant, car wash and lubrication facilities, that characterises many contemporary service stations. This and other new marketing techniques helped raise Ultramar's Canadian total product sales to 85,000 barrels per day by 1977.

While the market for gasoline and home heating oil gradually expanded during the mid 1970s, other products were not so successful. Residual fuel oil was a problem because of huge market surpluses and exports were severely restricted. This particular problem was somewhat reduced in 1972 when Golden Eagle signed a five-year contract, described in the previous chapter, to supply a new power station being built by the Hydro-Electric Power Commission of Ontario. Although this large contract was a major marketing achievement, its initial promise was not to be fulfilled. After two years, Ontario Hydro found they had overestimated the demand for electricity and bought themselves out of the contract.

Price problems and government intervention continued to affect marketing growth, particularly in the aftermath of the oil crisis of 1973/4. The Ontario company found that it had to buy products from Ontario refineries that used Canadian feedstock because Quebec products, which were still dependent upon imported crudes, were too expensive. At the same time government price controls in Canada took the form of support payments for imported crude to hold down the price of products and keep them level across Canada. These and other problems were clearly identified in an article published by *Eagle Eye* in 1976: 'Governments are playing an increasing role in our business. Our operations in Venezuela have been nationalised. Our holdings in Ecuador have been expropriated. A consortium of producing country governments (OPEC) fixes crude oil prices on a world-wide basis and determines the cost of the feedstock for our refineries. The Government of Canada restricts exports of products and also provides price support payments for imported crude oil to hold down petroleum prices. The United States and the United Kingdom in one form or another also regulate petroleum prices. Since there is little or no co-ordination between governments, it is often difficult for an international marketing company to chart the proper path through the maze of conflicting regulations and restrictions. Furthermore, the increasing demands by governments at all levels for more and more reporting on the different aspects of our business cause a severe strain on staff and impede operating efficiency.'

These difficulties continued to hinder expansion throughout the 1970s, but most were at least international in origin. However, there were others that were more particularly Canadian.

An element in the Canadian Government had always argued for nationalisation of the oil industry, and this element was powerful enough to organise a number of pro-Canadian restrictions. For example, it became government policy from 1976 to restrict the ability of non-Canadian companies to grow via acquisition, a policy that directly affected Ultramar's ability to sell sufficient products to enable the refinery to be operated close to capacity. Another problem was the constant battle with the National Energy Board who had drawn a rather arbitrary line down the Ottawa valley to mark the limit of product sales from Quebec refineries and imports. In theory all markets west of the line were to be supplied from western Canada. The problem was overcome by inter-company exchanges, much to the annoyance of the Energy Board.

For Canada a critical year was 1979. With sophistication of the Quebec refinery delayed, additional markets had to be found for heavy fuel oil and distillates. The only way this could be achieved was by acquisition and so negotiations were opened with Shell Petroleum to acquire its wholly owned subsidiary, Canadian Fuel Marketers (CFM), a broadly based energy company operating mostly in Ontario, Quebec and the Maritime Provinces. With sales of 90,000 barrels per day of oil products, with storage facilities for 10 million barrels, with 40 gasoline stations, and with interests in home heating and water purification equipment, Canadian Fuel Marketers seemed the ideal oil company for Ultramar. The purchase was finalised in January 1979 for a cash payment of Can.$54,000,000.

CFM's history dates back to the 1870s, when Andrew Dunlop Webster began selling coal in Quebec City. In partnership with his sons, George and Lorne, Webster expanded the business into other fields, becoming involved in import and export, and acting as agents for shipping and coal companies. From these roots grew a widely diversified business controlled by the Webster family, but composed of a large number of individual

174

Caminol service station in California in the early 1930s, showing the Beacon trademark

The Beacon refinery at Hanford, California

Senior members of the staffs of Shell, Canadian Fuel Marketers and
Ultramar at the sale of CFM to Ultramar by Shell on 23 August 1978

companies that were all run with a high degree of autonomy. Coal remained the
backbone of the business until the 1940s when the newly developed oil interests began to
dominate. A chain of terminals was established and the Webster group became an
essential part of the Canadian oil business, buying for storage and eventual distribution
the surplus distillates and heavy fuel oils that the refineries accumulated every summer.
Additional supplies were imported from the Caribbean and Europe. The pattern of
diversification and acquisition continued and by 1967 the group included 54 wholly
owned and active member companies and nineteen that were inactive. In addition, there
was a 50% interest in a further nine companies.

In 1967, Colin Webster, the founder's grandson, by then in his sixties, decided to sell
the business, and the transaction was concluded with Shell Petroleum of London. The
company formed by Shell to take over and rationalise the Webster empire was Fuel
Marketing Holdings (Eastern Canada) Ltd. The name was changed in 1968 to
Canadian Fuel Marketers Ltd. (CFM). The next few years saw an extensive
programme of reorganisation and consolidation, much of which was masterminded by
Laurie Woodruff who joined CFM in 1970 after many years of marketing experience
with Shell. In 1973 Woodruff became President, continuing to develop the group until its
purchase by Ultramar in 1979. For Ultramar, CFM was an important purchase. The
scale of operations meant that a far bigger controlled market became available, paving
the way for increased output from the Quebec refinery, and putting the whole of the
eastern Canadian operation into a more profitable position by lowering unit refinery
costs.

The purchase of CFM required the approval of FIRA, the Canadian Government
Foreign Investment Review Agency. Negotiations were long and arduous and were
carried out by David Elton, assisted by Jean Gaulin and Pat Guarino, with Ultramar

# MARKETING

finally securing approval by undertaking, inter alia, to turn eventually their Canadian operations into a public company, with the proviso that Ultramar recovered its investment plus interest. At the onset, the CFM staff, not sure of the direction that Ultramar was taking, were reluctant to accept their new role in an integrated management. They were used to Shell's laissez faire policy, which the latter followed because of its concern about violating the Canadian anti-monopoly statutes by virtue of its holdings in Shell Canada who competed in the same market. It shocked Ultramar to be informed by CFM that, if the latter was to follow established reporting procedures its new owners, Ultramar, would be 'provided only such information as is generally afforded to any shareholder'. Ultramar management was flexible and equal to the task and the various Ultramar interests in Canada were rapidly brought together under one title, Ultramar Canada, and under the control of a centralised management headed by Laurie Woodruff based in Toronto. Senior levels were staffed by the former officers of Golden Eagle, Neal and CFM. The results were immediately apparent. Average product sales doubled to 144,000 barrels per day, and over 300,000 homes in eastern Canada were now supplied with Ultramar heating oil. The bunkering market was also expanded with the opening of fuelling stations on the Detroit River and the Welland Canal, designed to win business from the 13,000 ships that used the Great Lakes transportation system each year.

Considerable effort was devoted to establishing the Ultramar brand name and corporate image. The old Golden Eagle and Arrow names were gradually phased out, replaced by a new unified style and logo. Various marketing techniques were used to familiarise the public with the new image, including an Ultramar blimp in Newfoundland for a smokey-glass promotion at gasoline stations, with over 1.5 million glasses being given away. In the event, 1979 was to prove to be Ultramar's most successful year to date in Canada. The product sales figures represented an all-time high that has not since been matched, largely because of the steady decrease in general market demand after 1980 and the effect of increased competition from electricity and gas.

The situation in the United States during the 1970s was rather different. The determining element was still the status of the Los Angeles refinery, which from year to year fluctuated from being a useful asset to a small liability. In 1972 a marketing campaign took the Golden Eagle name into Oregon, Washington, Arizona and Nevada, as well as California, and at the same time a gasoline shortage in California revived the idea of rebuilding and enlarging the refinery. Enthusiasm for this idea carried on into 1973 and resulted in the Los Angeles refinery coming back under Ultramar control. A party was held in Long Beach in 1974 to welcome back the staff into the Ultramar fold, but David Oreck and William Theisen decided to continue to operate Carson Oil as a separate company. The return of the refinery coincided with new government petroleum allocation regulations, but the price control system caused widespread instability in both wholesale and retail prices. Despite this, enthusiasm remained and by 1975 plans had been drawn up for the conversion of the refinery to a 30,000 barrel gasoline unit. The Annual Report stated that the aim was 'to transform us from a buyer and reseller of

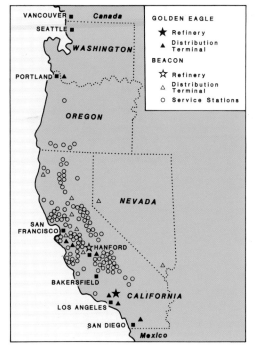

*Top left:* Golden Eagle and Beacon West Coast marketing network at the time of the Beacon acquisition

*Top right:* Dale Austin signing the agreement for Ultramar's purchase of Beacon in 1981

*Centre right:* Senior Beacon staff, *left to right:* David Bacigalupo, Virgil Anderson, Walter Dwelle

*Right:* Eugene K. O'Shea, General Counsel of American Ultramar Ltd.

An early horse drawn delivery tanker used by James Evans in Missouri in 1906.
Evans Tank Lines was later incorporated into Pittston Petroleum

gasoline to a manufacturer and supplier'. At the same time, an alternative scheme that involved the purchase of a Gulf refinery in San Francisco was considered. Within a year the picture had again changed completely. A major decline in gasoline sales had made the rebuilding idea seem largely irrelevant.

The following year saw another volte face. The market improved greatly and the overall picture was helped by an increase in cargo sales. The refinery rebuilding plans were brought out again and dusted down, ready for implementation. The general improvement was maintained through 1979, although work on the new refinery did not actually start.

Golden Eagle's success in California was based on the flexibility associated with a small company. A number of important fuel oil contracts with industrial users were established through the company's flexible approach to pricing, while the government aviation fuel contracts were maintained over a long period because Golden Eagle enjoyed a privileged position as a small, locally-based independent supplier. Golden Eagle was also helped by the Government Entitlements Program which was in force from 1974 to 1981, and whose regulations tended to favour smaller companies and protect them in a way that was otherwise not possible in a market economy dominated by major oil companies.

A new market was launched as a result of CFM's ownership of a 50% interest in Asphalt International, a Florida-based company. It was hoped to create in the United

The Pittston purchase agreement in 1983.
Hendrik Hartong and Dale Austin

William Mannion

The Bronx deepwater terminal of Metropolitan Petroleum, a forerunner of Pittston, in 1950

180

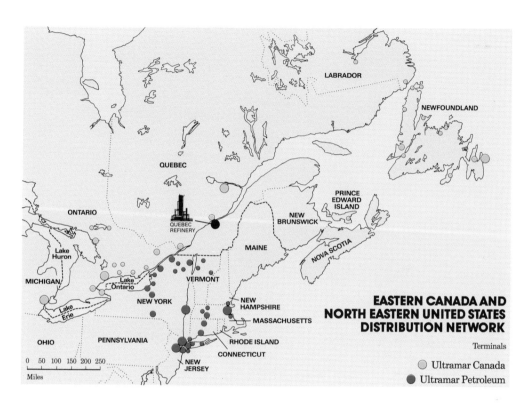

Ultramar's eastern Canada and northeast United States marketing network, 1985

States an equivalent of the successful Canadian asphalt business. In the event, Ultramar's interest in this company was sold at a profit about a year later.

In Canada, the upgrading of the Quebec refinery and the resultant increase in Ultramar's gasoline avails was unfortunately offset by a steady decline in market demand, and the early years of the 1980s have been marked by a reduction in total product sales. By 1983 the figure had fallen to 76,500 barrels per day, from its 1979 high of 144,000 barrels. The declining market in Canada was a general problem, influenced by price wars and, more particularly, by the entry into the market in 1982 of Petro-Canada, the new national oil company. Ultramar Canada tried to maintain its market share despite the decline, mainly by a policy of aggressive marketing and by improving services. Gasoline stations were revamped, with many more being converted to self-service operation backed by additional facilities and merchandising outlets.

In September 1983 the first Pipeline unmanned stations were opened, designed for

181

A convoy of Pittston trucks crossing into New York City in 1980

credit card operation. Other marketing activities were developed, notably automated, unmanned facilities for diesel fuel for commercial transport and marine fuelling, while, as already mentioned, the purchase in 1983 of Spur Oil, a subsidiary of Murphy Oil, added 150 branded outlets, mostly in the Montreal area as well as a marine terminal in Chicoutimi.

Another important marketing breakthrough occurred in 1983, when Ultramar received permission from the Canadian Government to import and process up to 25,000 barrels per day at the Quebec refinery for subsequent export to Ultramar Petroleum in the northeastern United States. However, the essential volume trend in Canada has been downwards, a trend epitomised by the decision to close the Holyrood refinery, which finally took place on 30 June 1983. Holyrood had particular significance for Ultramar. It was the first refinery Ultramar had constructed and its building was the keystone in the plan to diversify into the Canadian market. In 1981, the refinery had celebrated twenty-one years of continuous production, a period during which it had performed faultlessly despite being doubled in output capacity. It also provided a useful training ground for many Ultramar people who used the experience gained at Holyrood to good effect in other refineries. Although the emotional attachment to Holyrood was strong, there was in the end no other answer to the marketing difficulties of the 1980s. By 1983 Holyrood was too small, too old fashioned and too costly. Its output had declined over a number of years and by the early 1980s it was operating at under 50% of its capacity.

Pittston's Boston terminal in 1979

The high unit costs of its products, determined by the small size, meant that it was no longer able to produce fuel oil at competitive prices for the local industrial market. Expansion or redevelopment were impractical, particularly following the investment in Quebec City, and so the closure decision was made. There were some attempts to keep the refinery running under a different management but these ideas came to nothing. Holyrood is now a storage base, and plans for the development of the site are being drawn up.

Over the years Canada has been an essential part of Ultramar's development. For more than 30 years it has represented the major investment in both refining and marketing. Market conditions today and the likely deregulation of the industry present enormous challenges. Ultramar can face them positively. It has modern facilities, a strong image, innovative marketing and a well-balanced management team.

In the United States, the Los Angeles refinery expansion plans were finally abandoned in 1980, a year that saw the collapse of the gasoline market. Total product sales declined and the Annual Report admitted that 'our Californian business does not face a promising future'. However, the outlook was to be changed in the latter part of 1981 by the purchase of Beacon Oil.

Beacon was formed originally as the Caminol Company in 1931 by Walter Allen and four associates. It had a refinery near Los Angeles and gasoline stations that used the Beacon brand name with its distinctive lighthouse symbol. Later Caminol purchased a

Thames Matex, Essex, England, where
Ultramar Golden Eagle leased storage
facilities in 1968

A Summit service station in Sandhurst
acquired by Ultramar in 1968

Empress service station in Bletchingley,
one of the first Ultramar sites in England

David Elton and Peter Raven who developed Ultramar's marketing interests
in the U.K. photographed at the cricket match in AGM week in 1978

second refinery in Hanford, in the San Joaquin Valley of central California, and concentrated on building a strong market position in that region. Early pioneers in the field of merchandising at gasoline stations and in self-service techniques, Beacon soon became a popular brand, with a chain of stations in central and northern California. In 1967 the Caminol name was changed to Beacon Oil.

Ultramar was attracted to Beacon for a number of reasons. First, its 300 branded gasoline stations enabled Ultramar to move from gasoline wholesaling into retailing, and at the same time offered a new but developed market region. Second, the refinery at Hanford was small but efficient and was producing gasoline from locally produced West Coast feedstock, thereby making unnecessary once and for all the plan to rebuild the Carson refinery. Third, Beacon was a usefully diverse marketing operation, with interests in marine bunkering in San Francisco, fuel oil supplies to agriculture, aviation fuel, high-speed automobile lube outlets, a storage and distribution network with seven terminals linked by pipeline, barge, truck and rail, a modern and well-equipped headquarters building, property development and the Laurelglen Shopping Centre in Bakersfield. Equally important, the removal of government controls and the return to a free market early in 1981 had threatened to undermine or even destroy Ultramar's Californian business, a threat that could only be overcome by a change in market direction. The purchase of Beacon, by greatly increasing Ultramar's presence on the West Coast, effectively minimised the threat. At the same time there were advantages for Beacon, the most significant being the access to the international crude oil market that Ultramar offered. Also, Beacon was a family concern and the members of the family decided they did not wish to continue any longer in the business. Negotiations were concluded in 1981 and a cash price of about U.S.$62 million was paid.

During the early months of 1982 a rapid integration programme was carried out to merge Beacon and Golden Eagle, while retaining separate market identities and regions. Beacon's President, David Bacigalupo, became President of the merged business and headquarters were moved to Hanford. Frank Sisti, Golden Eagle's manager in California, who had been transferred from New York when David Oreck left, was transferred back to the New York office to help Dale Austin on the operations side. The total product sales figure of the merged companies rose dramatically to 50,000 barrels per day and, for the first time, Ultramar was in possession of a fully integrated marketing operation in the United States.

The importance of having acquired Beacon became even more evident in 1984, when the Carson refinery was unable to renew the jet fuel contracts and the reluctant decision had to be made to shut down the refinery at the end of 1984. This refinery had been built in the mid 1940s and acquired by Ultramar in 1960. The 77-acre property was sold at a profit. Some years earlier a 70-acre plot intended for expansion of the refinery had also been sold at a profit.

The market expansion programme was continued when Ultramar in 1983 acquired Pittston Petroleum, formerly known as Metropolitan Petroleum, for about U.S.$105 million. Formed over 150 years ago as a retail coal business in Boston, Pittston was one of the first companies to realise the potential of oil as an alternative fuel. By the 1930s it was already operating a large fleet of delivery trucks, supplying fuel oil to the New York area and to other parts of the northeast. From this grew a market network that covered New York, New Jersey, the New England States and the Canadian Province of Quebec. By 1983 Pittston had become the leading independent marketer and distributor of light and heavy fuel oils in the northeastern United States and eastern Canada, selling over 90,000 barrels per day. It had 27 terminals, 300 trucks and a fleet of eight barges.

As well as maintaining Ultramar's tradition of growth by acquisition, the purchase of Pittston, quickly renamed Ultramar Petroleum, made particular sense in a number of ways. Geographically it provided a continuous market in the northeastern United States and eastern Canada. Another benefit was the proximity of Pittston's operation to the Quebec refinery, allowing the gasoline and other refined products coming from the catalytic cracking unit to be distributed and sold directly into one of the largest markets in the world. Pittston also complemented Ultramar's shipping business, not only through its own barge fleet and marine distribution network, but also by creating the opportunity for profitable backhauls from Quebec to New York. Also important was the possibility of developing trading links between Canada and the United States following the relaxation of Canadian Government restrictions and the agreement that part of the Quebec refinery be treated as a free-trade zone. The first shipment, 200,000 barrels of Quebec products, was off-loaded in New York harbour in early 1984. Other cargoes are taken by truck across the border, further developing a trading pattern already established by Pittston's Canadian division.

By a process of rationalisation and expansion, Ultramar's position in the United States market has been altered during the last few years. On the West Coast, the acquisition of Beacon has given Ultramar a market position that can be steadily developed. No longer is the business dependent upon an ageing refinery, the fluctuations of the wholesale gasoline market, and the uncertainties of government aviation fuel contracts. Beacon has added stability as well as growth potential. On the East Coast, Pittston has added the missing dimension to Ultramar's established business, bringing together the United States and Canadian markets, and supporting the continued development of the Quebec refinery. At the same time, the rapid expansion of exploration activities in North America and the purchase of Enstar with its onshore and offshore oil interests will help to ensure that the growth of the North American market can be supported by an increased reliance on locally produced crude.

The various Canadian and U.S. acquisitions brought a wealth of new talent to Ultramar, especially on the marketing side. In Canada, with CFM, came Laurie Woodruff, now a director of Ultramar, Darrel McLaughlin, Dick Dickinson, André Roy and others. With Beacon came Dave Bacigalupo, Walter Dwelle and Pete Smith. With Pittston came Bill Mannion and Joe Tower. However, through the years Ultramar has also developed basically home-bred talent on the marketing and supply side, including Ted Hall, John Auld and Paul Thorne in the U.K., Joel Mascitelli in California, Roy Myers in Newfoundland and Peter Maitland, John Robertson, Orlie Belanger and John Wilson in eastern Canada. The overall coordinator of Ultramar Group marketing is David Elton, now based in London where he is also managing the London office.

Ultramar's other major market is the United Kingdom. In 1963, following the successful development of a fully integrated marketing operation in Canada, Ultramar began to look for other markets. Panama and the United States represented the next step, one that grew logically from the refinery infrastructure that was already in place in each country. For the first time, Ultramar also began to consider its home territory as a possible market. In 1963, Ultramar Golden Eagle Limited (UGE) was incorporated in London, while another subsidiary was set up in Ireland. These companies, however, remained inactive for several years.

It should be mentioned that for many years Ultramar had regularly marketed cargoes of crude oil and products to the U.K. and the continent of Europe. As early as 1958, storage facilities had been rented in Rotterdam and arrangements for marketing fuel oil had been established with Defrol and other German companies.

Towards the end of 1967 Ultramar began to take seriously the possibility of an entry into the British retail market. The Canadians were enthusiastic about the idea, an enthusiasm heightened by the Quebec refinery project and the need to develop new markets for its products. The best way to enter the market seemed to be the usual Ultramar technique of growth by acquisition, and so studies were made of the various British independent distributors, a number of whom had established service station networks that carried their own brand name. The most important of these were Jet, Trident and Summit. Paul Boyd came over from Canada and visited the various independents, to see if any sort of deal could be put together. Lengthy discussions were held with Trident, but they were not prepared to sacrifice their independence, while Jet, later to be linked with Conoco, were felt to be too big. During the summer of 1968 while

Home heating oil delivery truck in England, operated by an Ultramar subsidiary

An Ultramar service station in England during the Green Shield trading stamp boom of the early 1970s

Quickfill, a fully automated credit card operated services station for truck drivers

the issue was still unresolved, a manager and staff were hired, and storage was leased at Thames Matex, a riverside facility near Thurrock in Essex. In July the first shipment arrived and was received into storage. The next few months were marked by frantic efforts by Boyd and others to create some viable operation, culminating in the purchase of Herts & Beds Petroleum, a company with 56 service stations carrying its own Summit brand name, a truck fleet and storage facilities. This purchase marked the real start of Ultramar's marketing operations in Britain, and in January 1969 Herts & Beds Petroleum was renamed Ultramar Golden Eagle, taking over the company that had been formed in 1963.

The business grew rapidly. By March 1969 there were 88 Summit brand outlets and 13 carrying the Ultramar name, with total product sales of over 2,000 barrels per day. By the end of the year, the number of outlets had risen to 162, but the operation was running at a loss. With the benefit of hindsight, the first few years of Ultramar Golden Eagle do not seem to have been particularly successful. There was much enthusiasm but not enough organisation and the market was very competitive. At first the existing management, inherited from Herts & Beds Petroleum and led by Arthur Bills, were left to their own devices, but it became increasingly clear that they could not handle the process of rapid growth and integration into a larger operation. By now there was some grumbling by Ultramar's British directors to the effect that this operation was a waste of time and money. The operation suffered from being too close to home base and constantly under the eye of the Board. In 1970 two young Ultramar-bred managers, David Elton and Peter Raven, were given the task of bringing the British operation under control.

By 1971 the losses stopped and in 1972 Ultramar Golden Eagle recorded its first profit. The turn-round was achieved by management reorganisation, tight control, consolidation of marketing activities, giving up the heavy fuel oil market and entering the home heating oil business. Following the well-proven Canadian formula, a market was created by the purchase of a number of small heating oil distributors, including Corrie Fuel Supplies, Kent Petroleum, and Markim Fuel Oils. Other acquisitions, notably Channel Petroleum and Highway Petroleum, expanded both the gasoline network and heating oil sales. By the end of 1972, there were 226 outlets, using both Summit and Ultramar brand names, and an increasing number were promoting the self-service concept, encouraged by the popularity of Green Shield trading stamps. One of the more notable outlets was Cowley Ultraserve, near Oxford, whose launching celebrations were shared by Campbell Nelson's wife Pauline and Eva Rueber-Staier, a former Miss World and TV personality. Such was the publicity that traffic queues were up to two miles long and 18,000 gallons, a very large number at that time, were sold in the first two days.

The mid 1970s were a period of consolidation. The growth was not sustained, mainly because of the oil crisis of 1973/4. Government price controls brought new problems, while fluctuations in the value of the pound also affected profits. However, the number of outlets continued to grow, reaching 380 by 1975 and 430 by 1979, and these were gradually spread over a greater area. Many were restyled as Ultraserve self-service

Repps Ultraspar, a combined service station and convenience store

stations. Electronic blender pumps were first introduced in 1976. Despite this growth, Ultramar had to struggle to increase its market share.

Some growth came from the heating oil business as more local distribution companies were acquired. By 1979 there were 23 heating oil distribution companies operating under the Ultramar name. During this difficult period, Ultramar Golden Eagle managed to remain generally profitable. A significant contribution came from trading activities in the European bulk cargo market. It had grown sufficiently to warrant the leasing of one million barrels of storage in Rotterdam. Products were sold in barge lots to West Germany and other European destinations. However, in the late 1970s this market had begun to decline and the Rotterdam facility was cut back and eventually terminated.

Having survived the uncertainties of the 1970s, Ultramar Golden Eagle entered the 1980s in a strong position. It had been able to consolidate and expand its market share and in the early 1980s the total product sales increased sharply, reaching a high of 15,400 barrels per day. Although this total level of sales has not been maintained, the volume of retail sales has increased significantly each year.

Other areas of business have been able to contribute, particularly marine bunkering and cargo trading. Marketing in the United Kingdom has always somewhat stood on its own, partly for reasons of geography, and partly because of the nature of the British market. Despite the initial idea that the United Kingdom should be an outlet for Canadian products, Ultramar Golden Eagle has always purchased its supplies on the open market. Much now comes from the North Sea, via refineries operated by major oil companies on the British mainland. At the same time, the influence of North America is easy to detect. In November 1983 the first United States style combined service station and convenience store was opened. There had of course been earlier examples of cross merchandising at service stations, usually at the instigation of the lessee or owner. These had concentrated on giftware, snacks and automotive products.

Designed to be the start of a chain, and bringing together Ultramar and the Spar supermarket network, Ultraspar introduced convenience shopping to southern England. Open seven days a week, from 7 a.m. to 10 p.m., each store quickly attracted over 1,000

A tanker belonging to an Ultramar subsidiary delivers heating oil to Pembroke House, UGE's London headquarters

Charles Daly, Ted Hall and John Auld of UGE in March 1981

customers a day. Another new approach was reflected by the opening of the first of a chain of Quickfill outlets. Fully automated, and operated by a special credit card, the Quickfill concept was designed to give 24-hour diesel service for truck operators, essentially a new market for UGE.

Peter Raven and David Elton took on increased responsibilities in Ultramar's management structure and were succeeded by Ted Hall who took over the day-to-day management of UGE in the late 1970s. Recently Hall has been moved to the U.S. to supervise expansion of gasoline marketing in the northeastern United States. At the end of 1984, he was able to record success by the acquisition of Augsbury, a gasoline marketer in northern New York State. Meanwhile, Hall's position has been filled by Bob Walter, who was uprooted from his New York position as vice president of finance. Walter, like Frank Sisti, Peter Raven, Howard Pearl, Roger Nunns and so many other Ultramarians, began his Ultramar career as a teenager and was helped by the company's college education programme. Another change in London, unrelated to marketing, occurred in 1983 when Limebeer, who had been associated with Ultramar since its formation, ceased to perform the function of company Secretaries. Tim Hunt, who is the legal coordinator for Ultramar, took over this role.

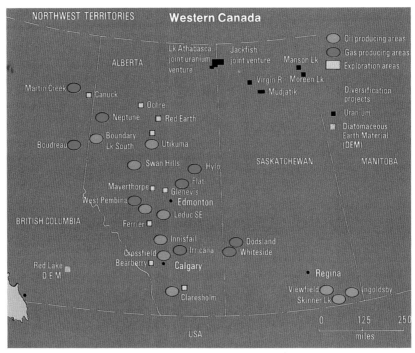

Ultramar's oil and gas exploration and production interests in western Canada in 1979

this area. The wells were shallow and small producers but the producing area was very large and other companies soon got the lion's share. Ultramar is still very active in this field and it continues to expand.

By the end of 1968, Ultramar had interests in just under five million acres in western Canada and exploratory drilling continued. Most of the wells were unsuccessful or uncommercial, but there were some important gas discoveries at Helmet in British Columbia and at Nosehill in western Alberta. Unfortunately, even then, much as now, natural gas in remote areas had virtually no marketability. In 1971, 344,000 acres in Quebec Province were added, and there was considerable wildcat activity to try to discover commercial oil reserves near the new refinery being completed at St. Romuald. During the early 1970s, the rate of exploration and drilling in Canada slowed, partly as a result of the conflict between the Canadian Federal and Provincial Governments in western Canada over their relative share of tax revenue from oil and gas production.

Over the next few years, activities in western Canada were eclipsed by events in Indonesia, the North Sea and Iran, which meant a reduction in financial support for large-scale exploration programmes in a part of the world which had given rather scant results. Some small oil discoveries were made at Swan Hills, Leduc, Boundary Lake South and Innisfail, but the overall pattern was one of slow-down rather than expansion. Large blocks of acreage were relinquished in the Arctic, in Newfoundland and Quebec,

Winter drilling,
Boundary Lake, Alberta

Seismic shooting
in western Canada

Neptune gas project in Alberta, western Canada

Well adjacent to Calgary airport. This well was drilled in 1961 and is still producing

Exploration drilling at Claresholm, western Canada, in 1980

and total holdings in western Canada were reduced to about one million acres. Some producing properties also were sold to raise cash for other ventures. Then, in the late 1970s, the pattern was again reversed. An accelerated acquisition and exploration programme was launched in an attempt to increase Canadian production. The rate of drilling was also increased but again with limited success. The following year a large offshore concession was added, over eight million acres in the Gulf of St. Lawrence.

To summarise, in western Canada Ultramar has had quite a few discoveries, but none has been particularly remarkable. In 1983, oil output totalled 1,700 barrels per day, a figure that had not altered significantly over many years. Gas production was running at about 6 million cubic feet per day. The potential gas figure was considerably larger, but the limited market demand for gas in Canada has kept the production level on a plateau. In 1984, Ultramar's oil production in western Canada climbed to about 2,500 barrels per day and projections for the future are brighter. Accelerated drilling in the last few years has resulted in a number of new producing areas. While attempts to discover major fields convenient for the Ultramar refineries have so far been unsuccessful, Canadian exploration and production is likely to remain an important and profitable part of Ultramar's activities.

In the United States, the pattern of exploration has been broadly similar. The rather limited activities of CPUS, headquartered in Dallas, continued into the mid 1960s, generally making only a small contribution to Ultramar's profits. During 1965 CPUS was absorbed into Golden Eagle Refining, the main operating company in the U.S.A. Division. During the next two years some drilling was carried out in California, Wyoming, Montana and North Dakota, but by the end of 1968 Ultramar had interests in only 56,203 acres, with production running at about 170 barrels per day. A small amount of gas was also being marketed commercially.

The end of 1968 saw the exploration efforts in North America being restructured. Golden Eagle Exploration was put on inactive status, and a new office was opened in Denver to develop prospects in the Rocky Mountain area of the United States. In fact, this restructuring seemed to bring about a reduction in activity and during the early 1970s exploration in the United States came to a virtual standstill. Between two and five wells were drilled each year, with few successes. The exploration emphasis and experienced personnel were switched to other areas of greater potential, such as Indonesia and the North Sea. In 1974 an old-established oil field, the Raisin City Field in California, was purchased in an attempt to increase production. Discovered in 1941, this field was thought to have considerable untapped potential, and a drilling programme was launched at the end of the year. In the event, this optimism was misplaced. The four wells drilled were dry. By 1976 the acreage had been reduced and many of the producing wells had been sold. Some of the land in California turned out to be quite profitable in real estate terms, but from an oil point of view it was a big disappointment.

In the early 1980s, Ultramar began a new and more intensive effort to increase its business interests in the United States, both upstream and downstream. Having now disposed of all the legacies of the previous two decades and learned some lessons, the

A well at the Raisin
City field in California.
Bill Dickson, operations
foreman for Golden
Eagle Refining, with
Joe Bryson, head pumper

Offshore production rig in
the South Chandeleur Sound,
St. Bernard Parish,
Louisiana, in 1982

Exploration drilling in
Liberty County, Texas,
in 1982

EXPLORATION AND PRODUCTION

Group was in a good position to start again. A new capital expenditure programme was under way and the acquisition of Beacon Oil in California in 1981 brought the United States once more into the limelight. The same year saw a dramatic increase in land holdings, with the company purchasing interests in 303,000 acres, and the start of an ambitious drilling programme. During the next three years nearly 150 wells were drilled, of which the majority were exploratory, and in which Ultramar mostly held only small percentage interests. A number of discoveries were made and, by the end of 1984, output had reached about 300 barrels per day, matching the production high point of the mid 1960s. In 1983 a new subsidiary, Ultramar Oil and Gas, was launched and a Houston office was opened. In 1984 the acquisition of 50% of the Enstar Corporation, with its exploration and production interests in the Gulf of Mexico, the Permian Basin in Texas, and the Rocky Mountains, as well as its daily oil production of about 4,500 barrels, greatly expanded Ultramar's presence in the United States. To summarise, exploration in the United States has followed a rather erratic pattern and has not been crowned with great success. However, until recent years, the investment was quite small. With the present enthusiasm of management, the build-up of a competent technical staff and the dedication of considerable funds, Ultramar's U.S. production should increase rapidly.

One of the most important decisions made by Ultramar during the late 1960s was to start looking for new areas for substantial oil production to replace Venezuela. By the end of 1968, there were interests in over 1.5 million acres around the Island of Eleuthera in the Bahamas, in nearly 3.5 million acres in the Gulf of Guayaquil, in Ecuador, and in four million acres on and offshore Jamaica. Not all areas were so exotic, however. Licences were acquired covering nearly 800,000 acres of Worcestershire and the Solway Firth in the U.K., and Ultramar also took a 5% interest in a consortium which had been awarded a block covering 100,000 acres of the Dutch North Sea. There was also exploration interest on the west coast of Africa, and a concession was applied for in the Benguela Basin of Angola.

At the end of 1969, Ultramar's management, spearheaded by Thompson and Bensen, saw a unique opportunity in Indonesia, and convinced the Board to take the plunge. The opportunity arose in the form of a Production Sharing Contract with exploration rights over 4.4 million acres in the East Kalimantan (Borneo) and Sumatra regions of Indonesia. It was a complicated contract, drawn up between Pertamina, the Indonesian National Oil Company, and Roy Huffington, who ran a Houston based oil company.

The basis of the arrangement was that Roy Huffington would form a consortium which would carry out a specified amount of exploration and drilling in several areas, with the consortium bearing all the costs. If commercial production was attained, the costs were recoverable out of revenue from production and the remainder would be split 65% to Pertamina and 35% to the consortium. This was later changed to 85% and 15% for oil, but remained at the old level for gas. Pertamina would pay all income taxes. The original consortium consisted of Huffco 20%, Austral Oil 10%, Vico 10% and Ultramar 60%; but Ultramar almost immediately brought in Allied Corporation to take 25% of its

199

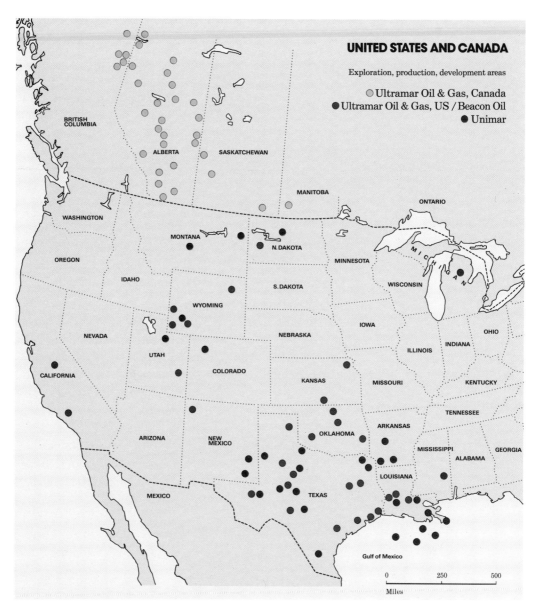

**UNITED STATES AND CANADA**

Exploration, production, development areas

◎ Ultramar Oil & Gas, Canada
● Ultramar Oil & Gas, US / Beacon Oil
● Unimar

Ultramar's exploration and production interests in Canada and the United States
following the acquisition of Enstar

200

60% stake. The composition of the consortium has changed several times through the years and in 1985 it is Huffco 20%, Ultramar 37.9%, Allied 37.9% and National Bulk Carriers (Ludwig) 4.2%.

With hindsight, it must be said that the entry into Indonesia was a critical decision, but at the time, of course, it was just one of a number of what seemed to some of the directors to be risky and expensive ventures.

The next few years were rather like a horse race, a kind of exploration stakes. There were a number of runners, one or two favourites with some kind of proven form, but no one could be certain about the result. An early leader seemed to be Ecuador. The first well was drilled in Ecuador in September of 1969 and discovered the Amistad gas field. This well yielded ten million cubic feet per day on test and was followed by a programme of exploration and development drilling. More discoveries were made, but they were not quite sufficient to justify commercial development of the gas. Output of 500 million cubic feet per day was deemed necessary to pay for the building of a liquefaction plant and for special ships to transport the gas. In 1971 and 1972 successful drilling continued, but then in November 1972 the Ecuador Government suddenly nullified the concessions without warning, on the grounds of some irregularities in the way they had originally been granted to the companies which had organised the consortium before Ultramar came in. With their multi-million dollar investment at stake, Ultramar had no choice but to attempt to renegotiate the concession. Discussions dragged on through 1973 and into 1974 but with no concrete result. The consortium fell apart, and it had to be accepted that the concession had been expropriated and the investment was therefore written off. To this day, the Amistad gas field has not been developed.

The Bahamas and Jamaica were extensively surveyed, but with less promising results. In the event, the Bahamas concessions were taken no further and were abandoned in 1973. Jamaica was more active. In 1972 a well was drilled but this was unsuccessful and the concession was also abandoned in 1973.

Angola never really got started. The discussions with the Portuguese Government over the Benguela Basin concession continued into 1971, and then in 1973 this was also dropped before any concession could be obtained. The area later became active and there is considerable drilling by other companies, but Ultramar could not at the time reach agreement on currency exchange and cost recovery matters.

The onshore and offshore U.K. concessions were a different matter. In 1971 acreage in the Hampshire Basin was added to the original Worcestershire and Solway Firth interests, and there was an extensive programme of seismic surveying. In 1973 Silloth 1A was drilled in the Solway Firth but proved to be dry and that concession was abandoned.

The same thing happened in Worcestershire the following year, but Hampshire remained in the race. The early 1980s were marked by an increasing interest in the oil potential of southern England. Patrick Sergeant wrote prophetically in the *Daily Mail* in April 1980: 'North of Southampton, in a kind of ecclesiastical Bermuda triangle, is a tract of land watched over by the Bishop of Winchester, the Bishop of Salisbury and the Bishop of Gloucester. Somewhere in that calm green countryside oil is to be found.'

The drillship *Sonda*
on exploration location
in the Gulf of
Guayaquil, Ecuador

Wildcat drilling at
Netherton, near Evesham,
Worcestershire, in 1974

Sonic testing in
Hampshire in 1982,
prior to the drilling
of Hoe 1

The visit of Lord Romsey to the Hoe 1 drilling site on the
Broadlands estate in Hampshire in June 1982

Drilling eventually took place in 1982 and 1983, the first on the edge of the Broadlands estate of the late Lord Louis Mountbatten, but both wells were dry. However, discoveries by other companies in the area have encouraged Ultramar to retain their interest. In 1984, a well, Stockbridge 1, was drilled near Winchester with Amoco as operator and gave encouraging results. Additional drilling will take place in the area during the next few years and there is optimism that an oil field can be developed.

The small interest in the Dutch North Sea has proved to be equally long-lasting. The first well was drilled in 1970 with Placid as operator. This was unsuccessful, as were the two subsequent wells, but the fourth well, drilled early in 1983, had a major gas success and a licence for commercial development has been granted. Ultramar has a 4.6% interest.

In 1969 Ultramar took part in a seismic survey covering one million acres on and offshore Puerto Rico and this continued into the following year before being given up. Later, in 1974, Puerto Rico came back briefly into the Ultramar limelight when the purchase of a refinery there was considered.

In the early 1970s, there was also a short-lived interest in Libya, described by Charles Quigley: 'Omar Haliq, a consultant to the Arab world and a personal friend, proposed a

203

Stockbridge 1, Hampshire, where Ultramar in partnership with Amoco made its
first onshore oil discovery in the U.K. in 1984

choice concession in Libya for Ultramar. In order to obtain it for little or no money, we
had to have partners. Knowing that Libya wanted a refinery of its own for prestige, the
plan was to build a small hydroskimming plant and then exchange it for a concession of
our choice. I confirmed Libya's interest in the plan by meeting their oil minister. In those
days his office had two chairs, one rug and one table and people waiting to see the
minister had to sit on orange crates. I had found out about the concession from the retired
geologist of a major oil company who had worked in Libya. It had been turned back to
the government as the poorest concession they owned. It was in this concession that
Occidental subsequently made their major discovery.' Ultramar did not have much
enthusiasm to get involved in Libya.

Interest in Greenland started in 1972, because of its proximity to the Quebec refinery,
and extensive offshore surveys were carried out in the western part of the country during
the next two years. In 1975 Ultramar took a 50% interest in a group which had been
awarded licences covering 610,000 acres offshore, with a three-year commitment
amounting to $750,000. Surveying continued but by 1977 enthusiasm was already on the
wane owing to the lack of success by other companies drilling in the same region and the
following year the concession was relinquished.

The entrance to the Stockbridge site in 1984

William Sheptycki, Managing Director
Ultramar Iran, in 1975

Duane MacFarland, *seated left,* signs on behalf of Ultramar the exploration and
production agreement with the National Iranian Oil Company
on 7 August 1974

The well at Band-e Lengeh, Iran, 1975

Ultramar's exploration policy was affected by external political events during the mid 1970s. The Arab-Israeli War of 1973 and the drastic oil price rises achieved by OPEC in its aftermath inevitably made the Middle East the focus of attention. Some of Ultramar's exploration plays, particularly those in the Caribbean, became less interesting because of the increase in transport costs that followed the crisis in the Middle East. As has been seen, a number of concessions were abandoned or relinquished during 1973. Ultramar had never been seriously interested in the Middle East, but after 1973 it seemed a good idea to develop friendships in that region. Contacts were established with a number of the recently-formed but powerful OPEC national oil companies and some successful trading took place over the next few years, particularly with Sonatrach, Algeria's national oil company. Another important contact was the National Iranian Oil Company, with whom discussions started in late 1973. These eventually were to involve more than trading and led Ultramar into its only serious Middle Eastern exploration play.

In August 1974 Ultramar signed a service contract with the National Iranian Oil Company covering an exploration licence for just under two million acres of the Lar block in southern Iran. In this case, Ultramar took the licence 100% on its own, an unusual move for a medium-sized company and particularly rare for Ultramar which almost always went with partners. The basis for the contract was

206

Lord Remnant and
Peter Leidelmeyer
travelling on the
River Musi in
Sumatra in 1972

A field exploration
party in Indonesia
in 1970

Drilling at Badak in Indonesia in the early 1970s

an agreed minimum exploration expenditure of $14 million over five years in return for the right to purchase oil from any field discovered on the block for a period of fifteen years.

Despite its late start, Iran rapidly took the lead in the exploration race. An office was opened in Teheran, and in January 1975 William Sheptycki, who had previously been general manager of Golden Eagle Oil and Gas in Calgary, moved there as Managing Director of the newly-formed Ultramar Iran Oil Company. Sheptycki, a geologist by education and training, had come to Ultramar from Texaco and climbed the rungs of the ladder to management status.

Seismic work started immediately and the results seemed to justify the enthusiasm and speed with which the Iranian project had been established. The Annual Report for 1975 was able to state: 'In Iran, geological and geophysical surveys have confirmed numerous major surface structures in our contract area. An exploration well began drilling in August.' Over the next year, Iran was to prove a major disappointment. The well was plagued with problems, making drilling both slow and expensive. Worse still, it proved to be a dry hole. A second well was drilled, which proved to be equally expensive and just as dry. By the end of 1976, all the early enthusiasm had evaporated: 'Our experience in southern Iran has been disappointing. Two expensive wells drilled on excellent surface features had no shows of hydrocarbons. Drilling by other operators in this general area has also been unsuccessful and a reassessment of the potential of the area is now under way. Meanwhile, we have stopped drilling in Iran.' The drilling never started again. In 1977 the concession was relinquished, the Teheran office closed, and the Iranian adventure came to an end. The sense of disappointment and loss that accompanied the withdrawal was later considerably mollified by subsequent events in Iran.

Even though Iran was briefly a front runner during the mid 1970s, the major discoveries in Indonesia in 1971 and the North Sea in 1972 overshadowed everything else. However, it must be admitted that through the early 1970s exploration outside of

208

General view of Badak in March 1975 showing the production facilities
in the foreground and the camp and warehouse in the background

Exploration camp in
Sumatra in 1973

209

William Sheptycki, Campbell Nelson and Robert Bland standing in front
of the Badak 1 discovery well in 1980

Venezuela showed few real signs of success and on more than one occasion the directors used the Annual Report to sound a warning note: 'To the end of 1973 the Group had invested about £12.5 million in exploring for oil and gas in Indonesia, the North Sea, Ecuador and northwestern Canada. These operations have yet to make a contribution to profits. The major part of our capital investment is now being channelled into exploration.' It has to be remembered that, at that point, income from Indonesia was still four years away, while the North Sea was to need a further ten years before making any return on investment.

At the outset, Indonesia must have seemed to many an uncertain speculation. Formerly the Dutch East Indies, the country had been an important oil producer before the Second World War, but there had been no dramatic growth during the post-war period. Output in 1948 was about ten million tons, most of which was absorbed by Japan, Australia and local markets. Expansion had also been hindered by nationalisation, but by the mid 1960s there were signs of growth, encouraged particularly by the Japanese who wished to reduce their traditional dependence upon Middle East oil. Ultramar's decision to enter Indonesia was well timed, probably the result of the combination of good luck and good judgment that seemed to be a feature of much of its activity. It was a time when Japanese interest in Indonesia was rapidly

Ultramar's Goodwill Mission to Indonesia in 1981. *Left to right:* President Suharto, the interpreter, Lord Remnant, Alan Furness (British Embassy), Campbell Nelson, Lord Catto, Sir John Buckley, John Gold and Suhartoyo

increasing, but many oil companies were still holding back from entering the area, deterred perhaps by the concept of a Production Sharing Contract as opposed to straight ownership of concessions. It should be remembered that Roy Huffington had not found it easy to sell the 60% share of the Production Sharing Contract which Ultramar took.

Unlike some other exploration plays, Indonesia developed slowly at first. Two years were spent in survey and evaluation, concentrating at first in the East Kalimantan area (formerly known as Borneo), and the first well, Badak 1, was not spudded until November 1971. This well was a major discovery, producing under test 2,300 barrels of oil per day, but, as later proved even more important, also showing substantial gas reserves. The programme of exploration and drilling was immediately speeded up, and gradually the size of the discovery became apparent. The wells drilled in 1972 established that the field contained oil, gas and condensate in commercial quantities. The gas, whose potential was apparently tremendous, was clearly going to be the most important element, and discussions were opened with Japan, the obvious market. During 1973 and 1974 activity increased dramatically. Development wells were drilled to establish the full potential of the Badak field, and exploration was pushed forward in other parts of East Kalimantan and in Sumatra. Discoveries were made in Semberah, Lamaru, Pamaguan and Nilam. By the end of 1974, 24 oil and gas wells had been

211

LNG carriers under construction at the General Dynamics shipyard,
Quincy, Massachusetts, in September 1976

completed, and output had been tested to 10,000 barrels per day of oil and over 500 million cubic feet per day of gas. A pipeline had been built to connect the fields with a deep-water terminal, capable of carrying 15,000 barrels per day, and in December 1973 a 20-year contract was signed between Pertamina and a Japanese consortium for the sale of gas in the form of Liquefied Natural Gas (LNG). During 1974 contracts were awarded to Bechtel for the construction of a liquefaction plant. The first oil shipments from Indonesia were also made in 1974.

The problems of building a sophisticated LNG plant in a primitive jungle region were described by Malcolm Haigh, vice president technical development, in an article published in the Ultramar magazine, *Eagle Eye,* in 1977: 'It's a far cry from the jungle of New York to that of Kalimantan, Indonesia, on the opposite side of the world. Whilst Singapore is the normal jumping-off point for visits to the actual jobsite at Bontang, the focal point for much of the project is in Jakarta on the island of Java. Being very close to the equator, the whole area has a generally hot and humid climate punctuated periodically by heavy rainfall which can be extremely enervating and is often compounded by jet-lag and "the trots". Whether you fly east or west from New York it's still a hell of a long distance and involves some 25-30 hours flying time each way coupled with transit through twelve time zones. From Singapore or Jakarta, a one and a half

212

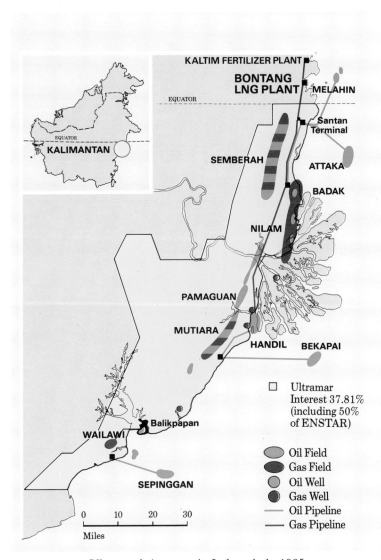

KALTIM FERTILIZER PLANT

**BONTANG LNG PLANT** MELAHIN

EQUATOR

Santan Terminal

SEMBERAH

ATTAKA

BADAK

NILAM

PAMAGUAN

MUTIARA

HANDIL BEKAPAI

☐ Ultramar Interest 37.81% (including 50% of ENSTAR)

Oil Field
Gas Field
Oil Well
Gas Well
Oil Pipeline
Gas Pipeline

Balikpapan

WAILAWI

SEPINGGAN

0   10   20   30
Miles

KALIMANTAN

EQUATOR

EQUATOR

Ultramar's interests in Indonesia in 1985

hour jet ride takes visitors onward to Balikpapan in East Kalimantan, and after that it's about half an hour by helicopter to the Badak field or an hour by Short Skyvan to the Bontang jobsite.

'It is well to remember that not too long ago this area was virgin jungle sparsely populated by orang-utans and head hunters with no infrastructure whatsoever. Without roads, all the material - about half a million tons - had to come in by sea from all over the world. A large number of expatriate and Indonesian personnel had to be transported, fed and housed and a permanent self-sustaining community had to be built to accommodate the 400-500 permanent staff and their families.

213

The LNG plant at Bontang

Malcolm Haigh at Bontang in 1977

# EXPLORATION AND PRODUCTION

'Building a sophisticated plant in such a remote area on an accelerated schedule has its own special problems not the least of which were simple communications and logistics. Nevertheless, equipment was landed on the beach at Bontang to build temporary construction facilities such as a cargo dock, roads and living quarters. It was not long before large earthmoving and construction equipment was off-loaded and activity was accelerated until more than 6,000 construction people and hundreds of pieces of equipment were engaged in building the plant. A localised dredging programme was also initiated to permit loading of 125,000 cubic metres (785,000 barrels) LNG ships without recourse to long sealines and causeways. Much has been written of the problems associated with funding of this project, the escalation of cost, the difficulties encountered by Pertamina and the many other worldwide changes so I will not dwell on these aspects. Suffice it to say that it is through the dedication of a great many people that today we have a fully operating plant processing what until recently was considered waste material into a valuable non-polluting product.'

Inevitably the emphasis during this period was on the Kalimantan region, but other areas were not ignored. One important discovery was made in Sumatra, Meruap 1, tested at 1,286 barrels of oil per day, but subsequent development was not successful, and work in this area stopped. At the same time, another partnership deal was set up with Pertamina, this time in conjunction with Conoco, covering just under a million acres in the East Kutai region of the Makassar Strait.

Ultramar could not have timed better the discovery of the oil and gas fields in Kalimantan. Just as the full potential of the discovery was being assessed, the Middle East oil crisis broke. The Arab cutbacks in oil supplies, and the subsequent disruption and price rises not only increased the value and significance of the Indonesian discovery, but also made the Japanese even more determined to replace their Middle East suppliers with more local sources.

The members of the consortium as well as Mobil Oil, who had made a comparable discovery at Arun in Indonesia, in 1972 and 1973, had been pursuing potential purchasers in the U.S. and elsewhere. Suddenly, they found themselves in the autumn of 1973 being heartily welcomed by the Japanese. The intensity of the negotiations paralleled the concern that was building up over the burgeoning world energy crisis. In the end most of the U.S. parties to the contract declined to make any announcements about the transaction lest they be criticised for disposing of an energy source in their control to other than U.S. consumers.

By 1975 the LNG plant was experiencing its first cost overruns, which resulted in new price negotiations with the Japanese consortium and the Bank of Indonesia, who were financing the project. The following year the Production Sharing Contract with Pertamina was also revised, at the behest of the Indonesian Government, who wanted more favourable terms. After complicated negotiations, the issue was resolved. The long-term cost recovery was stretched out and the profit element somewhat reduced, but without affecting the viability of the operation as a whole. During the summer of 1977 the LNG plant at Bontang was completed. There were two production trains, one of

The third and fourth LNG trains under construction at Bontang in January 1983

which started in July, the other in October, and the first cargo of LNG was delivered to Japan in August of 1977 on board the LNG carrier *Aquarius,* specially built for the service by General Dynamics in their Massachusetts shipyard. Linked by a pipeline to the Badak field, the Bontang plant is owned by Pertamina and is operated on a non-profit basis. The final cost of construction was $717 million, including a $260 million overrun.

As soon as the LNG plant was fully operational, the emphasis switched to the expansion of the Kalimantan fields. In 1978, fourteen new wells were drilled in Badak and two were drilled in the East Kutai concession under a farmout arrangement with Shell. There were already plans to expand the LNG plant, which by now had acquired all the necessary support facilities, including housing, schools, stores, a clinic and areas for recreation. The drilling successes the following year confirmed that there were sufficient gas reserves to double the size of the plant, while potential output was also increased by the Nilam field coming into production. Between 1979 and 1982 over 80 new wells were drilled, greatly expanding the Badak, Pamaguan and Nilam fields, and in 1981 construction started on two new production trains at Bontang. The only drilling

216

disappointments were in Sumatra and Kutai, where operations continued to be unsuccessful, resulting in both concessions being relinquished during 1981 and 1982.

In 1983 the two new production trains at Bontang came on stream, their completion somewhat accelerated because of an explosion and fire that had damaged one of the two original trains. The doubling in capacity of the LNG plant was matched by an expanded exploration programme which not only enlarged the existing fields, but also resulted in the discovery of a new oil field in the Mutiara region. There was now sufficient gas to supply local needs, for example a fertiliser plant north of Bontang, as well as to satisfy the Japanese contracts.

While the growth and success of the Indonesian venture had been developing steadily since the mid 1970s, Ultramar's other front runner, the North Sea, had a far less certain start. Interest in the North Sea was first aroused during the late 1960s, but at that time Ultramar had neither the finance nor the expertise to enter the water. It has to be admitted that at that time Ultramar was also influenced by geologists who did not believe in the North Sea as a prolific oil basin. The first step was the setting up of Ultramar Exploration Limited, a subsidiary company incorporated in London in July 1968 which, working closely with V. C. Illing and Partners, was to look at the opportunities offered by the North Sea. It is an interesting irony that the title of this subsidiary, and its association with Illing, were an echo of the earliest days of Ultramar's history during the mid 1930s. In the 1960s, Leslie Illing and John May were effectively the technical branch of the London company, and they helped Ultramar take its first tentative steps into the North Sea. These occurred in 1969, when Ultramar took a 6% interest in a Phillips Group consortium applying for licences in the third round of applications covering the U.K. sector. In 1970 the Group was awarded five blocks totalling 251,000 acres and a half interest in four other blocks. Survey work began and continued into 1971, when new licences covering the North Sea and the Shetlands were awarded. At the same time, Ultramar took an 8% interest in a small block in the Celtic Sea. In November 1972 the drilling of the first well started on block 16/29, 170 miles northeast of Aberdeen, and the following February Phillips, the operator, announced an oil discovery which tested at 3,500 barrels per day. The field was named Maureen.

The discovery of Maureen was a major event, but its commercial value was still uncertain. Ultramar could congratulate itself on its luck, for the first North Sea well in which it had a serious interest had hit the target, but successful commercial development was another matter. In a curious way there was another parallel with early days in Venezuela, for its first discovery there had raised a similar question. Oil had been found, but was there enough oil to justify commercial development? Between 1973 and 1976 a number of exploration and step-out wells were drilled to try to evaluate the scale of the Maureen discovery. Some were successful, some were unsuccessful, but there was still not enough information for a decision to be made. During 1976 and 1977, wells were also drilled on other blocks and there were two discoveries, Renee and Wendy. The latter tested at 4,760 barrels per day.

Despite the uncertainty about Maureen, Ultramar was now committed to the North

217

The Maureen production
platform under construction
at Loch Kishorn
and Hunterston in
Scotland in 1982

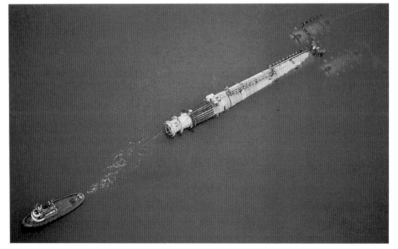

Part of the articulated
loading column for
the Maureen platform
complex being towed to
its position

The Maureen loading column in operation with the platform in the background, 1983

Sea and so, when the sixth licensing round was announced in 1978, it decided to play a more positive role. A new consortium was formed with Pan Canadian Petroleum and Houston Oil and Minerals, in which Ultramar was to be the operator, and in due course this group was awarded block 13/29 in the Moray Firth. An adjacent block, 13/30, was awarded to the Phillips Group. Survey work followed and then in 1981 Ultramar drilled its first North Sea well as operator, making a discovery in the Moray Firth which was tested to 4,142 barrels per day. The commercial potential of this oil accumulation is still being evaluated.

In the meantime, appraisal work continued on Maureen. By 1978 there was confirmation that the field was commercial and early in 1979 the U.K. Department of Energy gave its approval to the development plan. The target was 75,000 barrels per day

The Thistle field production platform in 1979

and a new type of platform was to be used, which would be built in Scotland. This would be a three-legged structure, with each leg formed as a vast vertical storage tank, with a total storage capacity of 650,000 barrels. It would be the world's first steel platform to combine flotation, ballasting and storage.

At the same time, a group in which Ultramar had a 25% interest purchased a small share in the Thistle field. This had gone on stream in November 1978, pumping through a pipeline to Sullom Voe in the Shetlands, but the field had great potential for expansion. This represented Ultramar's first step into North Sea production, paving the way for Maureen. The next four years saw the drilling of a number of development wells on Maureen and Thistle, while exploratory wells were also drilled on blocks awarded during the sixth and seventh licensing rounds. However, the most important year for Ultramar in the North Sea was 1983. First of all, the holding in Maureen was increased by the purchase of an additional 2.5%, for £28 million. Second, a 1% share in the established Forties field was bought for £30 million. Third, in September the Maureen field went on stream, producing over 70,000 barrels per day. Development had been slow and costly, but Ultramar could now call itself a real North Sea oil company, with significant interests in oil production. Not content to rest on its laurels Ultramar has had some successes in recent drilling in the North Sea. There is a heavy oil discovery in the 9/11 block and a gas discovery in block 49/5. The discovery in block 13/29 in the Moray Firth also remains to be evaluated. Only the future will tell which of these finds will be commercially developed. Ultramar will consider itself extremely lucky if all of them turn into commercially profitable fields.

Thus from the many entries that had started the exploration stakes during the late

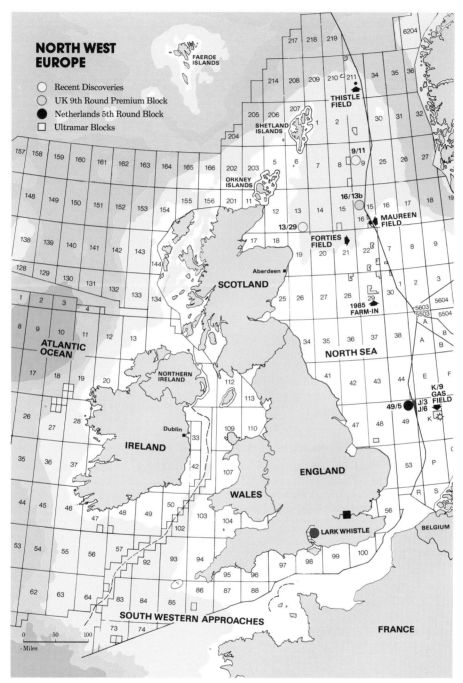

Ultramar's interests in northwest Europe in 1985

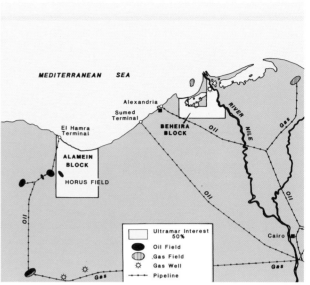

The Horus 1 well in the Alamein
field in Egypt in 1982

Ultramar's exploration interests in Egypt, 1985

1960s, there had emerged two clear front runners. Both had started relatively slowly, and in the case of Indonesia without too much popular support. In both cases early promise had been followed by slow and steady development, matched by increasingly heavy investment and then, during the late 1970s and early 1980s they had moved quickly into a dominant position, far ahead of the rest of the field. Together, Indonesia and the North Sea have transformed Ultramar from a small, well integrated but predominantly American oil company into a major international operation.

During the 1980s the exploration race will continue. At the moment Indonesia and the North Sea are the unchallenged leaders, but the search for oil and gas has already introduced a number of new challengers into the field. The first of these was Egypt. In 1978 a concession, held jointly with Murphy Oil, and covering over one million acres between Alexandria and El Alamein, was negotiated with the Egyptian General Petroleum Corporation. Two unsuccessful wells were drilled in 1979, followed by more surveying, and then in 1982 the Horus oil field in the Alamein block was discovered. The field is now being appraised for development. Another area of interest has been Australia. In 1979 a group, in which Ultramar had a 27.5% interest, took out an exploration licence covering over three million acres of the Gulf of Carpentaria, offshore Queensland. Following detailed surveys, this holding was relinquished. Perhaps more important were interests acquired in the Otway Basin off southern Australia and offshore Western Australia. The first wells have now been drilled in both regions, without any commercial success but with indications that follow-up wells may be warranted. Also an onshore area has been taken on in the Canning Basin. The Australian operation is headed by Hank Laska and Glen Muir, both transferred from

*Above and right:* Drilling
rig at Breaksea Reef,
South Australia

223

Canada, and Ultramar plans to expand its exploration activities. Other areas currently being worked on include offshore Ireland, where the first unsuccessful exploratory well was drilled in 1983, and Equatorial Guinea, where Ultramar has a 25% interest in a large offshore block. No doubt the continuing search for oil and gas will lead Ultramar into new regions during the second half of the 1980s.

As mentioned earlier in this chapter, perhaps the most interesting recent development has been the discovery of oil in Hampshire where Ultramar is a 50% partner with Amoco. It is too early to judge the importance of this find, but the next few years will probably see an accelerated drilling programme in southern England.

Exploration has made its own demands on the experience and training of Ultramar personnel and it is interesting to note how the company has handled this aspect of the business. For the first 25 years of Ultramar's existence, exploration and production was the basic business, and almost all of the second generation of Ultramar's top executives gained experience in the oil fields of Venezuela, including Lorbeer, Nelson, Thompson and Bensen. What they lacked in basic education in geology and petroleum engineering was often made up partly by special courses in geology or partly by the twelve-week cram courses in production technology given by the University of Texas at Kilgore, in the heart of the east Texas oilfield. Bensen, Lorbeer, Laska and many others went through these courses. Ultramar has from the start actively encouraged and supported education and programmes were set up to pay all or partial tuition, depending upon grades. This was initiated by Lorbeer, who seems to have been a frustrated teacher, and was formalised by Bensen.

However, with integration came a different set of skills and refining, marketing and shipping executives were hired or acquired through mergers. In the early 1960s, production and exploration was set up as a separate department and placed under Roy Brotherhood. He continued in that role until his retirement in the mid 1970s when Robert Bland took over. Bland, who along with William Sheptycki became a director of Ultramar in 1984, came to Ultramar from Conoco. The Ultramar exploration department now has three principal divisions, apart from Indonesia, the North Sea, Europe and Africa headed by William Sheptycki, the U.S.A. and Canada headed by Tony Lee, and Australia under Hank Laska. It is interesting that all these three men, as well as Alexander Stucken, Ultramar's resident manager in Indonesia, are Canadians who came up through the ranks in the Calgary office. The western Canadian operation, based in Calgary, has long been a training ground for Ultramar's geologists and technical personnel. Several of Ultramar's former managers in Venezuela also had their start there. The present resident manager in Calgary is Robert Ducharme. He is also chief geologist for the Group, maintaining the tradition of British-trained geologists being associated with Ultramar since its formation.

On the subject of geologists, it should be said that Ultramar certainly has never economised on the quantity. An early analyst of Ultramar in the late 1950s remarked that 'Ultramar seems to have a higher rate of geologists per barrel of oil production than any other serious oil company.' There was a constant stream of young British geologists

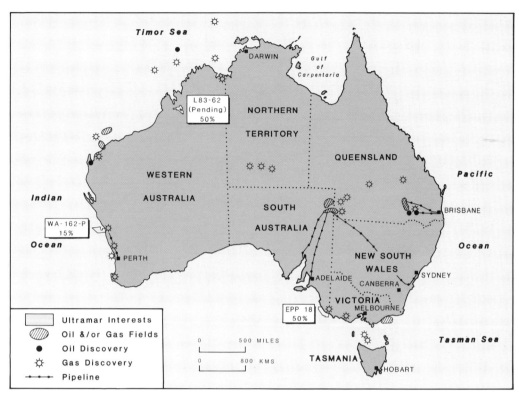

Ultramar's exploration interests in Australia, 1984

engaged by the Illing organisation and sent to Venezuela, western Canada or one of the U.S. offices but few of them stayed very long. Both Assheton in the early days, and Lorbeer when he became chief executive, complained to the Chairman of Ultramar that they seemed to have little control over the goings and comings of Ultramar's geologists. The Chairman replied that neither did he. There certainly was some bitterness on this score in the 1950s and early 1960s and Lorbeer suspected that geologists were being encouraged to leave because of differences of opinion with their superiors on technical points. Whatever the early problems, Ultramar's exploration and production team and policy has generally been successful and has certainly been instrumental in bringing the company to its present position.

The *Ultrasea* and the *Golden Dolphin* fitting out in the National
Steel shipyard in San Diego in 1974

# SHIPPING 11

Ultramar first became involved with shipping during the early 1960s, following a rapid policy of integration and the opening of the Holyrood refinery in Newfoundland. The transportation department was established by Lloyd Bensen as part of the marketing set-up. From late 1961, when Holyrood was opened, regular tanker movements between Venezuela and Canada were required and this was expanded to other areas once the Panama refinery was operational. Tankers were chartered on the spot market from voyage to voyage as the level of business in the early stages did not justify time-chartering. The increasing level of activity brought into being a separate transportation department which was initially managed by Al Marino, a professional hired upon his retirement from Amoco when the need for expertise arose. This department soon became highly proficient, which was to benefit Ultramar in years to come. At the same time a new subsidiary, Ultramar Liberia Limited, was incorporated in 1963, to look after supply and distribution and to pave the way for the entry into the shipping business.

Late in 1964 Ultramar became a ship-owner for the first time, with the purchase of the tanker *Eagle* for the Panama bunkering operation. By 1969 three specially built self-propelled bunkering barges were in operation in Panama waters. Apart from ship bunkering, the barges were used for transport and delivery duties in connection with the Panama refinery and also for the movement of marine diesel and fuel oil for other companies. The concept of self-propelled barges fuelling and provisioning ships standing in line to transit the Panama Canal was initiated by Ultramar. The success of the bunkering business may have encouraged Ultramar to consider ship-owning on a grander scale. In any case, by 1967 the company's shipping requirements had grown to such an extent that it was necessary to guard against the damaging short-term fluctuations of the spot tanker market. The initial answer seemed to lie in time-chartering and so an asphalt carrier, the *Leonidas,* was chartered for five years. Further time charters followed, ranging from one year to seven years. The most important of the ships to be chartered was the *Pennant,* for this was owned by Leo Berger and Peter Constas. From this charter grew a relationship that was to revolutionise Ultramar's shipping interests over the next decade.

Both alumni of the U.S. Merchant Marine Academy, Berger and Constas had been ship operators for a number of years. The steady growth of its shipping requirements

227

The *Pennant* at the Los Angeles terminal in 1967

The *Golden Falcon* leaving St. John's, Newfoundland, in 1978 on the last voyage prior to conversion into a floating dock at the Holyrood refinery

The *Capricorn* in 1971

combined with the uncertainty of the spot market convinced Ultramar that the best way to protect itself would be to have control over its own tanker fleet, and so a partnership agreement was drawn up with the Avon Steamship Company, an operation set up by Berger and Constas, for the acquisition and ownership of tankers. At this time Berger and Constas were keen to expand their ship-owning interests, but limited resources hindered their growth. What they needed was a partner with a good record of profits and an ambition to enter the shipping business. Ultramar was just such a company and so the association was well timed. The close relationship that developed was valuable to both sides. Berger and Constas saw in Ultramar a means to realise their ship-owning ambitions and a convenient source of finance, while for Ultramar Berger and Constas represented a pool of experience and expertise to guide them through the uncharted waters of the shipping world. For the next ten years the relationship was to be beneficial to both parties but, in the end, although the partnership remained, Berger's ambitions were to take him far beyond the relatively limited shipping needs of Ultramar.

During 1967 Ultramar became part owner of five medium-sized tankers by acquiring interests in four shipping companies that were already in operation, registered either in Bermuda or Liberia. These companies, each effectively contributing one ship to the Ultramar fleet, were put under the control of Avon Steamship Company. Notable among these ships were the *Golden Eagle* and the *Golden Falcon,* the first members of the tanker fleet to carry names that firmly identified them with Ultramar.

For the first few months the new shipping venture seemed rather shaky. During early 1967 tanker tonnage rates fell and the spot market weakened, but then the Arab-Israeli War and the Suez crisis that followed caused marine rates to rocket upwards. Once again, luck had favoured Ultramar, for the timing of the venture was almost perfect. As one commentator wrote at the time: 'This timely acquisition of ships saved the Ultramar Group many millions of dollars. In contrast, some less farsighted competitors took a real bath in the shipping market at that time from which they are still feeling the effects.' Even the Annual Report could not resist a mild gloat, albeit in rather more restrained language: 'An important development in 1967 was the acquisition of part ownership in a number of ocean-going tankers. This protected the operating companies against wide fluctuations in shipping rates which arose because of the Suez crisis. Acquisition of the tankers had been financed by United States banks.'

During 1968 the fleet was further expanded by the acquisition of a 50% interest in two tanker companies. The new enthusiasm for shipping also inspired the purchase of an interest in two dry-cargo ships, but this particular diversification did not pay off and the interest was sold in the following year. By the end of 1968, Ultramar was part owner of five tankers, ranging in size from 20,000 to 34,000 tons. In addition, future plans were announced in the Annual Report which, for the first time, carried a section headed 'Transportation'. These included the expansion of the fleet by the addition of four or five tankers in the 50,000/70,000 ton range when the Quebec refinery came on stream, and a detailed investigation of the St. Lawrence River to gain experience of tide effects and ice conditions. This pattern of activity was maintained for the next couple of years. The operation of the fleet reduced the company's dependence upon the spot market and, at the same time, valuable experience was gained in chartering the ships out to other operators when they were not required. The interests held in some companies were sold and others acquired, but the structure of the fleet did not alter significantly until 1971 when two tankers, the 39,000 ton *Golden Jason* and the 43,000 ton *Aigle d'Or,* were added. These two ships marked a radical change of policy for they were the first ocean-going tankers to be wholly owned by Ultramar, although still operated by Avon Steamship. Once again the purchase turned out to be well timed in relation to the international tanker market, but the purchase was more significant in other ways.

First of all, the size of the new ships was a reflection of the problems that were being encountered in navigating the St. Lawrence River to Quebec. Despite the promise of a dredging programme that had been part of the agreement that had brought the new refinery to Quebec, the draught was still limited to 35 feet. This resulted in light loading or lightering, causing considerable extra expenditure, and undermining the cost structure upon which the refinery operation had been based. In addition, some ships had been delayed or damaged by ice during a particularly severe winter. Second, the purchase gave the company experience in ship ownership, paving the way for the decision to commission the building of a new fleet during the latter part of 1971. It can be argued that Ultramar entered the ship-owning business too late. The pattern of growth that had marked the industry from the early 1950s had already reached its peak by 1970, when Ultramar's transport requirements had grown sufficiently to justify the establishment of a fleet. It is only fair to add that in some ways management felt the shipping business was not only fulfilling transport needs but was also a potentially useful diversification.

Another reason that encouraged Ultramar to swim against the tide was a change of policy by the United States Government towards the rules that covered ship subsidies. This was the passing of the Merchant Marine Act of 1970 by the United States Congress. The years following the end of the Second World War had been marked by a dramatic decline in the size of the United States merchant fleet, from 4,500 ships carrying about 60% of the world's seaborne commerce in 1945, to about 570 ships carrying under 5% of the seagoing trade during the late 1960s. The average age of the surviving U.S.-owned ships was seventeen years, and few new ships were being built in U.S. shipyards, a reflection of the financial reality that the American shipyard worker and the American seaman were more expensive than their foreign counterparts. This was not a new reality. The Merchant Marine Act of 1936 had recognised it by providing for the payment of government subsidies to U.S. shipowners operating vessels in foreign trade, subsidies designed to make U.S.-owned vessels competitive with foreign flag ships. The subsidy could cover both the construction differential and the operating differential. Despite the impetus given to shipyards and shipowners by the Second World War and its aftermath, the 1936 Act had become increasingly ineffective. As a result, a new Act was passed in 1970 which extended and enlarged the construction and operating subsidy programme, and set up the ambitious goal of 300 new U.S. flag ships to be built during the next ten years. For the first time, dry and liquid bulk carriers were included in the

The *Golden Swan* in 1972

The *Golden Robin* in dry dock for
repair from ice damage

231

Lord Remnant and Campbell Nelson at the launching of the
*Ultramar* in San Diego in February 1973

The launching of the *Golden Dolphin*
in San Diego in January 1974

232

subsidy programme. It was under this new Act that Golden Eagle Liberia, Ultramar's shipping subsidiary, entered into a contract for the building of a series of ships at National Steel's yard in San Diego, California.

At the end of 1971 construction started on the first two ships. These were to be 80,500 ton OBO carriers. The oil-bulk-ore combination carrier had been developed during the mid 1960s, and the first ship to carry the OBO classification was the *Naess Norseman*, launched in Germany in 1965. The function of an OBO is to compete economically on spot or time-charter markets under the same conditions as conventional tankers, ore carriers or bulk dry-cargo carriers, and so the ship has to be designed to perform the functions of all three types without compromising the best features of any one. This flexibility was seen as a way of overcoming expensive and time-consuming shipyard refits as the ship could be readily and quickly adapted by its own crew to suit market conditions. It would also take advantage of seasonal variations in freight patterns and minimise ballast voyages. The ships being built at San Diego represented the most advanced example of OBO technology and their cost was to be financed by maritime subsidies and an issue of U.S. Government guaranteed bonds.

During 1972 the reorganisation of Ultramar's fleet continued. Another medium-sized foreign flag tanker, the *Golden Swan*, was purchased outright. The foreign flag fleet, eight tankers with an aggregate tonnage of 300,000 tons, included the *Golden Falcon, Golden Eagle, Golden Jason, Golden Robin, Golden Swan, Aigle d'Or, Capricorn* and *Pennant*. The two OBO carriers were nearing completion in San Diego, and a further contract had been agreed for the construction of three 90,000 ton tankers, to be built to the same specifications as the OBOs, and under the same subsidy, finance and charter arrangements. The increasingly important role played by the shipping business in Ultramar's activities was reflected by the relatively large contribution made to Group profits, and by the setting up in Canada of Oceanic Tankers Agency Limited. Marine transportation was now a major Ultramar interest and had taken its logical place in the integration programme.

Expansion continued through the mid 1970s. On 17 February 1973 the first of the OBOs was launched at San Diego, amid cheers from 8,000 spectators. Named in the traditional manner as Captain Berger's wife, Arvie, cracked a bottle of Californian champagne against the bow, the *Ultramar* slipped down the ways. The largest ship built on the West Coast of America the *Ultramar* was 900 feet long 106 feet across (the maximum width for the Panama Canal) and each of the nine holds could contain a six-storey building. The following October saw the launching of the sister ship, the *Ultrasea*, the christening ceremony by Lloyd Bensen's wife, Edna, accompanied by the release of hundreds of colourful balloons. By this time the *Ultramar* had entered service, starting a ten-year sub-charter. Both ships were to be operated by Aries Marine Shipping, a company owned by Berger and Constas. The *Ultrasea* was put into service in 1974. While the focus of attention was naturally on California, Ultramar was rationalising the rest of its shipping interests. With the exception of the *Capricorn*, which was sold, all the seven remaining foreign flag tankers were bought outright, and placed under the control

Campbell Nelson, Peter Constas, Arnold Lorbeer and Leo Berger at the launching
of the *Golden Endeavor* in June 1974

of Golden Eagle Liberia. All vessels had by now been ice-strengthened. A number of additional tankers were also time-chartered and once again the market played into Ultramar's hands. Rates rose rapidly soon after the charters were contracted and some of the ships were subsequently sub-chartered to other companies at a profit.

In January 1974 the *Golden Dolphin,* first of the three 90,000 ton tankers, was launched at San Diego. At the naming ceremony, undertaken by Peter Constas's wife, Mary, the optimism of the moment was captured in a speech by John Vogel, President of the National Bank of North America: 'With ships like the *Golden Dolphin* the United States has begun to recapture a proud position among the merchant marine nations. It is good for our prestige, our economy and our balance of trade By the time she sails on her maiden voyage next summer, the *Golden Dolphin* will already have churned almost $100 million into the American economy.' The two sister tankers soon followed the *Golden Dolphin* into San Diego Bay, the *Golden Endeavor* launched in June 1974 by Helen Delich Bentley, the Chairman of the Federal Maritime Commission, and the *Golden Monarch* in February 1975, launched by Captain Berger's daughter, Phyllis. The names for the tankers and the two OBO carriers had been decided by a naming competition held among Ultramar's employees. Upon completion, the *Golden Dolphin* and the *Golden Endeavor* were taken into Ultramar's own service, while the *Golden Monarch* was sub-chartered.

This period represented a high point for Ultramar's shipping business. Many records were broken. The *Golden Dolphin* became the largest vessel ever to enter Quebec City, with a cargo of 643,000 barrels of crude, an event marred only by the continuing problems with the depth of the St. Lawrence which resulted in some of the cargo having

The *Golden Spray* in 1977

The *Golden Endeavor* unloading at the Quebec refinery in February 1981

OBO carriers under construction at the Puerto Real shipyard of Astilleros Españoles in 1982

The Spanish-built OBO carrier *Mercedes*

236

to be off-loaded onto lighters. In December 1974 the shipping department handled Ultramar's largest ever spot charter, the 285,000 ton tanker *Vespasian* carrying 2.1 million barrels of oil, but a few weeks later this was bettered by the chartering of the 370,000 ton *Hemland*. At the time this was the largest tanker ever spot chartered for a single voyage, and the largest vessel ever to sail into the western hemisphere. To handle all the complex aspects of the shipping business required a highly sophisticated marine transportation department, with many areas of responsibility. These included the operational control of vessels in the fleet and their scheduling, their bunkering and maintenance, ensuring that budgets are maintained and that all voyages are cost effective, chartering, both in and out, and being able to respond and even anticipate the fluctuations of the market, and supervising ship handling and facilities in port. Optimism was the order of the day and so, it is interesting to look, with hindsight, at some of the plans drawn up during this period of high ambition. These included bunkering and transport barges over four times the size of those used in Panama, a fleet of 380,000 ton tankers for worldwide trading, and many other projects.

Some of this optimism continued into 1976. A sixth U.S. flag vessel, another 90,000 ton tanker, was being built in San Diego and Ultramar took a 40% interest in the project. Named the *American Heritage* in honour of America's Bicentennial, the tanker was launched in April 1976 by Dale Austin's wife, Nancy, with all the usual ceremony. However, the ship was destined for only a short life in the Ultramar fleet for, within a few months of the launching, the interest in the *American Heritage* was sold, along with one of her sister ships, the *Golden Monarch*. During 1976 other ships were also sold from the fleet of foreign flag tankers, while others were laid up. Tanker rates were weak, and so it was often proving to be cheaper to spot charter than to use the wholly owned ships. The foreign flag tankers were also too small, and in some cases too old to be operated economically. As the market grew more uncertain, it became increasingly important to be flexible enough to cover all ends. Spot chartering and larger ships seemed to be the key to success, and so the smaller ships were gradually sold or scrapped, the last to go being the *Aigle d'Or* and the *Golden Swan*. One of Ultramar's longest-serving vessels was the *Golden Falcon*. In February 1978, the ship made her 114th and last trip to Holyrood. The scrap-yard awaited the 24-year-old tanker but at the last minute she was reprieved and turned into a floating dock at the Holyrood terminal. This allowed larger tankers to dock at the refinery because of the increased depth. The point was proved later when a 51,000 ton tanker was eased alongside the *Golden Falcon*. In her new role, the ship was to remain in the fleet until the final closure of Holyrood in 1983, by which time she had seen nearly twenty years of Ultramar service.

The requirement for a larger tanker was overcome by the time-chartering of the Swedish-built 120,000 ton *Golden Spray*. In 1977 the ship was purchased and put into regular service for the Quebec refinery. The depth problems in the St. Lawrence River had still not been overcome, but the *Golden Spray*, now the only wholly owned foreign flag vessel, was able to make several trips to Quebec during 1978.

The next few years were to see a complete reversal of Ultramar policy. To be fair it was the international oil and shipping industry which abruptly changed and Ultramar could not buck the tide. Large tankers became a liability, and so the *Golden Spray* was sold in 1979. Plans to dispose of the *Golden Dolphin* and the *Golden Endeavor* were discussed but market conditions were unfavourable. There was a world-wide tanker tonnage surplus, but at the same time there was a world shortage of small and medium size tankers because old ships in this category had not been replaced. This was underlined by the continuing difficulties in Canada. Dredging programmes on the St. Lawrence had either been ineffective, or had not been repeated often enough, with the result that the refinery had never been able to receive on a regular basis the size tankers for which it had been built. Its financial viability had been constantly undermined by the additional costs of trans-shipment, part loading and lighterage. Rather than continue to fight this battle, which had been in a state of trench warfare for nearly ten years, Ultramar decided to move away from the emphasis on large tankers, and switch to a medium-sized fleet which would not suffer from the St. Lawrence problems. With this in mind, negotiations were opened with a number of shipyards, but the order was eventually placed in 1980 with the Puerto Real Shipyard of Astilleros Españoles. The ships to be built were six 76,000 ton Panamax OBO carriers (Panamax being the maximum size to operate through the Panama Canal), and delivery was expected during 1982 and 1983.

The decision to invest in a new tanker fleet seems, with the benefit of hindsight, to have been somewhat unwise but at the time it was easy to justify. Ultramar's transport requirements would be fulfilled by about four of the new smaller OBO carriers and so it was logical to have six ships, each working at least 50% for Ultramar and the rest of the time in revenue-earning service. More important, experts throughout the world were in agreement that the early 1980s would be marked by a dramatic growth in the coal market. Every report, both official and unofficial, seemed to confirm this trend and so Ultramar, aware of the likely shortage of modern medium-sized tankers, felt safe in commissioning a fleet of ships that would be suitable for the coal trade. In the event, all the experts were proved to be wrong, and the predicted boom in coal never materialised, but this could not have been anticipated at the time. The Annual Report explained this new shipping policy in the following way: 'The new building programme is a major part of our plans to secure our in-house transportation needs with our own tonnage. In addition to providing a hedge against a volatile tanker market, the new vessels will be employed in the dry-cargo trade where profitable opportunities are foreseen in the mid 1980s.'

The decision to build the ships in Spain was influenced by several factors. First, in terms of merchant tonnage, Spain is high up the league of shipbuilding nations. Its major shipyards are government-owned and incorporate a wide range of marine engineering companies. Second, the Puerto Real shipyard is modern, having been constructed in the early 1970s, and can build a wide range of vessels, including tankers up to a theoretical size of one million tons. Its facilities and size meant that Puerto Real could build the Ultramar ships on production-line principles.

The *Golden Dolphin* unloading a Strategic Petroleum Reserve cargo

The *Ultramar* loading grain in
Louisiana for Bangladesh in 1982

# A GOLDEN ADVENTURE

The keels for the first two Spanish OBOs were laid in December 1981 and the programme proceeded on schedule for a while. The two ships were launched during 1982 and, still unnamed, were being fitted out. However, during 1982 the programme began to slip, and the completion date was moved forward to the middle of 1983. Delays continued and so in December of 1983 the contract with the shipyard was renegotiated, on the basis that the yard was unable to meet the contracted delivery dates. New dates were established, along with improved terms on price and financing from Ultramar's point of view, but this new agreement was not adhered to and so a Notice of Cancellation was served on the ships. Further discussions late in 1984 finally resulted in agreement and the first ship, named *Maureen* after the North Sea field, was delivered early in February 1985. The remaining ships are being delivered in the course of 1985 and have also been named after leading oil fields in whose discovery Ultramar participated - *Mercedes, Badak, Nilam, Dodsland* and *Palacio*.

Elsewhere, shipping operations continued, although there were some changes to the fleet. In 1981 the ten-year time charters for the two U.S. flag OBO carriers, *Ultramar* and *Ultrasea,* were terminated, and the ships came back into Ultramar service, joining the *Golden Endeavor.* At this time the ships underwent a refit to enable them to comply with new safety and pollution control standards. A new ship joined the fleet, the Panamanian registered *Grand Eagle,* an Aframax tanker on a five-year time charter. Apart from Ultramar's own activities, the ships became involved during the early 1980s in two U.S. Government-sponsored operations. The first of these was the Strategic Petroleum Reserve (SPR) programme. Following the problems and shortages in the United States that resulted from the oil crisis of 1973/4, the Government decided to establish a massive crude oil storage programme as an insurance policy against future emergencies. Huge underground reservoirs were established, and a fleet of tankers began to deliver cargoes of crude drawn from many different producing regions. The aim was to have one billion barrels in storage by the end of 1985 but the programme has slowed over the last two years. Ultramar has been drawn into the SPR programme as both supplier and shipper, with the U.S. flag ships carrying cargoes in 1981 and the following three years. More recently the attraction of the SPR business has not been lost on other ship-owners, and so the trade has become increasingly competitive. Rates have been cut to the extent that Ultramar's U.S. flag ships in 1984 could not compete commercially and so operated at a loss.

The Public Law 480 programme is a U.S. Government aid programme to Third World countries. Since 1982 Ultramar ships have carried a number of PL 480 cargoes, mostly grain from Louisiana. The delivery of one of these cargoes, 68,000 tons of grain to Bangladesh, was graphically described in a recent issue of *Eagle Eye*: 'When the *Ultramar* arrived and anchored off the coast, two daughter vessels steamed immediately alongside. The first ship, a Bengali flag vessel, named the *Banglar Upohar,* a 15,000 tonner, came on the *Ultramar*'s port side, while the second ship the *Sea Renown* (6,000 dwt) took her place on the starboard side. The *Banglar Upohar* and the *Sea Renown* had provided transport for the more than one hundred Bengali longshoremen who were

The *Ultramar*'s grain cargo being unloaded in the Bay of Bengal

to provide the labour for the *Ultramar*'s discharge. They brought with them all the provisions they would need during their stay, except for water which was supplied by the ship. Bags of rice and vegetables, firewood, pots and pans were all lowered over the side to men waiting on the *Ultramar*'s deck. Chickens were sent in bamboo cages, more often than not while standing on their heads, because their prison was lowered upside down. Even a goat was taken over the side by sling. This sling was less than reliable and its cargo fell unharmed twenty feet into the water. The goat seemed to prefer the Bay and was only reluctantly rescued. His attitude was more easily understood later, when it was discovered that he was the main ingredient of the curry everyone seemed to be enjoying so much.

'Coincident with the provisioning of the *Ultramar* (and the untimely end of the goat), stevedores were busily laying out the piping between the ships and starting up the vac-u-cators. Once everything was rigged, men climbed down into the holds to force the nozzles deep into the grain to provide better suction. As each hold neared completion, the remaining grain was swept towards the centre to provide an uninterrupted flow. The operation proceeded around the clock, with Bengalis sleeping and eating in shifts on deck.

241

Al Marino who pioneered Ultramar's
shipping department

Robert Haddow, Group senior vice
president, Transportation

'In all, six ships were chartered to perform the total of ten voyages that were necessary to unload fully the *Ultramar*. Due to an efficient operation and especially favourable weather, which generally permitted two daughter ships to be worked simultaneously with few interruptions, the *Ultramar*'s discharge was completed in only thirteen days.'

The 1980s have so far been a less than successful period for Ultramar's shipping interests, marked by continuing uncertainty about the future. The unprecedented slump in shipping rates that started in 1981 still shows no sign of recovery, and so Ultramar's policy is under constant revision in an attempt to balance the company's requirements against the fluctuations of the international market. The Spanish-built fleet begins a new chapter in Ultramar's shipping history. In the long term, the fleet is justified by the continuing shortage of new medium-sized tankers, a shortage that will become increasingly significant as the market recovers. According to Robert Haddow, president of Ultramar Shipping, the ownership of a small fleet can also be justified as an insurance policy, an investment that will cover Ultramar's needs. At the same time, as a result of the problems in Spain, Ultramar continues to operate the U.S. flag vessels which are expensive despite their efficiency and small crews (about 31 per ship). This fleet now comprises only three ships, *Ultramar, Ultrasea* and *Golden Endeavor,* with the fourth, the *Golden Dolphin,* having been lost in an explosion off Bermuda in March 1982, a disaster that cost nine lives. The *Golden Dolphin* was the second Ultramar ship to have been lost at sea, the first having been the *Golden Jay,* which sank in July 1972.

The expansion of Ultramar's shipping interests necessitated reorganisation and strengthening of the transportation department. In the early days, when chartering was the main activity, Al Marino was ably assisted by a number of Ultramar youngsters largely drafted from other departments, including Joseph Ament, Bart Murray, John

Tivnan and Al Forti. Later, after Marino had retired Robert Haddow was engaged to head shipping and reorganise the department. Haddow is a shipping professional who had worked for a number of companies and most recently had handled Burmah Oil's shipping department. He became a senior vice president of American Ultramar and a director of the parent company. He brought with him a number of professionals, for example, Gnana Supramaniam, Cesare Sorio, Robert Walsh, Jack Ostromogilsky and Jerry Eustace. Much of Ultramar's management talent has been in-bred, but the company has never hesitated to hire outsiders when specialised or professional help was required.

Shipping remains an essential part of Ultramar's business as a fully integrated oil company, but the pattern of development over the next five to ten years is hard to predict. At the moment, chartering seems more attractive than ship ownership but this could be reversed by any recovery in the international market. The story of Ultramar's diversification into the shipping business remains to be completed during the ensuing years.

Agricultural Genetics has developed a solution that when sprayed on crop stubble makes it
bio-degradable. As a result stubble burning may soon become obsolete

# DIVERSIFICATION 12

Diversification has different meanings to different people. For Ultramar the first 50 years have witnessed a steady progression from concession trading to oil and gas exploration and production, refining, distribution and marketing, transportation and ship ownership. Ultramar's activities and interests worldwide are now extremely diverse, but essentially they are mostly related to the energy business. However, during the early 1970s Ultramar, in common with many other fast-growing and profitable companies with international operations, began to look for ways to diversify out of their normal field of business. The idea was not entirely new, for as early as the 1930s Ultramar had dabbled in other fields. There was a search for minerals in the Dominican Republic and for copper and iron in central Venezuela. There was a scheme for cattle raising in the Orinoco delta, and for building a leisure resort at the Pamatacual terminal on the Venezuelan coast. In the 1960s there was the brief flirtation with the business of transporting fruit and dried cod between Panama and Newfoundland, described in Chapter Seven. There was also a flirtation with windmills as a substitute for oil in pumping and power stations. Most of these ventures never got off the ground, and those that did were not taken very seriously because they seemed to conflict with the company's main line of business. When cash was short, there was no point in spending it on projects that were unrelated to Ultramar's primary aim of becoming a fully integrated oil business, and surviving.

The radically changed situation that Ultramar found itself in during the 1970s enabled it to consider diversification as a serious possibility, and so the company began to look around for ideas. At a Management Meeting in San Diego, California, on the occasion of the launching of an American flag tanker, senior managers were each asked to present a paper with ideas on this subject. Some suggestions were patently light-hearted, but, writing in *Eagle Eye* early in 1974, Arnold Lorbeer gave a list of some of the ideas that had been brought up:

Initiate a small ship transportation network for the Canadian Arctic, Hudson Bay and western Greenland.

Manufacture white bricks in Venezuela.

Build condominiums in eastern Newfoundland.

Establish riding centres in suburbia, with indoor schooling rings.

The Hudson River Bridge under construction by the Fitzpatrick company in 1979

Ultramar Plaza, the condominium block in Panama under construction in 1980

The Miami rapid transit system under construction by the Fitzpatrick company in 1978

# DIVERSIFICATION

Develop a peat moss export business in the Port-au-Port Peninsula, Newfoundland.

Develop a chain of Homes-For-The-Aged and Retirement Homes, using centralised purchasing and management control.

Develop charcoal burners to generate carbon monoxide to power trucks.

Build or acquire chains of mortuaries, crematoriums, cemeteries and flower shops.

Develop small vineyards in the eastern United States.

Most of these ideas were obviously impractical, but others anticipated diversification projects that were to be brought about by other companies during the next few years.

The first serious attempts at establishing a diversification policy were made in 1976. The Annual Report for that year included a section headed 'Diversification', which gave details of Ultramar's purchase of an 80% interest in the Fitzpatrick Construction Company, referred to as 'a modest investment'. Fitzpatrick had been in the construction business in the United States for over twenty years, specialising in roads, bridges, docks and other heavy engineering projects. This company gave good advice to Ultramar in a number of areas, especially road building in Iran in connection with the exploration drilling programme. It also initially contributed a small profit through its own activities, which at that time included the building of parts of a rapid transit system in Atlanta, Georgia.

The next two years were to represent the high point of Ultramar's enthusiasm for diversification. The policy was clearly defined in the 1977 Annual Report: 'We are gradually and modestly broadening our profit base by diversifying into energy-related activities and developing new sources of earnings outside the oil industry.' The two years witnessed a flurry of activity. Fitzpatrick's projects included work on an ambitious sewage disposal programme in Long Island, New York, a barge loading pier, and a 50% interest in building a motorway bridge across the Hudson River, near Albany, New York. Other diversifications included the purchase of 50% of Servo Energy Systems, a maker of energy saving equipment, an option to purchase an interest in a Newfoundland construction company, a uranium exploration venture in northeast Alberta and northwest Saskatchewan in conjunction with a group of Canadian and United States companies and a scheme to mine and market diatomaceous earth in British Columbia, a product used for oil absorption, plant feed and animal bedding. Early in 1978 the list was increased by the purchase of Surgeonics Limited, a United States company making suppression equipment for computers and other electronic machinery. Surgeonics was moved to Mount Kisco, reorganised and its product range expanded. Its activities, and those of Fitzpatrick, were featured in *Eagle Eye*.

During 1978 and 1979 interest in most of these projects remained high. Fitzpatrick, although proving not to be as profitable as had been hoped, was working on the Hudson River Bridge, some road and dock contracts and the building of parts of a mass transit system in Miami. The uranium venture looked promising and the core drilling programme, backed by exploration techniques using Tracketch film which is sensitive to radon gas, showed positive indications of the presence of uranium deposits. Core drilling

| | Uranium Project |
| --- | --- |
| | Diatomaceous Earth Project |

Ultramar's interest in uranium and diatomaceous earth in western Canada in 1980

had also confirmed a large deposit of diatomaceous earth in British Columbia. A new venture was the decision to expand the selling and leasing of water softening and water conditioning equipment in eastern Canada, a business established by CFM during the early 1970s. By marketing water refining equipment through heating oil outlets, Ultramar quickly became the major distributor in the region, leasing over 6,000 units per year with a rental income of Can.$4 million. This business has continued to be profitable to the present day and is still growing.

Jacqueline Nowlan, a field geologist on the Virgin River uranium
project in Saskatchewan in 1979

   The next year saw a change of direction, and a noticeable reduction in enthusiasm for
the concept of diversification, a pattern that was to become more marked as the 1980s
progressed. This was underlined by the replacement of the heading 'Diversification' in
the Annual Report by the words 'Other Activities', which was to remain until 1983,
when it disappeared altogether. However, Ultramar in those years developed an interest
in real estate. In Florida, 900 acres were purchased for $8 million for eventual
residential development, and in Panama a condominium project was started. A sum of $7

Self-storage units opened in Ontario in 1981

million was also invested in two United States Venture Capital Funds in order to gain exposure to a number of new ventures with a concentration in the alternative energy and high technology industries. In other words, Ultramar, not impressed by its own efforts at diversification investment, was seeking guidance from more experienced channels.

Fitzpatrick's Hudson River Bridge project was formally opened on 14 August 1980 ahead of schedule; the search for uranium continued, but the diatomaceous earth scheme was abandoned after an economic study showed it to be impractical. The water refining equipment business continued to expand. There were also some new ventures in Canada. Surplus land was used at two Ontario terminals to construct malls of mini-warehouses which each had over two hundred small, self-storage units with good security designed to be leased to private individuals and small companies. This business is also still flourishing and additional mini-warehouses have been built. The main emphasis, however, seemed to be on real estate. The condominium block in Panama was completed, and land, previously acquired in California, was sold at a profit. In other fields, the interest in diversification was disappearing. In 1982, Surgeonics, which had never really flourished, was disposed of, and then, early in 1983, following several poor years in the construction industry, the interest in Fitzpatrick Construction was sold.

Against the trend was Ultramar's decision in 1983 to enter the fast-growing high

250

The Laurelglen Plaza shopping precinct developed by Beacon in Bakersfield, California

potential agricultural biotechnology industry and participate in a company set up to exploit opportunities for the application of new developments in agricultural biotechnology. It took a 26% interest in a new venture, the Agricultural Genetics Company (AGC), which had been formed by the British Technology Group in response to the British Government's concern about the lack of commercial development of major research discoveries. AGC has collaborative arrangements with government-funded research institutes and has specific rights to develop commercially research discoveries made by six institutes operated by the Agricultural Food Research Council. These institutes are concerned with the advanced technology of agriculture, and AGC aims to develop commercial applications for fields such as genetic engineering, pest control and the micropropagation of plants, as well as offering management and contract research facilities. During the last months of 1984, £17.5 million was raised to fund AGC to the end of the 1980s. As well as Ultramar and the British Technology Group, shareholders include three multi-national industrial companies and a wide variety of investment institutions. The potential returns from agricultural biotechnology are considerable in the long term, for agriculture is one of the few industries that can be compared in scale with oil.

With two or three exceptions, Ultramar's attempts at diversification have not been

Core drilling for the diatomaceous earth project

Aquafine water softening equipment marketed in eastern Canada from the early 1970s

A model of a windmill designed during the early 1970s as a possible alternative source of energy

particularly successful. The expertise and dynamism that management brought to the oil business over several decades has not been easily diverted into other fields. However, since by most standards the oil industry is no longer a growth industry and will very gradually phase out, the arguments for diversification are still strong. Ultramar will be considering many options in the search for successful ways of broadening the profit base. There is no pressure for immediate action because management believes that Ultramar has many decades of vigorous life ahead within the oil industry.

The Ultramar Race Day is a regular feature of the annual London AGM week,
and is held at Sandown, Kempton Park or Newbury race course

# ULTRAMAR LIFE 13

Despite its growth from a struggling oil-producing company centred in Venezuela to an international company operating on five continents, Ultramar through its 50-year history has had remarkable stability of management and consistency of business philosophy. There have been only six Chairmen of the Board in 50 years and only three chief executives. Alfred Meyer ran the operations from 1935 to 1954, Arnold Lorbeer succeeded him and was chief executive until 1974 and Lloyd Bensen followed. When Bensen took over as Chairman of Ultramar in 1985, Dale Austin became chief operating officer. Since Meyer, Nelson, Lorbeer and Bensen had close friendly relationships both in and out of the office, it was perhaps inevitable that their business philosophies would not diverge greatly.

Fundamental to Ultramar's policy has been the philosophy that there are three cornerstones to running a successful private business - capital, management and an environment which welcomes private enterprise. To obtain capital, a business must provide a reasonable return and a vision of future growth. To attract and retain competent management, a business must provide fair compensation and stimulating and attractive working conditions. To encourage an environment which welcomes private enterprise, a business must be a good corporate citizen.

Alfred Meyer seldom took a business trip without his wife. Georgette Meyer was a vivacious, enthusiastic lady who no doubt helped keep the lid on her strong-willed husband. Alfred Meyer believed that morale and performance of staff would be improved if the spouses and families were brought into the Ultramar environment and this philosophy has been continued by his successors.

Meyer believed that coordination and exchange of ideas were essential in running a business. He inaugurated periodic management conferences in Evian, France, before the Second World War, and the practice has been continued by Lorbeer and Bensen, except that the conferences now take place in different centres of Ultramar activity. Also important in Ultramar's policy-making machine is the annual AGM week in London, a carefully balanced blend of business and social activities.

Emphasis on education and schooling of Ultramar staff was pushed by Professor Illing in London and strongly endorsed by management. Even in the 1940s, in difficult days, countless youngsters were subsidised at the Royal School of Mines or at American universities and considerable management talent was developed.

Most of Ultramar's leaders were and are enthusiastic sportsmen. Aside from personal and team participation in various sports, Ultramar has been a leader in sports sponsorship. Ultramar Race Day has for many years been a regular feature at the annual London meeting. Horse racing has been followed by sponsorship in other fields, including motor racing and power boat racing. From motor racing came the idea of Racing for Charities. In America, a similar exercise has been the sponsorship of the Guiding Eyes for the Blind Golf Tournament. The employees in various countries introduced an increasing range of sporting activities. Curling, bowling, softball, basketball, rugby, cricket and ice racing are among the sports played by company teams.

By the early 1970s the diverse nature of Ultramar life worldwide had made clear the need for a regular means of communication between various offices and areas of activity. So *Eagle Eye,* the Ultramar house magazine, was born. Since the spring of 1973, *Eagle Eye* has reported three times a year on Ultramar people and events, documenting history in the making. In the process *Eagle Eye* has become a useful record of Ultramar's moves towards a unified house style. Symbols, trademarks and other elements of the Ultramar image are gradually being coordinated.

Essentially the story of Ultramar is the story of its people. Fifty years of Ultramar life is a record of their contribution.

Arnold Lorbeer's retirement as Chairman was celebrated in London in January 1985.
*Left to right:* Lord Remnant, Arnold Lorbeer, David Elton

In 1952 a lunch was held to celebrate Alfred Meyer's 75th birthday. *Left to right, standing:*
Arnold Lorbeer, Campbell Nelson, Morris Frank, unknown, unknown, unknown, Paul Fekula,
*seated:* Fred Sealey (Texaco), Jim Assheton, Bill Clark (Texaco), Alfred Meyer, Ralph Gutman,
Paul McCullough (Texaco), Professor V. C. Illing

257

2 Broad Street Place, Ultramar's London office until 1980

Morgan House, *centre,* where Ultramar's London office is now located

In September 1972 American Ultramar moved from New York City to
these offices in Mount Kisco, New York State

American Ultramar moved to new offices in Tarrytown, New York State, in 1985

Social occasions and celebrations. *Top left and right:* Ultramar dinners in New York in the late 1960s and Montreal in the early 1970s, *centre left and right:* American Ultramar's 50th anniversary celebrations in 1979 (Edna Bensen holding a 'Golden Eagle' and Georgette Meyer blowing out the candles), *lower left:* Campbell Nelson's retirement, January 1981, *lower right:* Bert Ault reads a poem to celebrate Arnold Lorbeer's birthday

260

Ultramar has been actively involved in sports sponsorship and sporting charities for many years. *Top left:* Jockey Lester Piggott at the Ultramar Race Day, *top right:* the launching of the Ultramar Racing Team in London in 1976, *centre left:* Guy Edwards, who drove frequently for Ultramar Team Racing, enjoyed several successful seasons, *centre right above:* the Racing for Charities scheme raised money for the Mental Health Foundation and the Order of St. John from successes on the motor racing circuits, *centre right below:* Mike Seebold driving a power boat sponsored by Ultramar, *right:* since 1978 American Ultramar has sponsored the annual Guiding Eyes for the Blind Golf Tournament at Mount Kisco

Ultramar's sporting life. *Left to right from the top:* Golf in Montreal, cricket during the AGM, rugby football in Kent, softball in Mount Kisco, ice racing at the Quebec Carnival, American football at Mount Kisco, women's softball in Canada

262

San Diego was the location for the annual management conference in 1973. *Left to right:*
Malcolm Haigh, Blaine Beal, Jean Gaulin, Blake Stewart, Frank Sisti, Roy Myers

Ultramar's non-executive directors, 1982. *Left to right:* Sir Kenneth Barrington, Michael Beckett,
Lord Remnant, Donald McCall, Sir Leo Pliatzky

During the last 50 years Ultramar's Annual Report and Accounts has developed from a simple financial statement into a full colour brochure, reflecting both the company's growth and the increasing scope of its activities. Early Reports were small and austere, but there has been a steady move towards a more elaborate approach while at the same time making it more readable for shareholders. Maps were added in the mid 1940s, illustrations in the late 1950s and full colour dates from 1969. The Report and Accounts today is Ultramar's most important promotional document

Ruth Brenner, general manager Public Relations, has edited Ultramar's house magazine *Eagle Eye* since its launch in 1973

Designed to keep all the Ultramar offices in touch with each other, *Eagle Eye* has been published in both English and French three times a year since 1973. Today the magazine is enjoyed by over 15,000 readers worldwide, and provides both insiders and outsiders with a view of Ultramar people and events

# UNIVERSITY EDUCATION AWARDS

Ultramar has historically given financial backing for education at all levels. Staff members have been encouraged to seek advanced technical degrees, to enrol in intensive management development courses at Harvard University and elsewhere, or to attend shorter sessions in specialised courses, such as production technology or petroleum economics.

In Canada, Ultramar has for over 20 years been granting annual $1,000 University scholarships to deserving children of employees, retired employees or deceased employees of the Canadian Ultramar group of companies. Awards are made on the basis of scholastic record and the degree of difficulty in their choice of studies. Below is a random selection of Canadian students who have received awards.

Hélène Manseau, daughter of Alain Manseau, Supervisor, Reconciliation, Montreal Division, was granted a University Award in 1978. Hélène graduated in Mathematics from the University of Montreal. She now works for the Ministry of Justice as Assistant to the Director, Statistical Services.

Isabelle Houde, daughter of Guy Houde, General Manager, Development, Montreal Division, was granted a University Award in 1978. Isabelle graduated from the University of Montreal with a Doctorate in Oral Surgery and presently practises at a clinic in Montreal.

Susan Airth, daughter of Jim Airth, Vice-President Refinery Sales, Head Office, Toronto, was granted a University Award in 1978. Susan graduated from Queen's University, Kingston, with a Bachelor of Science. Susan also obtained a Degree in Education from Weston University. She is presently teaching Chemistry and Biology at Frontenac High School in Kingston.

Donna Batten, daughter of Gordon Batten, retired Newfoundland employee, was granted a University Award in 1977. Donna graduated from Memorial University, Newfoundland, with an Honours Degree. Donna majored in Computer Science at Queen's University, Kingston, and graduated in 1980 with a Master of Science Degree. In 1981 she was hired and works at the University, where she teaches Computer Science.

The emergence of the Ultramar trademark. *Left to right:* Golden Eagle and Aigle d'Or symbols as used during the 1960s, the Ultramar symbol of the 1970s and the current design, now in universal use. In the United Kingdom Ultramar products were marketed under the Summit symbol. Symbols of companies either associated with Ultramar or acquired by Ultramar, Beacon Oil, Aquafine Water Refiners, the flag of the Aries Steamship Company, the symbols of Arrow Petroleum, Canadian Fuel Marketers and Enstar

The Ultramar Board of Directors in 1985. *Left to right, standing:* William Sheptycki, David Elton, Eugene O'Shea, Campbell Nelson, Richard Webb, Peter Raven, Robert Bland, *seated:* Robert Haddow, John Du Cane, Sir Leo Pliatzky, Arnold Lorbeer, Dale Austin, Lloyd Bensen, Lord Remnant, Laurie Woodruff, Ronald Utiger, Michael Beckett

# THE NEXT FIFTY YEARS 14

Although Ultramar is celebrating its fiftieth anniversary, it is the last 25 years that have witnessed the most dramatic changes. It has been a period of rapid growth and expansion as the policy of integration was developed; a period that has seen Ultramar's emergence as a significant international oil company.

This 25-year period has also been marked by a steady increase in the importance of the main Board in London, largely because of the addition of experienced executives within the Group and by recruitment of talented outsiders. As the second 50 years begin, the Group's management is headed up by Lloyd Bensen, who became Chairman in 1985, and by Dale Austin, group chief operating officer.

The heads of some of the principal operating divisions in 1985 are directors of the parent company. Finance is headed by Peter Raven, legal affairs by Eugene O'Shea, exploration and production by Robert Bland and shipping by Robert Haddow. In addition, the manager of Ultramar's important eastern Canadian Division, Laurie Woodruff, is a director, as are David Elton, head of the London Office and group marketing coordinator, and William Sheptycki, the manager of the exploration and production Division in the North Sea, Europe and Africa. On the non-executive side, special effort has been made to obtain talent with wide commercial and financial experience. Lord Remnant, who has been a director since 1970, is the Deputy Chairman of the Group. He has a financial and accounting background. Two very popular non-executive directors, Sir Kenneth Barrington and Donald McCall, who each served on the Ultramar Board for over fifteen years, retired in 1983 and 1984 respectively. Continuing the relationships with Morgan Grenfell and Consolidated Gold Fields are Richard Webb and Michael Beckett respectively while Sir Leo Pliatzky, John Du Cane and Ronald Utiger have become directors in more recent years and have brought a wide range of experience in government and industry. Finally, there are still Campbell Nelson and Arnold Lorbeer, both ex-Chairmen of Ultramar, with the latter having been chief executive from 1954 to 1974 and retiring as Chairman at the end of 1984.

The increasing complexity of Ultramar's operations worldwide has been reflected by the intricate financing arrangements that have been a feature of the last two decades. Since the mid 1960s additional monies have been provided by stock issues, by Eurodollar and Swiss franc loans, by non-recourse borrowing, by conventional bank loans and by various ingenious financial arrangements devised by Campbell Nelson, Richard Thompson, Bertram Ault, Peter Raven and others. The dramatic change in Ultramar's financial rating during the last two decades has been underlined by Max Bayer, vice president finance and administration for Ultramar Canada:

'When I joined Golden Eagle Refining of Canada in the early 1960s we had a hard time convincing our bankers that a $2 million loan was justified. We had to pay a rate of interest that was higher than prime, and provide documents that were many times more voluminous than those we need today. Now our credit line with five major Canadian banks totals over $430 million, and we have no trouble arranging additional financing for special projects like the Quebec cat cracker. I can also remember the excitement and the plaudits I received in 1963 when I discovered we could reduce our taxes by $5,000. Today we are involved in negotiations with Federal and Provincial departments that entail tens of millions of dollars.'

For the year 1984 the Ultramar Group had record results, with sales revenue of over £3,200 million, profits before tax of about £285 million and net profits of just over £127 million. However, it is also apparent to the Board and to senior management that the company has reached a sort of plateau, although earnings over the next few years may increase considerably. New strategies and plans are required to stimulate greater growth and progress as Ultramar moves into the second half of its first century. There are naturally differences of opinion among Ultramar's leaders as to the course to follow for the future. There is some feeling that Ultramar, as a significant but still relatively small integrated oil company, has attained its optimum size, and that further expansion would require the infusion of fresh expertise and a new style of management. This philosophy would rather put the emphasis on improving efficiency and the rate of return on present invested capital without adding large segments of new business. There is also some reluctance to move away from the traditional lines of the oil business. At a recent Management Meeting, the Board members and senior managers were asked to write down where they wanted Ultramar to be ten to fifteen years from now and how they would achieve it. The answers were far from uniform, but there was hammered together a composite *Corporate Strategy For Ultramar* which has been widely circulated within the organisation and which contains the following paragraphs:

'Ultramar will continue to be primarily an oil company and will strive to maximise profits in its present business lines. We shall seek to increase our oil reserves and production relative to our refining and marketing. We shall remain alert to investment opportunities outside of oil and gas, provided we are satisfied that we have the management skills to handle such investments.

'The company will grow largely by the reinvestment of internally generated funds, but the use of shares and borrowed funds is not ruled out, especially for an acquisition.

'Geographically, we are aiming to diversify our profits so that roughly we will have 25% from each of the United Kingdom, the United States, Canada and the Pacific Basin. In absolute terms, we look for a net profit of at least £200 million by 1990 and a growth rate of between 10% and 15% in subsequent years. Cash dividends should increase in line

270

with the increase in earnings per share so that, over a period, they will be between 30% and 35% of net profits.

'People are our most important asset and we must have a programme which will exploit the available talent and provide for orderly succession at the various management levels. We must also continue to encourage innovative thinking and avoid getting stifled in bureaucracy.'

The immediate aim then is to create a more balanced business in which Ultramar's four main areas of activity, Canada, the United States, Indonesia and the United Kingdom contribute about equally to the results. Since the decision to integrate was made in the late 1950s, Ultramar has tried to avoid the temptation to put too many eggs in one basket, although Indonesia has outperformed the other Divisions. There was a slight variation from this policy in 1984 with the acquisition of Enstar. In the spring of that year the Board approved a proposal for Ultramar to join with Allied Corporation in making a tender offer for Enstar Corporation, a company listed on the New York Stock Exchange. It was Ultramar's first experience in the frenetic world of public takeovers and it proved to be a complicated operation. Although the terms of the tender bid were agreed with Enstar's Board, it was attacked by dissident shareholders who engaged in multiple litigation stretching from Texas to Alaska. Those involved in the takeover were kept hard at work day and night from May to September when the deal was finally concluded, and they returned to their more conventional spheres of activity with considerable relief. In a disclosure statement to Ultramar's shareholders, the acquisition was described as follows:

'As a result of this merger, the Ultramar Group now has a 50% interest in Enstar's assets and operations, the principal of which are:

(i)    a 23.125% interest in the Huffco Indonesian Joint Venture in which Ultramar and Allied each already hold 26.25% interests,

(ii)    a U.S. exploration and production company which at the end of 1983 had reserves totalling approximately 25 million barrels of oil equivalent and which is currently producing about 4,700 barrels per day of oil and 50,000 mcf per day of gas, and

(iii)    An Alaskan natural gas pipeline and distribution utility and other miscellaneous small assets and operations.'

Enstar is currently in the process of selling its Alaskan utility and the miscellaneous assets. In future, its business will consist wholly of the participation in the Indonesian Joint Venture and the continuation of its U.S. exploration and production activities. The Ultramar Group's share of the initial cash outlay for the acquisition was $155 million. However, this is being reduced considerably as a result of the sale of assets and the refinancing of Enstar's existing loans.

For a relatively modest outlay the Enstar acquisition has given the Ultramar Group a 50% interest in a sizeable U.S. domestic exploration and production operation with a good spread of prospective acreage. The acquisition improves the Group's

271

operational balance by increasing its overall oil and gas production and will also allow Ultramar (in conjunction with Allied) to control the future of its most significant operation, the Indonesian Joint Venture.

The Enstar takeover represents somewhat of a shift in style by Ultramar. Previous acquisitions were all by friendly negotiations and on a smaller scale. Moreover, Enstar reinforces Ultramar's position as an oil and gas producer in two of its four preferred geographical areas of activity.

Canada has in recent years been Ultramar's major investment. Recent acquisitions, supported by the sophistication of the Quebec refinery, have given Ultramar a strong market position in eastern Canada and the northeastern United States. In the past few years, the Canadian Division has been affected by poor profit margins and lack of balance between upstream and downstream operations. To create a more balanced situation requires a greater emphasis on exploration and production. An accelerated drilling programme has led to some recent successes in western Canada and production is expected to build up.

A feature of the 1980s has been the increasing importance of the United States to Ultramar. By a policy of acquisition, Ultramar has established a firm base in refining, marketing and production. There has also been a dramatic increase in exploration drilling since the opening of the Houston office in January 1983, and it is hoped to increase United States oil and gas production substantially by the end of the decade.

The importance of Indonesia in Ultramar's position today cannot be overstated. Oil and gas reserves are sufficient for significant increases in production, but the market for LNG is no longer buoyant, as a number of new factors have come to play since the early 1980s. In the short term another LNG train may be built, while a sixth is also possible if sufficient new markets can be found. Possible candidates for new LNG markets in the Pacific Basin include Korea, Taiwan, China and Thailand, as well, of course, as Japan. At the same time, oil and gas condensate production is likely to be expanded.

Expansion of production in the United Kingdom will be harder to achieve because of the high costs in the North Sea, but Ultramar will continue to grow, both by acquisition and by drilling. Ultramar is associated with several groups applying for the ninth round licences which will be announced in the course of 1985. The company will no doubt continue to apply for licences in future rounds. In the long term, if means can be found to develop the more marginal North Sea fields economically, then Ultramar will benefit. Ultramar has substantial interests in a number of discoveries of this kind, for example, the 13/29 block and the possibly large accumulation of heavy oil in the 9/11 block. In many ways the United Kingdom represents a well-balanced market, with good co-ordination between upstream and downstream activities, and so it is bound to remain a major interest for Ultramar. It is also a useful base from which to develop other exploration plays in The Netherlands, Denmark, Ireland and the Mediterranean. There is also a considerable future for onshore exploration and development in England.

Although Ultramar's future will be concentrating on the above four main areas, there will always be flexibility for taking advantage of new promising opportunities. Australia,

Egypt, West Africa and the Caribbean are all in the sphere of Ultramar's activities. A prominent objective is to search for another Indonesia, 'another large elephant' as Lloyd Bensen has been quoted as saying, to highlight Ultramar's next 50 years.

# ULTRAMAR
# 50 YEARS OF FINANCIAL GROWTH

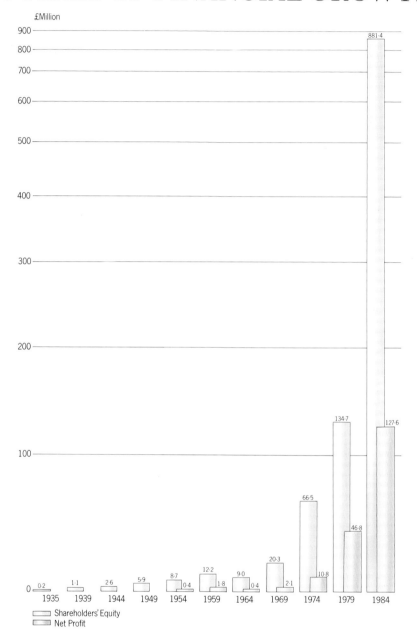

£Million

Bar chart showing Ultramar's financial achievement over the fifty years. The blue column represents equity in millions of pounds at the end of each five-year period. The red column shows net profit in the final year of each five-year period.

# DIRECTORS
# PAST AND PRESENT

*WALTER MACLACHLAN   1935–44   *British*
RALPH MICKLEM   1935–45   *British*
RICHARD P. L. THOMPSON   1935–43, 1963–69   *British*
ALFRED MEYER   1937–64   *American*
ROLLAND BEAUMONT   1938–40   *British*
CYRUS T. POTT   1938–45   *British*
SIR CECIL RODWELL   1938–47   *British*
JOHN A. ASSHETON   1940–55   *British*
*ALFRED J. BRETT   1940–49   *British*
J. O. MAY   1940–44   *British*
HERBERT ORAM   1943–59   *British*
R. S. G. STOKES   1944–46   *British*
LORD HARLECH   1945–49   *British*
R. D. PETERS   1945–57   *British*
*SIR EDWIN HERBERT (LORD TANGLEY)   1946–73   *British*
*CAMPBELL NELSON   1947–   *British*
MALCOLM MACLACHLAN   1948–49   *British*
SIR KENNETH MEALING   1950–68   *British*
R. H. A. NEUSCHILD   1949–66   *British*
*ARNOLD LORBEER   1955–   *American*
JOHN M. SHAHEEN   1960–65   *American*
BASIL R. GOODFELLOW   1964–72   *British*
J. DONALD MCCALL   1966–84   *British*
*LLOYD E. BENSEN   1965–   *American*
JOHN A. OWERS   1965–83   *British*
DALE H. AUSTIN   1969–   *American*
SIR KENNETH BARRINGTON   1970–83   *British*
LORD REMNANT   1970–   *British*
EUGENE O'SHEA   1975–   *American*
LAURIE D. WOODRUFF   1979–   *Canadian*

* *Chairman*

275

# DIRECTORS PAST AND PRESENT

MICHAEL E. BECKETT  1981–  *British*
ROBERT S. HADDOW  1981–  *American*
SIR LEO PLIATZKY  1981–  *British*
DAVID O. ELTON  1981–  *British*
PETER L. RAVEN  1981–  *British*
RICHARD M. WEBB  1983–  *British*
RONALD E. UTIGER  1983–  *British*
JOHN P. DU CANE  1983–  *British*
ROBERT BLAND  1984–  *American*
WILLIAM SHEPTYCKI  1984–  *Canadian*

# INDEX

Acción Democrática party (AD: Venezuela)
 70, 98, 125
Agricultural Food Research Council 251
Agricultural Genetics Company *244*, 251
*Aigle d'Or* (tanker) 230, 233, 237
Aigle d'Or trade mark *263*
Airth, Jim 150
Airth, Susan, University Award 1978 *266*
Aitken, John 161, *162*
Alfonso, A. *22*
Alfonzo, Juan Pablo Pérez 70, 125
Algeo Oil Concessions Corporation 16, 30
Allan, James *112*, 139, *140*, *144*, *145*, 161
Allen, Walter 183
Allied Corporation 199-201, 271-2
Ament, Joseph *121*, *132*, 134, 159, 242
*American Heritage* (tanker) 237
American Ultramar
 anniversary celebration *260*
 name changed 119
 offices *259*
Amistad field (Ecuador) gas production (1969) 201
Amoco (U.K.) Exploration Company
 203, *204*, *205*, 224, 227
Amuay refinery (Venezuela) 117
Anderson, Virgil *178*
Anglo-Persian Oil *see* British Petroleum
Anglo South American Bank 15
Angola 199-201
Anzoátegui 16, 19, 26, 27, 35
Anzoátegui Royalties 55
 *see also* Venezuelan Royalty Companies
Apex Trinidad Oilfields Limited 26, 94, 119
Aquafine 248, 250, *253*, 267
*Aquarius* (LNG carrier) 216
Arab-Israeli war (1973) 152, 206
Archambault, Raynald 150
*Aries* (LNG carrier) *192*
Aries Marine Shipping 233, *263*

Arrow Petroleum 164, 166, 171, 173, 177, *263*
asphalt 159, 161, *162*, 166, 181
Asphalt International 179-81
Assheton, John (Jim: director of Ultramar)
 41, *42*, 63-4, 65, 66, *71*, 86, 88, 102, 225, *257*
 joins Ultramar 39-40
 retires 89
Astilleros Españoles (Puerto Real) *236*, 238
*Atlantic Marchioness* (tanker) *100*, 117
Atlantic Refining (Atlantic Richfield)
 59, 60, 63, 79, 81, 118
Augsbury, acquired by Ultramar 191
Auld, John 187, *191*
Ault, Bertram 109, *120*, 122, *132*, 137, *260*, 270
Austin, Dale (director of Ultramar)
 109, *120*, *121*, 122, *132*, 139, *140*, 143, *144*,
 *178*, *180*, 186, 255, 261, 262, *268*, 269
 joins board 137
Austin, Nancy (Dale Austin's wife) 237
Austral Oil 199
Australia 210, 271
 exploration 222-4
 Ultramar's interests in *225*
Avon Steamship Company 229-30

Bacigalupo, David *178*, 186, 187
*Badak* (OBO carrier) 240
Badak (Indonesia) *209*, *210*, 211, 213, 216
Bahamas, the 85, 199-201
Bailey, Dan 31, *62*
*Banglar Upohar* (ship) 240-1
Bank of Indonesia 215
Bank of Montreal 156
Barbados 33, 84
Barbula well (Venezuela) *65*
Barinas 35, 118, 126
Barrington, Sir Kenneth (director of Ultramar)
 144, *262*
 joins board 137
 retires 269

277

# INDEX

Batten, Donna, University Award 1977    266
Bayer, Max    270
Beacon Oil acquired by Ultramar    183-6, 187, 199
Beacon refinery (USA)    *175*, 185
Beal, Blaine    150, 157, *263*
Beatty, A. Chester    17
Beaumont, Rolland (director of Ultramar)
   joins board    39
   resigns    55
Bechtel    212
Beckett, Michael (director of Ultramar)
   *263*, *268*, 269
Bedford, G.    *151*
Belanger, Orlie    187
Bell, David    119
Bensen, Edna (Lloyd Bensen's wife)
   *123*, 233, *261*, *260*
Bensen, Lloyd (Chairman of Ultramar 1985)
   52, *88*, 89, 94, 95, 97, 101, 109, *120*,
   *121*, 122, 123, *136*, *145*, 159, 165,
   199, 224, 255, *268*, 269, 273
   background    87-8
   joins board    137
   forms transportation department    227
Bentley, Helen Delich    234
Berger, Arvie (Leo Berger's wife)    233
Berger, Leo    133, 227-9, 233, *234*
Berger, Phyllis (Leo Berger's daughter)    234
*Bermuda Bianca* (tanker)    157
Bertrand, J. J. (Prime Minister of Quebec)    *142*
Betancourt, Rómulo    70, 98, 99
Bethlehem Steel (USA)    134
Bills, Arthur    189
Bland, Robert (director of Ultramar:
   exploration and production)    *210*, 224, *268*, 269
Board of directors, Ultramar's    *268*
   changes
     1939/45    55-7
     1946    64-6
     1950s    89
     1963    121
     1970    137
     1980s    269
Bogatá    15, 55, 91
Bontang (Indonesia), *192*, 212, 213, *214*, 215, 216,
   *216*, 217
Boundary Lake, Canada    194, *195*
Boyd, Paul    109, *112*, 118, 122, *142*, *145*, 187, 189
Boylan, Ebert    25, 27, *42*, 51, 63, 87
   letter to Servello    *18*
   and CPSA formation    37-8
Bracken, Brendan    65
Brandt, Alfredo    15-16
Brenner, Ruth    109, *264*

Brett, Alfred (Chairman of Ultramar 1944-6)    55, 64
   becomes Chairman    57
   resigns chairmanship    65
   resigns directorship    74
British-Borneo Petroleum Syndicate    26
British Newfoundland Exploration Ltd    193
British Petroleum Co.    21, 119, 149, 150
British Technology Group    251
Brotherhood, Roy    44, 49, 57, *62*, 63, 89, 93, 97,
   *120*, 122, 224
   letter of employment    *31*
   in Venezuela    23, 31-5, 69-70
Brouillette, R.    *151*
Bruce of Melbourne, Lord    75
Bryson, Joe    *198*
Buckley, Sir John    *211*
*Buen Provecho* (Dorothy Kamen-Kaye)    51
bulk storage in Canada    *140*
bunkering    161, 169, 177, 185
   barge launching    *133*
   in Panama    130, 133-5, 159, 227
   ship    *169*
Burmah Oil    243

Camaz-Placer    63
Caminol Company    *175*, 183-5
Campbell, Pepper and Laffoley (lawyers)    146
Canada
   early developments    91-5, 119
   exploration    193-7, 210
     and production interests    *194*, *200*
   gas production (1983)    197
   marketing    161-6, 171-7, 181-3
   oil production
     1962    119
     1983    197
   product sales
     1977    173
     1979    177
     1979/83    181
   Ultramar's interests in    *90*, *116*
   *see also* Newfoundland and Quebec refinery
Canadian and Caribbean Oil Company
   (Can-Carib)    117
Canadian Fuel Marketers (CFM)    154, 187, 248
   acquired by Ultramar    174-7
   symbol    *267*
Canadian Government 139, 140, 152, 154, 155, 157,
   174, 182, 186, 194
Canadian Ice Company    163
Canadian Imperial Bank of Commerce    113, 156
Canadian National Energy Board    157
Canadian National Railways    150
   locomotive    *167*

# INDEX

Canpet Exploration Limited, formed by Ultramar
    93-4, 111, 119
Cape Verde Islands     113
capital, Ultramar's
  increases
    1938     37
    1940     41
    1960     106
  surplus distribution     78
Capozzi, Ralph     *121*
*Capricorn* (tanker)     *228*, 233
Caracas (Venezuela)     89
Caracas Petroleum Corporation     15-25 *passim*
  manages Ultramar's interests     29-37 *passim*
  merges with Ultramar     37
Caracas Petroleum Sociedad Anónima (CPSA)
    15, 131
  formed by Ultramar     37
  negotiations with Texaco     40-1
  office     *36*, *89*, 97
  *see also* Mercedes field
Caracas Petroleum US Limited (CPUS)
    95, 111, 119, 169, 197
Caribbean area and West Indies     16
Caroll, Jack     *110*
Carson Petroleum     169, 177
Carson refinery (USA) *see* Los Angeles refinery
Caston, John     63
Cattier, Jean     104
Catto, Lord     *211*
Cazenoves (brokers)     29, 74
Central Mining and Investment Corporation
    19, 25, 38-9, 43, 57, 64, 70, 73, 74, 86
Cerro de Pasco     97
CFM *see* Canadian Fuel Marketers
Chalbaud, Major Carlos Delgado     70
Channel Petroleum acquired by Ultramar     189
Clark, Bill     *257*
Clarke, Phil     94
Colombia     15, 35, 39, 41, 91
Compañía de Petróleos Bolívar (Colombia)     35
concessions, Ultramar's in Venezuela     *60*, *82*
Conoco (Continental Oil Company)     113-14, 131,
    135, 187, 215, 224
Consolidated Gold Fields     17, 19, 25, 39, 73, 74, 89,
    94, 119, 269
Constas, Mary (Peter Constas's wife)     234
Constas, Peter     227-9, 234, *234*
Continental Oil Company *see* Conoco
Cornwall Petroleum acquired by Ultramar   118, 163
Corrie Fuel Supplies acquired by Ultramar     189
Cowley Ultraserve     *158*, 189
CPSA *see* Caracas Petroleum Sociedad Anónima
CPUS *see* Caracas Petroleum US

Creole (Exxon) constructs Guárico Road     59-60
crop burning     *244*
Cull, Eric     17, 65
Cull & Company (merchant bankers)
    17, 19, 26, 27, 29, 55, 89, 121
  *see also* Morgan Grenfell
Cullingham, Keith     91, *94*, 95, 122
CVP (Corp Venezolana del Petroleo)     129

*Daily Mail*     201
Daly, Charles     *191*
Dao, Dr     84
Defrol     187
Deutsche Bank     15
Di Tomaso, Nick     *172*
diatomaceous earth     247-50
  drilling     *252*
Dickinson, Dick     187
Dickson, Bill     *198*
diversification, Ultramar's     245-53
Djalaloff, Vahan     27, *48*, 59, *62*, 63, 64, *65*, 88, 95
  doubts about expenditure     51-2
  dies     131
*Dodsland* (OBO carrier)     240
Dominican Republic     15, 161, 245
drilling rigs
  Australia     *223*
  Badak     *208*
  Boundary Lake     *195*
  Claresholm     *196*
  diatomaceous earth     *252*
  Matagorda county     *96*
  Mercedes     *46*, *47*, *62*, *73*
  Oritupano     *80*
  South Chandeleur Sound     *198*
  Texas     *95*, *96*, 198
  Venezuela     *36*
  Worcestershire     *202*
Du Cane, John (director of Ultramar)     *268*, 269
Ducharme, Robert     224
Dunmore, Harold     *71*
Dwelle, Walter     *178*, 187

*Eagle* (tanker)     *130*, 134, 135, 227
*Eagle Eye* (Ultramar house magazine)
    166, 174, 212, 240, 245, 247, 256, 264, *265*
Eagle Lake site (Canada)     *92*
Eagle Oil Company     105
East Kalimantan
    199, 211, 212, 213, *213* (map), 215, 216
East Kutai     215, 216, 217
Ecuador     174, 199-201, *202*, 210
Edwards, Guy     *261*

Egypt 273
  exploration 222
  Ultramar's interests in *222*
Egyptian General Petroleum Corporation 222
El Rincón Británico (The British Corner) 51
Elton, David (director of Ultramar: marketing
  coordinator)
    173, *185*, 187, 189, 191, *257, 260, 268, 269*
  and CFM purchase 176-7
Enstar
  symbol *267*
  Ultramar's interest in 187, 199, 271-2
Equatorial Guinea 224
Esso *see* Exxon
Eureka-Dodsland (Canada) 94, 119, 193
Europe, Ultramar's interests in *221*
Eustace, Jerry 243
Evans Tank Lines 179
exploration
  Australia 222-4
  camp *209*
  Canada 93, 193-7
  Egypt 222
  Indonesia 199-201, 210-17
  Iran 206-8
  Newfoundland 193
  North Sea 217-22
  UK 199-203
  uranium 247-8
  USA 197-9
Export Credits Guarantee Department 144
Exxon 13, 19, 39, 117, 142, 150

*Falcon* (tanker) *130*, 134
Farquharson, Bob *172*
FCI *see* Finance Corporation for Industry
Federal Maritime Commission 234
Fekula, Paul *257*
Ferraro, Mr *22*
Ffoulkes-Jones, Roger (Gogs) 69, *87*, 89, 98
Fifer, Harvey 109
Fina *see* Petrofina
Finance Corporation for Industry (FCI)
    66, 71, 73, 74, 75, 77
*Financial Times* 66
First National City Bank 77, 107, 113
Fitzpatrick Construction *246*, 247, 250
Fling, J. *22*
Fluor Canada 156-7
Foreign Investment Review Agency (Canada) 176
Forrester, Mildred *87*
Forti, Al 243
Frank, Morris Henry 41, 64, *72*, 94, 95, 104, *257*
  dies 122

Fraser, Chick 109, *112, 115*
Freshfields (solicitors) 26, 29, 122
Fuel Marketing Holdings (Eastern Canada) Ltd 176
Furness, Alan *211*
Futterman Corporation 118

Gallegos, Rómulo 70
Garde-Hansen, Hans 94, 122
Garriga, Gorgias *126*, 131
gas
  compressor *80*
  pumping station *83*
  separators *67, 115*
  *see also* Liquefied Natural Gas
gas production
  Amistad field (1969) 201
  Canada (1983) 197
  Mercedes 8 and 9 (1943) 49
  Mercedes field
    1958 79-81
    1960 118
  USA (1962) 119
Gaulin, Jean 150, 176, *263*
Gauthier, A. E.: acquired by Ultramar 163
General Dynamics (USA) 212, 216
Gerard Hebert acquired by Ultramar 163
Gilbert, David *91*
Gillies-Guy *172*
Gold, John *211*
Gold Fields American Development Company
  (subsidiary of Consolidated Gold Fields) 94
*Golden Condor* (bunkering barge) 134
*Golden Dolphin* (tanker) 226, *232*, 234, 238, *239*, 242
*Golden Eagle* (tanker) 229, 233
Golden Eagle advertising *162*
Golden Eagle Exploration 193, 197
Golden Eagle Liberia 233-4
Golden Eagle Oil formed by Ultramar 171
Golden Eagle Oil and Gas 119, 208
  *see also* Canpet
Golden Eagle Refining Company 105, 197
Golden Eagle Refining Company of Canada
  formed by Ultramar 139, 270
Golden Eagle trade mark *267*
*Golden Endeavor* (tanker) 234, *235*, 238, 240, 242
*Golden Falcon* (tanker) *162, 228*, 229, 233, 237
*Golden Jason* (tanker) 230, 233
*Golden Jay* (tanker) 242
*Golden Monarch* (tanker) 234, 237
*Golden Owl* (bunkering barge) *124*, 135
*Golden Petrel* (bunkering barge) 134, *134*
*Golden Robin* (tanker) *231*, 233
*Golden Spray* (tanker) *235*, 237-8
*Golden Swan* (tanker) *231*, 233, 237

# INDEX

Gómez, General Juan Vicente        12-13, *14*, 15
Goodfellow, Basil (director of Ultramar)        *136*
    joins board        137
Gorham, Ed        44
*Grand Eagle* (tanker)        240
Greenland        204, 245
Greig, Mr        31
Guaranty Trust        15
Guardia, Hector        *22*
Guárico  25, 26, 27, 35, 38, 41, 43, 45, 47, 49, 59, 60
Guárico Oilfields (Venezuela)        38-9, 43, 49
Guárico Road described        59-60, *62*, 84
Guarino, Pat        176
Guayabo 2 (Venezuela)        *38*
Guiding Eyes for the Blind Golf Tournament        *261*
Gulbenkian, C. S.        17, 19
Gulf Oil        21, 102, 150, 179
Gutman, Ralph        *257*

Haddow, Robert (director of Ultramar: shipping)
        242, *268*, 269
    joins board        243
Haigh, Malcolm        148, *151*, *163*, 212, *214*, *263*
Haliq, Omar        203-4
Hall, Ted        187, 191, *191*, 262
Hampshire (UK)
        201, *202*, 203-4, *203*, *204*, *205*, 224
Hanford (California)        175, 185, 186
Harlech, Lord (director of Ultramar)
    joins board        65
    resigns directorship        74
Hartong, Hendrik        *180*
Hawco, John        *163*
Hawk, Mr        *22*
*Hemland* (tanker)        237
Herbert, Sir Edwin *see* Tangley, Lord
Herts & Beds Petroleum acquired by Ultramar        189
Hesketh, Ed        *62*, 63, 89
Hicklin, John        29
Higgins, George        33, *33*, *40*, 57
Highway Petroleum acquired by Ultramar        189
Hobson, Dr        33, 87
Holman, Mr        39
Holyrood refinery (Newfoundland)
    *100*, *109*, *110*, *111*, 115, 123, *129*, 132, 142, 143,
        148, 159, 161, *163*, 227, 237
    capacity        117
    closed        182-3
home heating services        *162*, *164*
Horus 1 well (Egypt)        222, *222*
Houde, Isabelle, University Award 1978        266
Houston Oil and Minerals        219
Hubbard, Douglas        27, 55, *91*, 93
Hudson River Bridge        *246*, 250

Huffco        199, 201
Huffco Indonesian Joint Venture        271
Huffington, Roy        199, 211
Humble Oil        113
Hunt, Tim        191
Hydro-Electric Power Commission of Ontario
    *see* Ontario Hydro

Illing, Leslie (V. C. Illing's son)        85, 87, 217
Illing, Professor Vincent C.        *20*, *24*, 26, 27, 29, 30,
        33, *36*, 41, 45, 55, 63, 65, 66, 74, 95, 122,
                255, *257*
    background        21-2
    and CPSA independent drilling        67-8
    disagreements        84-8
    dies        131
Illing and Partners, V. C.        87, 217, 225
Imperial College        95, 122
incentives for staff        55, 113
Indonesia        194, 197, 224, 271, 273
    exploration        199-201, *207*, *208*, *209*, 210-17, 222
    Ultramar's interests in        *213*
International Fuels acquired by Ultramar        163
International Mining Company        105
Ipire field (Venezuela) oil production        63, 125-6
Iran        154, 155, 194
    exploration        205-8, *206*
Ireland        224, 272

Jackson Pixley (auditors)        29
Jamaica        199-201
Japan        132
    and LNG        210-12, 215-16, 272
Jet        187
Jiménez, Major Marcos Pérez        70, 98
Jiménez Government        81, 83, 97, 98
Julian, Chauncy C.        105
Julian Petroleum Company        105, *106*

Kamen-Kaye, Dorothy (M. Kamen-Kaye's wife)
        51, *62*
Kamen-Kaye, Maurice        27, 31, 37, 38, 41, 45, 51,
                52, *58*, 59, *62*, 63
    Venezuelan introduction        22-3
    resigns        87
Kane, Jean        *123*
Kay, Frank        81, 83, 84, *91*, 98, *126*
Kent Petroleum acquired by Ultramar        189
Khan, Mr        *22*
Kimber, J. R.        *171*
Knudsen, Orin        122, 137
Kuwait National Petroleum        111

Langevin, Ray                          150, *151*
Larazabal, Admiral                          98
Laska, Hank                *92*, 94, 193, 222-4
Laurelglen Plaza (USA)              185, *251*
Lawder, Arthur      17, *25*, 27, 30, 37, 39, 63-4
Lee, Hazel                                  88
Lee, Tony                                  224
Legan, Steve                              *112*
Leidelmeyer, Peter                        *207*
*Leonidas* (asphalt carrier)               227
Libya                                    203-4
Limebeer and Company (secretaries and
    accountants)       26, 27, 29, 66, 99, 191
Liquefied Natural Gas (LNG)   212-17 *passim*, 272
    Bontang plant                        *214*
    carriers                        *212*, 215
    trains                               *216*
    *see also* gas
Liquifuels                                165
living conditions in oilfields  22-3, *26*, 31-5, 49-50,
                                    52-3, 81-4
LNG *see* Liquefied Natural Gas
Lorbeer, Arnold (Chairman of Ultramar 1980-4)
      52, *58*, 63-4, 66, 88, *88*, 89, 95, 97, 98, 101,
      104, *108*, 111, 117, 120, *120*, 121, 122, 123,
      126, *135*, 137, *144*, *145*, *171*, 224, 225, *234*,
      245-7, 255, *257*, *260*, *268*, 269
Los Angeles refinery (USA) *also known as*
    Carson refinery     *102*, 105, 109, 114, 159, 166,
      169-71, 177, 179, 183, 185, 186, *198*, *239*, 240
Louisiana (USA)                            97
Lundrigan's Construction Limited           114

McCall, Donald (director of Ultramar)      *263*
    joins board                           137
    retires                               269
McCullough, Paul                          *257*
MacFarland, Duane                         *205*
Maclachlan, Malcolm (son of W. Maclachlan:
    director of Ultramar)
    joins board                            65
    resigns                                89
Machlachlan, Walter (Chairman of Ultramar
    1935-44)                   26, 29, 65, 94
    dies                                   57
McLaughlin, Darrel                        187
McLean, Dan                               150
McManus, Joe                         *165*, 166
Maitland, Peter                      173, 187
Mannion, William                     *180*, 187
Mannville site (Canada)                    *92*
Manseau, Hélène, University Award 1978     266
Maracaibo (Venezuelan lake)  11, 12, *12*, 15, 16, 43
Marchand, Jean                            *145*

Marino, Al                       159, 227, 242-3
marketing
    Canada              161-6, 171-7, 181-3
    eastern network                       *181*
    Golden Eagle and Beacon West Coast network *178*
    Newfoundland                          161
    UK                                 187-91
    USA              166-71, 177-81, 183-7
    northeast network                     *181*
Markim Fuel Oils acquired by Ultramar      189
Marks, Ruth                            27, 63
Marsh, James                       *22*, 27, 63
Marx, Hermann    17, 29, 30, 55, 64, 65, 66, 89
Mascitelli, Joel                          187
*Maureen* (OBO carrier)                    240
Maureen field (North Sea)            217, 219
    loading column                        *219*
    oil production (1979)                 220
    production platform                   *218*
May, J. O. (director of Ultramar)          57
May, Dr John                63, 68, 69, 87, 217
Mealing, Sir Kenneth (director of Ultramar)
                                89, *108*, 115
Melamid, George                           103
Mendoza, Lorenzo                           15
Mercantile Bank                     15, 17, 27
*Mercedes* (OBO carrier)             *236*, 240
Mercedes Chain Lots          38, 49, 60, 79, 85
Mercedes field (Venezuela)
    development         41, 43-55, 59-70, 77-87
    shortage in production      70, 71, 73, 75
    gas
        compressor                         *80*
        pumping station                    *83*
        separator                          *67*
    oil production
        1957                               79
        1960                              118
    rigs                              *46*, *47*
    road building                         *62*
    roughnecks                             *48*
Merchant Marine Act (USA)
    1936                                  230
    1970                                  230
Metropolitan Petroleum of New York  103, *180*, 186
Mexican Eagle                              40
Mexico                       13, 40, 85, 86, 96
Meyer, Alfred (director of Ultramar)  *42*, 63-4, 65,
      66, *71*, 73, 74, 78, 89, 104, 120, 123, 255
    background                          13-22
    concession certificate               *14*
    and Ultramar's early years   26-41 *passim*
    joins board                           35
    made Honorary President              121

Meyer, Alfred—*contd.*
 75th birthday *257*
 dies 131
Meyer, Georgette (A. Meyer's wife)
 16, *71*, 255, *260*
Miami rapid transit system (USA) *246*
Micklem, Hugh 17
Micklem, Lieutenant Colonel Ralph (director of
 Ultramar)
 joins board 29
 resigns directorship 64
Miller, Berta *22*
Ministry of Mines and Hydrocarbons (Venezuela)
 125
Mobil Corporation 59, 122, 215
Mobile Mike *168*
Monagas 26, 35
Morgan, Henry (pirate) 11
Morgan, J. P. (bank) 75, 77
Morgan Grenfell (merchant bankers) 17, 29, 55,
 64, 66, 73, 74, 89, 144, 269
 *see also* Cull & Company
Morgan House *256*
Mottershead, George 163, 165, *165*, 166, *171*, 173
Mueller-Carlson, Dr 35
Muir, Glen 150, 222-4
Murphy Oil 157, 182, 222
Murray, Bart 132, 137, 242
Myers, Roy 161, *163*, 187, *263*


*Naess Norseman* (OBO carrier) 233
National Bank of North America 234
National Bulk Carriers 113-14, 131, 135, 201
National Energy Board (Canada) 174
National Iranian Oil Company (NIOC) 205-8
National Provincial (bank) 144
National Steel (USA) *226*, 233
Neal Petroleum acquired by Ultramar
 163, 165, 166, 171, 177
Nelson, Campbell (Chairman of Ultramar 1971-80)
 27, 52, *72*, 73, 74, *88*, 89, 97, 99, 101, 106,
 *108*, 122, 123, *135*, *140*, *144*, *145*, *171*, *210*,
 *211*, 224, *232*, *234*, 255, *257*, *260*, *261*,
 *268*, 269-70
 released from army 57
 joins board 66
 becomes managing director 120
 becomes Chairman 137
 retires *260*
Nelson, Pauline (C. Nelson's wife) *158*, 189, *261*
Nelson, Walter *163*
Neptune gas project (Canada) *196*

Neuschild, R. H. A. (director of Ultramar) 89
New Consolidated Gold Fields *see* Consolidated
 Gold Fields
Newfoundland 132, 245, 247
 exploration 193, 194
 marketing 161
 Ultramar's developments 114-18
Nilam (Indonesia) 211, 216
*Nilam* (OBO carrier) 240
Norman Wells (Canada) *116*
North Sea exploration
 194, 197, 199, 203, 210, 217-22, 224, 272
Nowlan, Jacqueline *249*
Nunns, Joan 123
Nunns, Roger 123, 191


OBO *see* oil-bulk-ore
Oceanic Tankers Agency Limited 233
Oficina (Venezuela) 21
oil-bulk-ore (OBO)
 combination carriers 233, *236*
 Panamax carriers 238-40
oil production
 Canada
  1962 119
  1983 197
 Ipire field 125-6
 Maureen (1979) 220
 Mercedes field
  1958 79
  1960 118
 Mercedes 2 (1941) 45
 Mercedes 4 (1942) 47
 Mercedes 7 (1943) 49
 Oritu 4 (1959) 79
 Oritupano field (1960) 118
 Palacio field (1940s) 69
 Refineria Panama (1965) 131
 Texas 95
 USA
  1962 119
  1968 197
Ontario Hydro *151*, 152, 154, 173
OPEC (Organisation of the Petroleum
 Exporting Countries) 125, 129, 154, 174, 206
Oram, Herbert (director of Ultramar) 55
 dies 89
Orange Grove, Texas (USA) *95*
Oreck, David 109, 122, *168*, 169, 177, 186
Oriental Oil Company 16
Orinoco Oilfields 16, 17, 19
Orinoco River 44, 53, 245
Oritu 14 (Venezuela) oil production (1959) 79

Oritupano field (Venezuela) 102, 109, *115*, 126, 129
  drilling                                          *80*
  pipeline                                           79
  pooling agreement                                  79
  production (1960)                                 118
  tank farm                                         *78*
Oronel, Victor                                      *22*
O'Shea, Eugene (director of Ultramar: legal
  affairs)                       137, *178*, *268*, 269
Ostromogilsky, Jack                                243
Oviedo y Valdés, Gonzalo de (conquistador)          11
Owers, John (director of Ultramar)
                               98-9, *136*, *140*, *260*
  joins board                                      137

*Palacio* (OBO carrier)                            240
Palacio field (Venezuela)               63, 69, 73, 85
  camp             49, *50*, 52, 59, *62*, *65*
Pamaguan (Indonesia)                          211, 216
Pamatacual (Venezuela)       55, 60, 69, *76*, 79, 84,
                                      *85*, 129, 245
Pan Canadian Petroleum                             219
Panama                   106, 131-7, 159, 249-50
Panama Refining and Petrochemical Company
  acquired by Ultramar                          105-7
Payardi refinery (Panama)   *107*, 113-14, 131, 135,
                              136, 139, 159, 227
Pearl, Howard                                      191
Pemberton, Doug                                    *162*
Pembroke House                                     *191*
*Pennant* (tanker)                       227, *228*, 233
Pepper, John                                       146
Perri, Edna *see* Bensen, Edna
Perri, Nina (J. Ament's wife)                      *123*
Pertamina (Indonesian National Oil Company)
                               199, 212, 215, 216
Peters, R. D. (director of Ultramar)                74
  joins board                                       65
  dies                                              89
Petro-Canada                                       181
Petrofina                                     113, 150
Petroleum Scientific Services Limited               63
Phillips Petroleum Company    59, 107, 217, 219
Piesse, Mr                                          39
Piggott, Lester (jockey)                           *261*
pipelines, oil
  Mercedes field         53-5, 59, 60, *61*, 69, 79
  Oritupano                                         79
Pipeline self-service system           *170*, 181-2
Pittston Petroleum acquired by Ultramar
                               157, *179*, 186-7
Placid (company)                                   203
Pliatzky, Sir Leo (director of Ultramar)*263*, *268*, 269
Pointe à Pierre refinery (Trinidad)                 64

political instability in Venezuela      69-70, 97-9
Polk, Jack          *108*, 109, *112*, 115-17, 122, 161
Poole, W. G.                                        *62*
Port-au-Port Peninsula (Newfoundland)
                                      123, 193, 247
Portuguesa                                          25
Potier, Gilbert                                 66, 99
Pott, Cyrus (director of Ultramar)
  joins board                                       39
  resigns directorship                              64
Prebble, Frank                              *91*, *92*, 93
Procon (GB)                                    143-4, 146
production, gas *see* gas production
production, oil *see* oil production
profits and losses, Ultramar's
  1959/60                                          109
  1960/61/62                                     117-18
  1964                                             122
  1984                                             270
Public Law 480 (USA)                               240
Puerto La Cruz        53, 55, 59, 79, *80*, 84, 103
Puerto Rico                                        203
Punzón-Grico                                        63

Quebec refinery      123, 136, *138*, 139-57, 163, 166,
    171, 174, 176, 181, 182, 186, 187, 194, 204, 229,
                              *235*, 237, 270, 272
Quickfill outlets                             *188*, 191
Quigley, Dr Charles   102, 109, 115, 117, 139, *140*,
                                 141, 159, 203

Raffinerie Belge de Petroles                     102-3
Raisin City field (USA)                       197, *198*
Raven, Peter (director of Ultramar: finance)
                    173, *185*, 189, 191, *268*, 269-70
Reagan, Ronald                                     104
Refineria Panama                              113, 131
Remnant, Lord (deputy Chairman of Ultramar)
              *207*, *211*, *232*, *257*, *261*, *268*, 269
  joins board                                      137
Reyes, Francisco                       97-8, 126, *126*
rigs, drilling *see* drilling rigs
Rivct, Gaston                                      150
Robertson, John                               *172*, 187
Robbins, Edward                                    *121*
Robinson, William     95, 122, 126, *126*, 129, *136*
  dies                                             137
Roblecito camp (Venezuela)    45, 49-53, *52*, *53*, *61*,
                              69, *74*, 79, 81, 84, 126
  bachelor quarters                                 *54*
  golf course                                       *86*
  hospital                                          *56*
  labourers' apartments                             *56*

Roblecito camp—*contd.*
staff houses                                            *54*
swimming pool                               84, *86*
warehouse                                               *56*
Rodwell, Sir Cecil (director of Ultramar)
joins board                                              39
resigns directorship                              65
Rogers, John                                             150
Romsey, Lord                                            *203*
Ronde Lake (Canada)                          *116*, 119
Rothschild (International) Limited       144
Rotterdam                                          187, 190
Roy, André                                              187
Royal Bank of Canada                       15, 156
Royal Dutch/Shell    12, 13, 40, 59, 79, 85, 86, 87,
                    118, 154, 165, 174, 176, 177, 216
Royal School of Mines         21, 31, 63, 91, 255
*see also* Imperial College
Rueber-Staier, Eva (former Miss World)  *158*, 189
Russell, Dennis                                          94
Russell, Gilbert                                         17

St. Helena                                          113, 159
St. Joseph's Lead                                       97
St. Romuald         142, 143, 146, 151, 157, 194
*see also* Quebec refinery
SA Petróleos Las Mercedes formed by Ultramar
and Texaco                      43, sold 129, 135
*see also* Mercedes field
SA Petrolera Manapire formed by Ultramar
and Texaco                       43, 47, 49, 59
sales, product
Canada
1977                                             173
1979                                             177
1979/83                                        181
Summit outlets (1969)                   189
sales revenue, Ultramar's (1984)            270
Sandt, Mrs Ralph (A. Meyer's daughter)  *71*, 123
Sandt, Ralph                                             123
*Santa Rosa*, SS                                         71
Santo Domingo                                         18
*Sea Renown* (ship)                                   240-1
Sealey, Fred                                     45, 84, *257*
Seebold, Mike                                           *261*
seismic
party                                                 *36*
rig                                                    *38*
shooting                                             *195*
Selection Trust                            19, 25, 73, 89
self-storage units                           250, *250*
Sergeant, Patrick                                      201
Servello, Thomas: letter from Boylan        *18*

service stations        117, 161, 166, 173, 174, 181-2,
                                              185, 189-91
Bletchingley                                         *184*
California                                            *175*
Canada                                               *112*
Cowley                                         *158*, 189
England                                              *188*
Los Angeles                                        *103*
Newfoundland locations                     *160*
Ontario (Arrow)                                  *164*
Panama                                             *127*
Pipeline                                      *170*, 181-2
Quebec (Spur)                                   *172*
Quickfill                                      *188*, 191
Repentigny                                         *170*
Repps Ultraserve                              *190*
Sandhurst                                           *184*
Thunder Bay (Ontario)                       *167*
Servo Energy Systems, Ultramar's interest in   247
Shaheen, John (director of Ultramar) *105*, *108*, 113,
                                              114-15, 123
background                                        103-6
resigns directorship                           121-2
share issues, Ultramar's
convertible debenture stock (1950)        75
equity
first certificate                                *30*
1935                                             29
1943/44/45                                    55
1946                                             64
1968                                            144
loan stock
1947                                             66
1960                                            113
Shell *see* Royal Dutch/Shell
Sheptycki, William (director of Ultramar) *205*, 208,
                                         *210*, *268*, 269
joins board                                        224
shipping activities, Ultramar's        159, 227-43
Sinclair Oil                                59, 103, 111, 113
Sindicato de Petróleos Bolívar *see* Compañía de
Petróleos Bolívar
Sisti, Frank                           *121*, 186, 191, *263*
Six Day War                                      127, 229
Smallwood, Premier (of Newfoundland)  *108*, *110*,
                                          113, 114-15, 117
Smith, Pete                                            187
Snam Progetti                                        143-4
Société Française de Recherches au Venezuela
                                                 16, 19, 27
Société Petrolière Française de Caracas      18-19
Socony *see* Mobil Corporation
Solway Firth (UK)                               199, 201
Sonatrach (Algerian national oil company)    206

*Sonda* (drillship) — 202
Sorio, Cesare — 243
Spar supermarket network — 190-1
Spencer, William — 120-1
Spens, Mr — 31
sports sponsorship, Ultramar's — 255, *261*
Spur Oil acquired by Ultramar — 157, *172*, 182
Squire, Cecil — *168*
Standard Oil Co. (Indiana) — 101
  *see also* Amoco
Standard Oil Co. (New Jersey) *see* Exxon
Stewart, Blake — *144*, 148-50, *263*
stock issues *see* share issues
Stockbridge (UK) — 203, *204, 205*
Stoker, D. N. — *171*
Stokes, Brigadier (director of Ultramar)
  joins board — 55, 57
  resigns directorship — 65
Strategic Petroleum Reserve (SPR) — *239*, 240
Stucken, Alexander — 224
Suez crisis — 99
Suharto, President (Indonesia) — *211*
Suhartoyo — *211*
Sumatra — 199, *207*, 209, 211, 215, 217
Summit — 187, 189
  symbol — *267*
Sunset International Oil Company — 105
Sunset International Petroleum — 105
Sunset Oil Company — 105
Sunset Pacific Oil Company — 105, *106*
Supramaniam, Gnana — 243
Surgeonics Limited acquired by Ultramar — 247, 250

Tangley, Lady (Lord Tangley's wife) — *71*
Tangley, Lord (Sir Edwin Herbert: Chairman of Ultramar 1946-70) — 66, *71, 72*, 73, 74, 77, 79, 106, 117, 119, 122, *143, 145*
  becomes Chairman — 65
  disagreement with Illing — 85-7
  life peerage — 65, 121
  resigns chairmanship — 137
terminals — 161, 182
  Bay Roberts — *160*
  Boston — *183*
  Bronx — *180*
Texaco — 31, 118, 135, 136, 208
  crude oil contract — 64, 99, 101, 102, 123, 159
  negotiations with CPSA — 40-1
  partnership with Ultramar — 43-55, 59
  *see also* Mercedes field
Texkan Oil Company — 95-6
Thames Matex — *184*, 189
Theisen, William — 109, *168*, 169, 177

Thistle field (North Sea) — 220, *220*
Thompson, Margaret (R. Thompson's wife) — *87*
Thompson, Richard (director of Ultramar) — 27, 87, *87*, 89, 98, *120*, 122, 123, 199, 224
  joins board — 29
  resigns directorship — 55
  released from RAF — 63
  rejoins board — 121
  resigns directorship — 137
Thorne, Paul — 187
Tivnan, John — *121, 123*, 159, 242-3
Tolima Land Company *see* Texaco
Tom, Dorothy — *135*, 136
Tower, Joe — 187
Triad *see* British Petroleum
Trident — 187
Trinidad — 19, 21, 33, 39, 57, 63, 64
Trinidad Leaseholds — 63, 85
trucks
  coal — *172*
  heating oil delivery — *188, 191*
  horse drawn — *179*
  Panama — *127*
  Pittston — *182*
  promotional — *167, 168*
Tucker, Millard — 78

UGE *see* Ultramar Golden Eagle Limited
*Ultramar* (OBO carrier) — *232, 233, 239*
  in Bangladesh — 240-2
Ultramar Canada Limited — 177, 181
  formed — 94-5
Ultramar Company Limited (formerly Ultramar Exploration Company Limited)
  annual report, first *31*, development *264*
  board *see* board of directors, Ultramar's
  capital *see* capital, Ultramar's
  capital surplus distribution — 78
  corporate strategy — 270-1
  diversification — 245-53
  exploration — 193-225
  financial achievement (chart) — 274
  financial problems post-war — 71-5
  formed — 41
  future intentions — 269-73
  as integrated oil company — 101-23
  intra-company marriages — 123
  London offices — *258*
  marketing — 159-91
  partnership with Texaco — 43-55, 59, 118
  profits *see* profits and losses, Ultramar's
  sales revenue (1984) — 270
  share dealing permission — 39, *171*

Ultramar Company Limited—*contd.*
  share issues *see* share issues, Ultramar's
  shipping activities     227-43
  sporting life     256, *262*
  sports sponsorship     255-6, *261*
  Venezuelan interests nationalised     129-31
  world-wide activities     *128*
Ultramar de Venezuela SA formed     131
Ultramar Exploration Company Limited
  formed     11, 25, 29
  *see also* Ultramar Company Limited
Ultramar Exploration Limited formed     217
Ultramar Golden Eagle Limited (UK)     187-9
  formed     121
Ultramar Iran Oil Company formed     208
Ultramar Istmica SA formed     136
Ultramar Liberia Limited formed     121, 227
Ultramar Oil and Gas formed     199
Ultramar Panama formed     111, 131-2
Ultramar Petroleum     157, 182, 186
Ultramar Plaza (Panama)     136, *246*, 249-50
Ultramar Race Day     *254*
Ultramar Racing Team     *261*
Ultramar Shipping     242
*Ultrasea* (OBO carrier)     *226*, 233, 240, 242
Unare-Zurón     79, 118
Union Corporation     19, 25, 39, 65, 73, 74
United Kingdom
  exploration     199-203
  marketing     187-91
  Summit product sales (1969)     189
United States of America
  exploration     197-9
    and production interests     *200*
  Government
    controls     99, 106, 109, 177, 179, 185
    and shipping     230, 233
  marketing     166-71, 177-81, 183-7
  oil and gas production (1962)     119
  oil production (1968)     197
  Ultramar's developments in     95-7, 119-20
uranium exploration     247-8, 250
Utiger, Ronald (director of Ultramar)     *268*, 269

Velutini, Dr     *22*
Venezuela
  oil background     11-27
  political instability     69-70, 97-9
  States     *17*
  transport     *28*
  Ultramar's withdrawal     125-31
  *see also* Mercedes field
Venezuelan American Corporation     16
  certificate of authority     *18*
Venezuelan Petroleum Law (1943)     49
Venezuelan Royalties     55
Venezuelan Royalty Companies     26, 27, 55, 101, 109, 113, 119, 126, 131
Vengref refinery (Venezuela)     79, 101, 103
*Vespasian* (tanker)     237
Vico     199
Vogel, John     234

Walsh, Robert     243
Walter, Bob     123, 191
Walter, Gina (Bob Walter's wife)     123
Webb, Richard (director of Ultramar)     *268*, 269
Webster, Andrew Dunlop     174
Webster, Colin (grandson of A. D. Webster)     176
Webster, George (son of A. D. Webster)     174
Webster, Lorne (son of A. D. Webster)     174
Whitehall Group     40
White Weld (bankers)     104
Williams Bros     60
Wilson, Joe     68
Wilson, John     187
Wilson Company acquired by Ultramar     163
windmill     245, *253*
Wishaw, Charles     122
Woodruff, Laurie (director of Ultramar: Canadian Division)     *172*, 176-7, 187, *268*, 269
Woodson, Bill     *42*
Worcestershire (UK)     199, 201

Zamora *see* Barinas
Zuloaga, Nicomedes     15

Ultramar Worldwide